Promise Unfulfilled

Promise Unfulfilled

Juvenile Justice in America

Cathryn Crawford, editor

with Lorraine Boissoneault

International Debate Education Association

New York, London & Amsterdam

Published by
The International Debate Education Association
400 West 59th Street
New York, NY 10019

We are grateful for the generous support of the Children and Family Justice Center of the Bluhm Legal Clinic of the Northwestern University School of Law.

Library of Congress Cataloging-in-Publication Data
Promise unfulfilled: juvenile justice in America/Cathryn Crawford, editor; with Lorraine Boissoneault.
   p. cm.
   ISBN 978-1-61770-039-2
   1. Juvenile justice, Administration of—United States.   2. Juvenile corrections—United States.   I. Crawford, Cathryn.   II. Boissoneault, Lorraine.
   HV9104.P76 2012
   364.360973—dc23   2012005652

Composition by Brad Walrod/Kenoza Type, Inc.
Printed in the USA

IDEBATE Press

Contents

**Chapter 5: Populations Overreferred to the
Juvenile Justice System** 153

ACKNOWLEDGMENTS

We are grateful for the support provided by the International Debate Education Association. Its selection of juvenile justice as a topic for a book reflects an appreciation of the importance of exposing teenagers and young adults, arguably the best experts on adolescence, to the subject so that they can help inform the continuing debate on how to approach youth who are alleged to have engaged in delinquent acts. The attorneys and staff at the Children and Family Justice Center of Northwestern University School of Law helped identify topics for inclusion in this book and authors to provide the articles. Toni Curtis and Heather Lyster assisted us administratively. Laura Yoder, then a second-year law student at Northwestern University School of Law, provided research support and assumed principal responsibility for the chapter on indigent defense, including helping draft the introduction to that section.

Martin Greenwald and Eleanora von Dehsen provided significant substantive and technical support from the beginning to completion of this project. Without their vision and expertise, this book would not exist.

Finally, in acknowledgment of the significant contributions she has made to reforming the juvenile justice system and the critical role she plays in ensuring that juvenile defenders across the nation have sufficient resources, and are well-trained and ably supported, we dedicate this book to Patricia Puritz of the National Juvenile Defender Center.

Introduction

In 2006, Adam* was a 15-year-old African American boy living on the South Side of Chicago with his single mother and two siblings. During the summer, neighborhood gang members began pressuring him to join their gang. When he refused, they warned him that they would "take care of him" on the first day of school. Having been exposed to gang violence throughout his youth, Adam was terrified. He first tried to convince his mother to let him stay home from school. When his mother refused, Adam borrowed $50.00 from his girlfriend to buy a gun. Guns were easily obtainable in his neighborhood, and, while the one Adam purchased was held together by a rubber band, he was sure that he would only need to show it to be left alone.

On the first day of school, in Adam's ninth-period gym class, the gang members made good on their threats. Adam sat on the bleachers with a borrowed phone begging his brother to come and get him when approximately 20 teenagers converged and began beating him with their fists. After falling to the floor, Adam pulled the gun out of a sock in his front pocket and waved it in the air. This action had the desired effect and the boys fled. Adam, too, ran and, as he raced out the gym's emergency exit, the firearm discharged, striking another teenager in the foot. Adam was arrested a few moments later.

The prosecuting attorney was responsible for deciding whether to bring charges against Adam and in which court. Because Adam was only 15 years old, the prosecutor could elect to bring various charges (such as battery with a firearm) in juvenile court, where Adam would be held accountable for his actions without facing the long-term consequences associated with an adult criminal conviction. Another option available to the prosecutor was to file the most serious eligible charge—attempted murder—in juvenile court and then ask the juvenile court judge to hold a hearing to determine whether Adam should be transferred to adult criminal court. At that hearing, the prosecutor and Adam's defense attorney would present evidence about Adam's individual qualities (nonviolent, studious, etc.) and background (e.g., whether he had any prior involvement with the court, his school performance, and behavior at home) and the circumstances of the alleged offense. After hearing all of the evidence, the judge would decide whether Adam should be tried in juvenile court, where the maximum sentence

---

*Name changed to maintain confidentiality.

would be incarceration until Adam was 21, or in adult court, where the *minimum* sentence was incarceration for 26 years.

The prosecutor bypassed juvenile court altogether by employing a different tactic: charging Adam with "aggravated battery with a firearm in school," a seemingly less serious charge that nevertheless required automatic prosecution in adult court. The prosecutor then added the charge of attempted murder. Adam, who had never been in trouble before, was facing a maximum sentence of 87 years in adult prison without ever seeing a juvenile court judge.

Adam's case highlights a number of problems with juvenile justice systems across the country. As a minority youth, Adam was much more likely to be arrested, charged, prosecuted, and incarcerated than his Caucasian counterparts. Because he came from a low-income family, Adam could not afford an attorney and was dependent on the state to provide him with one. Because he lived in a state that had passed "zero tolerance" laws in the 1990s and 2000s in reaction to high-profile yet aberrational incidents such as the Columbine shooting, Adam was automatically sent to adult court. Because the prosecutor had unlimited discretion in making the charging decision, Adam was not able to present evidence to a judge that the offense was the result of impulsive teenage behavior and that he was less likely to reoffend than he was to grow into a mature, productive member of society. Consequently, a judge was never given the opportunity to decide whether Adam's case would best be handled in juvenile rather than adult criminal court.

THE PREMISE OF JUVENILE COURT

Arguably, the most appropriate venue for Adam's case was juvenile court. The fundamental premise of juvenile court is the belief that children who commit a crime, no matter how serious, deserve a second chance to redirect their energies, and to grow out of adolescence without the stigma and consequences of a criminal conviction. To that end, the proceedings and records of many juvenile courts are closed to the public. Juvenile court has a different terminology: an accused minor is a respondent rather than a defendant, a respondent is adjudicated delinquent rather than convicted, a minor receives a disposition rather than sentence. In the overwhelming majority of states, the court's jurisdiction ends when a person turns 21 years old—thus, a term of probation or incarceration cannot extend past a respondent's 21st birthday.

The creation—and continuation—of a separate juvenile court reflects society's understanding that adolescence is a transitory period during which children are more likely to engage in impulsive and risky behavior. It further reflects a belief that a youth should not be defined by a single act, no matter how serious. As the U.S. Supreme Court noted in its seminal *Roper v. Simmons* decision, which held that children under the age of 18 could not be sentenced to death,

> The susceptibility of juveniles to immature and irresponsible behavior means "their irresponsible conduct is not as morally reprehensible as that of an adult." Their own vulnerability and comparative lack of control over their immediate surroundings mean juveniles have a greater claim than adults to be forgiven for failing to escape negative influences in their whole environment. The reality that juveniles still struggle to define their identity means it is less supportable to conclude that even a heinous crime committed by a juvenile is evidence of irretrievably depraved character. From a moral standpoint it would be misguided to equate the failings of a minor with those of an adult, for a greater possibility exists that a minor's character deficiencies will be reformed. Indeed, "[t]he relevance of youth as a mitigating factor derives from the fact that the signature qualities of youth are transient; as individuals mature, the impetuousness and recklessness that may dominate in younger years can subside." *Roper v. Simmons*, 543 U.S. 551, 570 (2005) [internal citations omitted].

While an alarming number of children are removed from juvenile court for adult criminal prosecution, the majority of youth who commit criminal acts in all 50 states and the District of Columbia are prosecuted in juvenile courts. In most jurisdictions, youth under the age of 18 are eligible for juvenile court. Eleven states allow for youth under the age of 17 to be prosecuted as juveniles and two (New York and North Carolina) define juveniles for the purpose of court jurisdiction as people under the age of 16. Regardless of how *juvenile* is defined, many people agree that juvenile courts are the appropriate venue for addressing delinquent youth. However, questions abound as to the proper scope and focus of these courts.

CHANGES AND TRENDS

Juvenile courts have undergone significant changes since the first one was created in Cook County, Illinois, more than a century ago. Many more laws have since been passed that criminalize what is arguably normal adolescent behavior. Actions that once resulted in a trip to the school principal's office are now the basis of delinquency charges. Many schools actually have police officers as part of the staff. As a result of zero tolerance policies, children who get into a schoolyard fight or talk back to a teacher can find themselves standing in front of a judge on felony charges. Increasingly, schools use the courts to rid themselves of children who are entitled under federal law to specialized attention and instruction. The "school-to-prison pipeline" is a well-documented and disturbing trend across America.

Moreover, while the juvenile court traditionally emphasized rehabilitation, the current trend is to focus more on punishment. This has led to much more severe and lasting consequences for youth charged with committing delinquent acts. Children convicted of sex offenses (including those deemed "Romeo and Juliet" offenses because they involve consensual sex between two minors) face compulsory lifetime registration as sex offenders. Several states have imposed mandatory prison sentences, removing judicial discretion in sentencing. Minors adjudicated delinquent may be disqualified from public housing, the military, licensure in certain professions, and receipt of student loans. Children may be expelled for acts that occurred off school grounds. Whereas juvenile court records used to be sealed, they are increasingly being made available to schools, police, and the public. Children who are processed through the juvenile justice system are finding that employers have access to information about, and make decisions based on, their arrests and adjudications.

In some jurisdictions, however, juvenile justice stakeholders are attempting to improve the courts, while simultaneously creating alternative options for youth in conflict with the law. For example, schools have developed "peer juries" to handle school-based offenses. Community-based panels provide a venue for an offender to meet with the complaining witness and, under the direction of community members, negotiate an agreement that allows the youth to take responsibility for his actions and make the complaining witness "whole" while avoiding the delinquency system. Advocates in Philadelphia have developed a youth/police training curriculum aimed at helping each constituency better understand and interact with the other. These efforts reflect a growing understanding that the courts are not always the most appropriate forum to address a youth's behavior.

Despite these growing efforts to change the system, the reality is that in many communities, particularly urban ones, juvenile courts are the first, rather than last, resort. Most of these courts are riddled with systemic problems. In jurisdictions across the country, youth of color are disproportionately represented at all stages of the proceedings, the disparities widening the deeper children are drawn into the system. Children appear in court without lawyers or with lawyers who are overwhelmed and underresourced. Some prosecutors, judges, and even defense lawyers suspend constitutional protections, such as the standard of proof beyond a reasonable doubt, out of a misguided belief that helping a child trumps due process rights. While the juvenile justice systems have a number of well-intentioned actors, the system is often ill-equipped to properly assess and/or address the needs of the youth in it, often resulting in adverse and long-lasting consequences for youth and their communities.

THE BOOK

The American juvenile justice system has failed to provide a consistent, fair, and productive venue for addressing the needs of youth in conflict with the law. This book is intended to provide the foundation for both understanding some of the challenges of the system and for identifying solutions. Through contributions from an assortment of advocates, academics, and policy experts, we address some of the most pressing issues in the juvenile justice system. Through the articles, the readers will also be introduced to other juvenile justice topics and concerns worthy of consideration.

Part 1: An Overview of the American Juvenile Justice System

To appreciate the challenges of the system, we must understand its origins. The articles in the first section explore the history of the juvenile court, paying attention to trends in approaching youthful offenders and the corresponding challenges. The first article, "The History of Juvenile Justice," produced by the American Bar Association, serves as a primer on the juvenile court, providing a basic overview of its development and an explanation of how it functions. The second article, "Punishment and Control: Juvenile Justice Reform in the U.S.," by Melanie Taylor, Donna M. Bishop and Scott H. Decker, is a more in-depth exploration of the system by academics, focusing particularly on the last 20 years. The authors provide and interpret key crime statistics, helping the reader gain insight into the demographics and characteristics of youth in the justice system. The authors also discuss policy trends (both cause and effect) and attempt to forecast expectations. The article provides critical information to those seeking a more nuanced understanding of the trends within the system.

Part 2: Understanding and Addressing Disproportionate Minority Contact

Any analysis of the juvenile justice system must include a discussion about the racial and ethnic disparities that persist, as these are arguably the greatest barrier to a truly just system. Youth of color are overrepresented at every stage of the juvenile court proceedings, from arrest to incarceration. While the federal government has conditioned a state's receipt of certain funds on its documentation of racial and ethnic demographics of the youth in the court system, insufficient progress has been made in accurately recording this information and addressing the disparities. Many system stakeholders are unwilling or unable to accept that addressable causes exist for these inequities, opting instead to cite factors such as poverty and poor education systems as the cause.

We explore these disparities in Part 2. The first article, "Disproportionate Minority Contact," produced by the National Conference of State Legislatures, provides the startling statistics that reflect a genuine state of crisis, theories about potential causes, and examples of the different ways that jurisdictions are trying to remove these disparities. While the situation is bleak, some hope is provided by foundations and other funders that have made this issue a focus and priority and are financially supporting advocates engaged in efforts to reduce disparities. The second article, "Decisions that Drive Disparity: Minority Overrepresentation in the Juvenile Justice System," by Ashley Nellis, offers a more in-depth analysis of the causes and solutions. The third article, "Dreams Denied: The Over-Incarceration of Youth of Color," is written by the leading expert on this issue, James Bell of the Burns Institute. Mr. Bell presents a brief historical perspective, helping us understand that this is not a new problem, but it is an escalating one. He then outlines steps that can be taken to reduce or even prevent disparities, leaving room for guarded optimism that we can successfully address this crisis.

Part 3: Effective Juvenile Defense

Another challenge faced by youth who stand accused of committing crimes is access to competent counsel. One of the most important rights a youth has is the right to be represented by an attorney. Children in delinquency court generally cannot afford to hire a lawyer and are dependent on the state to provide legal counsel. These children are often represented by lawyers who have excessive caseloads and limited resources. Such children face additional barriers to competent representation. For example, many are represented by lawyers who are not trained in the specialized practice of juvenile defense. In several jurisdictions, the prevailing view is that juvenile court is less serious than adult court and, consequently, does not necessitate investigation, expert assistance, and, in some instances, even lawyers. Parents, often faced with missing another day of work and/or having to pay for a lawyer, sometimes pressure their children to accept plea offers even before an attorney has had the opportunity to explore deficiencies in the state's case. Another common problem is the suspension of important constitutional protections because of a perception that the court is supposed to help the child, regardless of guilt or level of culpability. Finally, some children have the misfortune of being represented by lawyers who believe that they, and not the clients they represent, are in the best position to decide the goals of representation and litigation.

These and other systemic challenges are fully explored in Part 3. The section begins with "The Importance and Role of the Juvenile Defender," by Samuel Goldberg, a fellow at the National Juvenile Defender Center, an organization dedicated to improving quality of counsel for children. The article explores the evolution of the juvenile defender, providing insight into the critical function of attorneys in delinquency proceedings. Relying in part on findings from juvenile indigent defense assessments conducted in various states across the country, the author identifies some of the most pressing challenges juvenile defenders face and explains their significance. The next article, "The Challenges of Defending Juveniles in Delinquency Court," by Tamar R. Birckhead, offers a deeper look at the consequences of substandard juvenile defense practices. The author examines many of the problems identified in the first article, considers additional ones, and offers some solutions. The third and final article in the section, "'Whose Side Are You On Anyway?': Best Interest Versus Expressed Interest Representation of Minors In Delinquency Court," is by Jacqueline L. Bullard, a juvenile public defender. The author examines a serious but easily solvable barrier to effective representation: role confusion among juvenile defenders. Lawyers representing adult defendants understand their ethical obligation to let the client determine the objectives of the representation, including whether to plead guilty and whether to testify. Some lawyers representing children in delinquency proceedings believe that they, rather than their clients, are in the best position to make these and other judgments. The article provides insight into the genesis of the misunderstanding and makes a strong case for resolving it in favor of children directing litigation. Taken together, these three articles give a greater appreciation of the importance of the defense attorney in delinquency proceedings.

Part 4: Prosecuting and Sentencing Children as Adults

The changes in juvenile laws are most bleak when examining the prosecution of youth in adult courts. As noted earlier, juvenile courts historically focused on rehabilitation over punishment. By the mid-1960s, several states had provisions allowing for children accused of the most serious crimes to be prosecuted in adult court after a judicial determination. Underlying these "discretionary transfer" provisions was the concern that juvenile court was simply not appropriate for a very small number of youth who committed serious (and generally repeated) offenses.

Lawmakers believed that, in such cases, it would be appropriate for a judge to assess the facts of the crime and the child and make a reasoned, individualized decision about whether a minor should remain in juvenile court.

In the 1980s and 1990s, however, the landscape changed significantly. Because of an increase in juvenile crime, which peaked in the mid-1990s, and the advent of the myth of the "super predator" (immoral and violent youth roaming the streets), states began enacting "adult time for adult crime" statutes. Illinois, the birthplace of the juvenile court, is fairly representative. For close to 100 years, the court was designed to accept all youth under 17, regardless of the crimes they were alleged to have committed. In 1982, the state adopted the Automatic Transfer statute, excluding youth who were accused of a limited number of serious crimes (murder, armed robbery with a firearm, and aggravated criminal sexual assault) from juvenile court jurisdiction without the benefit of a hearing before a judge. The purpose of establishing the Automatic Transfer statute in 1982, according to the Illinois Supreme Court, was to strike "the balance in favor of societal security [over the potential to rehabilitate] by vesting exclusive jurisdiction over these alleged juvenile offenders within the criminal court." *People v. Clark*, 518 N.E.2d 138, 143 (Ill. 1987).

While this provision was originally intended only to prosecute the "worst of the worst" juveniles in adult court, this is no longer the case. Like many jurisdictions, Illinois consistently expanded the class of youth that can be prosecuted as adults. Where the laws originally required judges to conduct individualized determinations about whether a minor should be prosecuted as a juvenile or adult, these decisions are more often in the hands of prosecutors, who have almost unlimited discretion in charging decisions. Unfortunately, many states do not keep statistics on the number of youth eligible for juvenile court who are transferred each year. In 2007, 29 states reported a total of 14,000 transfers; data from the remaining 21 states was not collected or made available. The 2004 data suggest that, nationwide, 23,000 youths were transferred to adult court that year. Combining all of the youth who are excluded from juvenile court jurisdiction because of statutory age limits with those who are transferred, an estimated 200,000–250,000 youth under the age of 18 are prosecuted in adult court annually.

Part 4 provides a historical and contemporary analysis of this phenomenon. Both of the selected articles provide a brief history of the prosecution of children as adults in the United States. "State Trends: Legislative Victories from 2005 to 2010—Removing Youth from the Adult Criminal Justice System," by Neelum Arya, assesses the individual and societal consequences of sending children to adult courts and jails. The author reveals current trends suggesting that a shift back toward affording more children the protection of juvenile court is underway. However, a universal abolition of prosecution of children as adults is unlikely absent a ruling from the U.S. Supreme Court.

While recent polls show that the majority of Americans favor rehabilitation of youth over punishment, questions remain about whether any distinctions should be drawn between children and adults prosecuted in adult criminal court. The most recent debate surrounds sentencing youth to life without the possibility of parole. Currently, 2,500 individuals in the United States are serving life without parole for acts committed when they were under the age of 18. This number was higher before the U.S. Supreme Court ruled in 2010 that sentencing juveniles to life without parole for offenses other than homicide is unconstitutional. As we were completing this project, the Supreme Court agreed to hear two cases involving 14-year-old children who were sentenced to life without parole for committing homicides (in one case, the child was not the person who actually killed the victim, but was convicted on an "accountability" theory, meaning that he was held responsible for the actions of the actual killer). The second article in this section, "Extreme Sentencing of Youth in the United States: The Imposition of the Sentence of Life without the Possibility of Parole for Youth," offers compelling reasons, both legal and moral, to end this practice.

Part 5: Populations Overreferred to the Juvenile Justice System

The final section addresses three groups of juveniles who are arguably over-referred to juvenile court and whose needs would be better served outside the court system: children with school discipline problems, children with mental health issues, and girls. The articles in Part 5 provide a very brief glimpse into some of the challenges faced by these populations, which collectively account for a significant majority of the youth in the delinquency system. It is important to keep in mind that the racial and ethnic disparities explored in Part 2 persist with these populations, particularly youth facing severe school discipline.

As noted above, schools are increasingly referring children who exhibit problem behavior to the courts. At the same time states were passing laws making it easier to transfer children to adult court, many school districts embraced "zero tolerance" policies that generally expanded the types of behavior that could lead to school discipline and mandated automatic suspension or expulsion for a number of disciplinary violations. In some cases, court referral was also required. Schools, especially urban ones, began placing police officers, metal detectors, and security cameras in schools. Not surprisingly, these zero tolerance policies, combined with increased scrutiny and contact with police, resulted in a drastic spike in suspensions and expulsions accompanied by a significant increase in the number of petitions in juvenile court for school-based offenses.

As the adverse and disparate effects of these zero tolerance policies have been revealed, some jurisdictions have undertaken reform efforts. The article "Still Haven't Shut Off the School-to-Prison Pipeline: Evaluating the Impact of Florida's New Zero-Tolerance Law," by the ACLU of Florida, the Advancement Project, and the Florida State Conference of the NAACP, analyzes the effects of a Florida law aimed at reducing the reliance on courts to address school disciplinary problems. The findings, which are not encouraging, are representative of what is happening in school districts across the country. The authors propose recommendations that, although directed to Florida, could potentially benefit any jurisdiction trying to block the school-to-prison pipeline.

Youth with mental health problems are also overrepresented in the system, as schools, police, and, in some instances, parents find referring such children to court to be easier than referring to them a treatment provider. In fact, in some communities, the only way a child can access mental health services is through a juvenile court referral. "Addressing the Mental Health Needs of Youth in Contact With the Juvenile Justice System in System of Care Communities: An Overview and Summary of Key Issues," by Joseph J. Cocozza, Kathleen R. Skowyra, and Jennie L. Shufelt, details the high incidence of youth in the delinquency system who have mental health problems and explains why finding alternative ways to address the needs of these children is critical. The authors offer a model approach and provide program examples that can be replicated in other communities.

We conclude this section and the book with an article about girls, whose numbers in the juvenile justice system are increasing. "In Reframing the Response: Girls in the Juvenile Justice System and Domestic Violence," Francine T. Sherman explores the range of factors that result in girls being improperly referred to delinquency court and argues that their and society's needs would be better served by other means. The article includes a poem by a girl who was involved in the juvenile justice system—a poignant reminder that the subject matter we are studying involves real and individual children, something too often forgotten.

Despite the current imperfect state of the American juvenile justice system and the ample room for it to be improved, juvenile court still plays a critical role in giving youth the opportunity to address their errant behavior and mature into responsible adults. Consider Adam, the boy who brought the gun to school. Adam had the rare and fortunate opportunity to be represented by lawyers and students from a law school legal clinic who had access to extensive resources. Despite objections from the prosecutor, the judge released Adam from detention and allowed him to move to another state with his family. During the year and a half that his case was in litigation, Adam prospered in his new home and high school. He proved that, given the chance, he could overcome a very bad decision and excel in a supportive environment. Ultimately, the prosecutor agreed to dismiss the adult criminal charges in exchange for Adam's agreement to plead guilty in juvenile court and spend the summer of his junior year in a juvenile prison. His lawyers worked with the juvenile department of corrections to ensure that Adam would be placed in a facility that was geared toward rehabilitation rather than punishment. This allowed Adam to take responsibility for his actions without subjecting him to the burden of a felony conviction. Because he had been adjudicated as a delinquent, Adam's records were sealed and ultimately expunged.

Adam recently wrote:

My experience in the juvenile justice system changed my view of life in words I can't fairly articulate. It provided me the opportunity to learn lessons from my peers and intellectually develop as a teenager. Juvenile court presented me a second chance, a sense of hope that I could do better and move forward with my life. I went on to graduate high school with honors, receive a scholarship at a four-year university, where I served as class president, intern on Capitol Hill, and acquire a grant to establish a partnership between my university and a local public school providing mentoring and economic resources for disadvantaged youth. Now, I will graduate from college with a work history and academic record that will make me competitive for not only top PhD programs in the nation, but also leading national and global fellowship programs. It was the hope inspired by my juvenile adjudication that helped provide me the fuel and energy needed to pursue my career as teacher and community organizer. If my juvenile record had not been expunged, I would not have had the hope in my heart needed to help propel me to do the work and service that I do every day.

Adam was accepted to a top tier graduate school.

Adam's case illustrates the importance of maintaining a separate and supportive juvenile court. While the American juvenile justice system is rife with problems, most people agree that individuals should not be subject to the adult criminal system for acts committed as juveniles. Behavioral science has demonstrated that youth act impulsively, with little or no regard for long-term consequences. Studies confirm that youth who are processed in juvenile court are less likely to reoffend and will likely outgrow the characteristics that contribute to their errant behavior. At the same time, juvenile court is not the appropriate venue to address all adolescent behavior. Efforts should be expanded to keep children out of the juvenile court system and in communities and schools. It is our hope that this book will serve as a road map for understanding the realities and challenges of juvenile justice system and for navigating a path for positive change.

SOURCES

Advancement Project. "Test, Punish, and Push Out: How Zero Tolerance and High Stakes Testing Funnel Youth Into the School to Prison Pipeline," March 2010, http://www.advancementproject. org/digital-library/publications/test-punish-and-push-out-how-zero-tolerance-and-high-stakes-testing-fu.

Arya, Neelum. "State Trends: Legislative Victories from 2005 to 2010, Removing Youth from the Adult Criminal Justice System." Washington, DC: Campaign for Youth Justice, March 2011, http://www.campaignforyouthjustice.org/documents/CFYJ_State_Trends_Report.pdf.

Griffin, Patrick, Sean Addie, Benjamin Adams, and Kathy Firestine. "Trying Juveniles as Adults, an Analysis of State Transfer Laws and Reporting." Washington, DC: Office of the Juvenile Justice and Delinquency Prevention, 2011, https://www.ncjrs.gov/pdffiles1/ojjdp/232434.pdf.

Justice Policy Institute. "Education Under Arrest: The Case Against Police in Schools," November 2011, http://www.justicepolicy.org/uploads/justicepolicy/documents/educationunderarrest_fullreport.pdf.

National Education Policy Center. "Discipline Policies, Successful Schools, and Racial Justice," October 2011,. http://nepc.colorado.edu/publication/discipline-policies.

National Juvenile Justice Network newsletter. "Advances from the Field," October 27, 2011. http://www.njjn.org.

Chapter 1:

An Overview of the American Juvenile Justice System

To understand the juvenile justice system, one needs a basic knowledge of its creation and development. The juvenile justice system has undergone significant changes since the first court was established in Cook County, Illinois, in 1899. While the original goal of that court was to offer children a second chance to overcome errant behavior, a perceived rise in crime and fear of the adolescent "super-predator" in the mid-1980s and 1990s led to a shift in policies toward harsher punishments. More recently, many states have endorsed the "balanced and restorative approach" in which the court attempts to (1) provide youth with the opportunity for reform and development; (2) hold youth accountable for their actions; and (3) protect the community. A principal challenge is determining which of these goals is paramount and how to balance them.

The first article in this book, "The History of Juvenile Justice," outlines the origins of the juvenile court and introduces the reader to basic concepts surrounding the juvenile court system. It examines several important U.S. Supreme Court cases that led to changes in how juvenile courts function. "Punishment and Control: Juvenile Justice Reform in the U.S." by Melanie Taylor, Donna Bishop, and Scott Decker, gives a deeper analysis of the changes juvenile court has undergone, especially in the last 20 years. By showing some of the prevailing trends in public opinion, social and economic factors in crime, and statistics, the authors give a more nuanced picture of the juvenile justice system. The authors undertake a critical analysis of the various approaches of juvenile court systems and suggest that policy continues to be driven by public misperceptions and cost to the detriment of our youth.

The History of Juvenile Justice

by ABA *Division for Public Education**

If you are a young person under the age of 18 and get into trouble with the law, you will probably have your case heard in the juvenile justice system. But this was not always the case. The idea of a separate justice system for juveniles is just over one hundred years old.

ORIGINS OF THE JUVENILE JUSTICE SYSTEM

The law has long defined a line between juvenile and adult offenders, but that line has been drawn at different places, for different reasons. Early in United States history, the law was heavily influenced by the common law of England, which governed the American colonies. One of the most important English lawyers of the time was William Blackstone. Blackstone's *Commentaries on the Laws of England,* first published in the late 1760s, were widely read and admired by our nation's founders.

"Infants" and "Adults" at Common Law

In one section of his *Commentaries,* Blackstone identified people who were incapable of committing a crime. Two things were required to hold someone accountable for a crime. First, the person had to have a "vicious will" (that is, the intent to commit a crime). Second, the person had to commit an unlawful act. If either the will or the act was lacking, no crime was committed. The first group of people Blackstone identified as incapable of committing a crime were "infants." These were not infants in the modern sense of the word, but children too young to fully understand their actions.

Blackstone and his contemporaries drew the line between "infant" and "adult" at the point where one could understand one's actions. Children under the age of seven were as a rule classified as infants who could not be guilty of a felony (a felony is a serious crime such as burglary, kidnapping, or murder). Children over the age of 14 were liable to suffer as adults if found guilty of a crime.

Between the ages of seven and fourteen was a gray zone. A child in this age range would be presumed incapable of crime. If, however, it appeared that the child understood the difference between right and wrong, the child could be convicted and suffer the full consequences of the crime. These consequences could include death in a capital crime. (A capital crime is a crime for which one

❏ Malice Supplies the Age

In this excerpt, 18th-century English lawyer William Blackstone describes the English common law doctrine "malice supplies the age."

> But by the law, as it now stands,...the capacity of doing ill, or
> contracting guilt, is not so much measured by years and days, as by
> the strength of the delinquent's understanding and judgment. For
> one lad of eleven years old may have as much cunning as another
> of fourteen; and in these cases our maxim is, that *malitia supplet
> aetatem* ["malice supplies the age"]. Under seven years of age indeed
> an infant cannot be guilty of felony; for then a felonious discretion
> is almost an impossibility in nature: but at eight years old he may be
> guilty of felony. Also, under fourteen...if it appear to the court and
> jury, that he...could discern between good and evil, he may be
> convicted and suffer death. Thus a girl of thirteen has been burnt
> for killing her mistress: and one boy of ten, and another of nine
> years old, who had killed their companions, have been sentenced
> to death, and he of ten years actually hanged; because it appeared
> upon their trials, that the one hid himself, and the other hid the
> body he had killed; which hiding manifested a consciousness of
> guilt, and a discretion to discern between good and evil....Thus
> also, in very modern times, a boy of ten years old was convicted on
> own confession of murdering his bedfellow; there appearing in his
> whole behaviour plain tokens of a mischievous discretion: and, as
> the sparing this boy merely on account of his tender years might be
> of dangerous consequence to the public, by propagating a notion
> that children might commit such atrocious crimes with impunity,
> it was unanimously agreed by all the judges that he was a proper
> subject of capital punishment.

William Blackstone's *Commentaries on the Laws of England*, Book IV, Chapter 2 ("Of the Persons Capable of Committing Crimes")

might be executed. For examples of children sentenced to death in Blackstone's time, see the sidebar "Malice Supplies the Age.")

A New System of Justice for Juveniles

During the nineteenth century, the treatment of juveniles in the United States started to change. Social reformers began to create special facilities for troubled juveniles, especially in large cities. In New York City, the Society for the Prevention of Juvenile Delinquency established the New York House of Refuge to house juvenile delinquents in 1825. The Chicago Reform School opened in 1855. The reformers who supported these institutions sought to protect juvenile offenders by separating them from adult offenders. They also focused on rehabilitation—trying to help young offenders avoid a future life of crime.

In 1899, the first juvenile court in the United States was established in Cook County, Illinois. The idea quickly caught on, and within twenty-five years, most states had set up juvenile court systems. The early juvenile courts shared with reform schools the same desire to rehabilitate rather than of punish juvenile offenders. They were based on the legal doctrine of *parens patriae* (a Latin term that means "parent of the country"). The *parens patriae* doctrine gives the state the power to serve as the guardian (or parent) of those with legal disabilities, including juveniles.

In line with their "parental" role, juvenile courts tried to focus on the "best interests of the child." They emphasized an informal, nonadversarial, and flexible approach to cases—there were few procedural rules that the courts were required to follow (see sidebar "Original Goals of the Juvenile Courts"). Cases were treated as civil (noncriminal) actions, and the ultimate goal was to guide a juvenile offender toward life as a responsible, law-abiding adult. The juvenile courts could, however, order that young offenders be removed from their

---

❑ Original Goals of the Juvenile Courts

In 1909, Judge Julian Mack, one of the first judges to preside over the nation's first juvenile court in Cook County, Illinois, described the goals of the juvenile court:

> The child who must be brought into court should, of course, be made to know that he is face to face with the power of the state, but he should at the same time, and more emphatically, be made to feel that he is the object of its care and solicitude. The ordinary trappings of the courtroom are out of place in such hearings. The judge on a bench, looking down upon the boy standing at the bar, can never evoke a proper sympathetic spirit. Seated at a desk, with the child at his side, where he can on occasion put his arm around his shoulder and draw the lad to him, the judge, while losing none of his judicial dignity, will gain immensely in the effectiveness of his work.

Julian Mack, "The Juvenile Court," *Harvard Law Review*, vol. 23 (1909), 120.

homes and placed in juvenile reform institutions as part of their rehabilitation program. [...]

JUVENILE JUSTICE AND DUE PROCESS OF LAW

Beginning in the 1960s, the United States Supreme Court heard a number of cases that would profoundly change proceedings in the juvenile courts. The first of these cases was *Kent v. United States*, 383 U.S. 541 (1966). Morris Kent first entered the juvenile court system at the age of 14, following several housebreakings and an attempted purse snatching. Two years later, his fingerprints were found in the apartment of a woman who had been robbed and raped. He was detained and interrogated by police and admitted to the crimes. Kent's mother hired a lawyer, who arranged for a psychiatric examination of the boy. That examination concluded that Kent suffered from "severe psychopathology" and recommended that he be placed in a psychiatric hospital for observation.

The juvenile court judge had authority to "waive jurisdiction" in Kent's case to a criminal court, where Kent would be tried as an adult. Kent's lawyer opposed the waiver and offered to prove that if Kent were given proper hospital treatment, he would be a candidate for rehabilitation. The juvenile court did not respond to the motions made by Kent's lawyer and, without a hearing, waived jurisdiction to the criminal court.

The Worst of Both Worlds?

The U.S. Supreme Court agreed to hear Kent's case and in a majority opinion authored by Justice Fortas, ruled that Kent was entitled to a hearing and to a statement of the reasons for the juvenile court's decision to waive jurisdiction. In its opinion, the majority also expressed concerns that the juvenile courts were not living up to their promise. In fact, the majority speculated "that there may be grounds for concern that the child receives the worst of both worlds [in juvenile courts]: that he gets neither the protections accorded to adults nor the solicitous care and regenerative treatment postulated for children." A particular concern was whether juvenile courts had received the resources, personnel, and facilities they needed to adequately serve youth charged with violations of the law.

A year after the *Kent* decision, the case of Gerald Gault, a 15-year-old Arizona boy, led to a major change in the way young people's cases were processed by the juvenile courts. Gerald was accused of making an indecent phone call to a neighbor. At the time, he was also under 6-months' probation because he had been with another boy who stole a wallet from a woman's purse. When Gerald's neighbor complained of the call, police arrived at his home and took him into custody. They left no notice for Gerald's parents.

Before Gerald's hearings, neither Gerald nor his parents received notice of the specific charges against him. At the hearings, there were no sworn witnesses and no record was made of the proceedings. Not even the neighbor who had made the complaint about the phone call was present. At the end of the hearings, the judge committed Gerald to Arizona's State Industrial School until he turned 21, unless he was discharged earlier by "due process of law." This meant that Gerald might have to spend up to six years at the school. An adult convicted of using vulgar or obscene language would have received a maximum penalty of a $50 fine and imprisonment for no more than two months.

Gerald's parents petitioned for their son's release. They argued that he had been denied due process of the law (see sidebar "What Is Due Process?") and that his constitutional rights to a fair trial had been violated. The case eventually made its way to the Supreme Court, which ruled in favor of Gerald in *In re Gault*, 387 U.S. 1 (1967).

Writing for the majority of the Court, Justice Fortas stated that "neither the Fourteenth Amendment nor the Bill of Rights is for adults alone." Juveniles subject to delinquency hearings were entitled to key elements of due process to ensure the fairness of their hearings, including:

- Notice of the charges against them.
- A right to legal counsel.
- The right against self-incrimination.
- The right to confront and cross-examine witnesses.

Blurring the Lines Between Juvenile and Criminal Justice

The Supreme Court's decision in *In re Gault* was not unanimous. In a dissent, Justice Stewart warned that by requiring many of the same due process guarantees in juvenile cases that are required in criminal cases, the Court was converting juvenile proceedings into criminal proceedings. In doing so, he argued, the Court was missing an important distinction. The object of juvenile proceedings was the "correction of a condition." The proceedings were not adversarial; juvenile courts functioned as public social agencies striving to find the right solution to the problem of juvenile delinquency. The object of criminal courts, in contrast, was conviction and punishment of those who commit wrongful acts.

Justice Stewart noted that in the nineteenth century, before juvenile courts were established, juveniles tried in criminal courts were given the same due

❏ What is Due Process?

Due process of law means that every person who is party to a legal proceeding is entitled to certain safeguards designed to ensure that the proceeding is fair and impartial. The Bill of Rights in the U.S. Constitution defines many due process rights, including:

- The Fifth Amendment's guarantees that:
  - No one can be deprived of life, liberty, or property without due process of law.
  - No one can be compelled to be a witness against herself or himself (self-incrimination) in a criminal trial.
  - No one can be tried for a serious crime unless indicted by a grand jury.
- The Sixth Amendment's rights to:
  - A speedy and public trial.
  - An impartial jury.
  - Notice of the nature and cause of an accusation.
  - Confrontation of adverse witnesses (the right to cross-examine witnesses).
  - Compel witnesses in one's favor to appear in court.
  - Assistance of legal counsel for one's defense.
- The Seventh Amendment's right to trial by jury in most civil (non-criminal) cases.
- The Eighth Amendment's protections against:
  - Excessive bail.
  - Cruel and unusual punishments.

Beginning in 1967, with its decision in *In re Gault*, the U.S. Supreme Court extended many, but not all, of these due process rights to young people involved in juvenile court proceedings.

process as adults. They were also subject to the harshest punishments for their crimes, including the death penalty. Juvenile courts were not perfect, Justice Stewart agreed. But by blurring the distinctions between juvenile proceedings and criminal proceedings, the Court was "invit[ing] a long step backwards into the nineteenth century."

Three years after the *Gault* decision, the Court took another step toward making procedure in the juvenile courts more like criminal courts. *In re Winship,*

397 U.S. 358 (1970), involved a 12-year-old boy charged with stealing a $112 from a woman's purse. The juvenile court decided that "a preponderance of the evidence" established that the boy had committed the theft. To say that someone is guilty of a crime by a "preponderance of the evidence" means that the available evidence (for example, the testimony of witnesses) makes it more likely than not that the person committed the crime. In a standard criminal trial, however, the government has to prove "beyond a reasonable doubt" that the accused committed the crime. "Beyond a reasonable doubt" is a higher standard than "preponderance of the evidence"—it means that the available evidence leaves you firmly convinced of a defendant's guilt.

One reason that the "beyond a reasonable doubt" standard of proof is required in criminal cases is that a person convicted of a crime can be sentenced to serve time in prison. In the *Winship* case, the boy charged with stealing from the purse faced up to six years in a juvenile training school. In defending use of the "preponderance of the evidence" standard, supporters of the juvenile court emphasized that the purpose of the training school was not to punish but to rehabilitate the boy. They also argued that it is not necessarily in the best interests of a troubled juvenile to "win" a case if the juvenile is truly in need of a court's intervention. A majority of the Court rejected these arguments, stating that "good intentions do not themselves obviate the need for criminal due process safeguards in juvenile courts." This was particularly true in cases where the juvenile's loss of liberty during confinement in a juvenile training school would be comparable to the punishment of imprisonment imposed when an adult is convicted of a crime.

Chief Justice Burger dissented from the majority opinion, joined by Justice Stewart. By moving the juvenile courts closer to procedures used in the criminal trials of adults, the dissenters argued, the Court was also moving away from the original idea of juvenile courts as benevolent and less formal institutions equipped to deal flexibly with the unique needs of juvenile offenders. "I cannot regard it as a manifestation of progress," Chief Justice Burger asserted, "to transform juvenile courts into criminal courts, which is what we are well on the way to accomplishing."

Trial by Jury and Juvenile Justice

The trend toward extending the due process rights of adult criminal trials to juvenile court proceedings slowed in 1971, with the Supreme Court's ruling in *McKeiver v. Pennsylvania*, 403 U.S. 528 (1971). In *McKeiver*, the Court ruled that juveniles are not entitled to trial by jury in a juvenile court proceeding.

An important factor in the Court's decision was its refusal to fully equate a juvenile proceeding with a criminal proceeding, even if the juvenile's case involved offenses that would be felonies or misdemeanors under the state's criminal laws and the juvenile court ordered the youth confined to a secure rehabilitation facility. The Court acknowledged that juvenile courts had not lived up to their promise, in part because of a lack of adequate resources. But the Court was also "reluctant to disallow the States to experiment further and to seek in new and different ways the elusive answers to the problems of the young." Trial by jury, the Court feared, would effectively abolish any significant distinction between juvenile and criminal proceedings. "If the formalities of the criminal adjudicative process are to be superimposed upon the juvenile court system," the majority opinion concluded, "there is little need for its separate existence. Perhaps that ultimate disillusionment will come one day, but for the moment we are disinclined to give impetus to it."

Three justices joined a dissenting opinion in *McKeiver*. They argued that when a juvenile is tried for offenses based on violations of a state's criminal law, and when the juvenile faces possible commitment to a state institution for delinquents, a jury trial should be required. "Where a State uses its juvenile court proceedings to prosecute a juvenile for a criminal act and to order 'confinement' until the child reaches 21 years of age . . . ," the dissenters stated, "then [the juvenile] is entitled to the same procedural protection as an adult." [. . .]

*The **American Bar Association** provides law school accreditation, continuing legal education, information about the law, programs to assist lawyers and judges in their work, and initiatives to improve the legal system for the public.

Punishment and Control: Juvenile Justice Reform in the U.S.

*by Melanie Taylor, Donna M. Bishop, and Scott H. Decker**

INTRODUCTION

A separate justice system for juveniles has existed in the USA for over 100 years. It was originally intended to function as a social welfare system with dual aims: to shield young delinquents from the corrupting influence of seasoned adult offenders, and to provide delinquents and status offenders with the guidance and treatment necessary to make the often difficult transition through adolescence to become law abiding adults. Over the last century, and most especially since the 1960s, juvenile justice policy has shifted dramatically, undergoing a series of reforms that have reshaped the system and challenged the principles on which it was founded.

In this chapter we examine trends in juvenile justice policy and practice in the USA, with a special focus on changes that have taken place in the last 20 years. The first section provides background on the context within which juvenile justice operates in the USA. We explain that juvenile justice in the USA varies greatly across state and local jurisdictions as a result of increased "federalization" of juvenile justice policy. In this first section, we also present a picture of juvenile crime and juvenile court processing to further contextualize the challenges presented to those who work in the juvenile justice field. Later, we describe juvenile justice policy trends and their intended and unintended consequences. We focus initially on punitive reforms, what motivated them and what research has demonstrated regarding their effects. We then turn to a discussion of current efforts for delinquency prevention. In the final section of this chapter, we step back and assess the juvenile justice system as a whole. We look at the uneasy mix of social welfare and social control that characterizes juvenile justice policy and practice in the USA today, and the very uncertain direction of juvenile justice policy in the future.

CONTEXT FOR UNDERSTANDING POLICY

Historical Context

Twenty years ago, Carter[1] noted that in order to comprehend juvenile justice in the United States, it is essential to understand three points. First, the size of the system(s) is enormous. All fifty states, the District of Columbia—and to some extent the federal government—have separate systems of juvenile justice.

Within minimum constitutional standards set by the US Supreme Court, each jurisdiction is free to establish its own juvenile justice policies and practices. States are not *required* to have a separate justice system for juveniles, although all established separate systems by the mid-1920s and have maintained them ever since. Second, the systems are extremely complex internally and externally. This is especially true of the interaction of the system with other public and private forms of control, including schools, mental health, public health, and agencies of government. Third, Carter underscores the dynamic character of the system(s), noting the significance of paying close attention to trends in those systems.

Social and Demographic Context

A key to appreciating the main policies of prevention, treatment, punishment, and procedural/individual rights is to understand something of the context of the juvenile population, the seriousness and extent of juvenile crime, and the nature of the juvenile justice system. The population of 15–17 year olds, the primary population "served" by the juvenile court, is increasing at a dramatic pace. In 2009 it was estimated that there were nearly 13 million juveniles in this age range, a number similar to that recorded at its peak in the midst of the post World War II baby boom of the 1970s.[2] This increase is projected to be dramatically higher among minorities.

The USA is characterized by much cultural diversity: racial and ethnic minorities make up approximately one-third of the youth population. According to the U.S. Census Bureau, in 2009 the composition of the 15–17 year old age group was 66% White non-Hispanic, 15% White Hispanic, 12% Black, 4% Asian, and 1% American Indian. Complicating this picture is the fact that a large fraction of juveniles live in poverty (roughly 20%), with minority youth being more likely to be in poverty than whites.[3] Family structure has also changed for juveniles in the USA: fewer youths live in homes with two parents than was the case in the past. In 2010, three-quarters of White children lived with two parents, 67% of Hispanic children lived with both parents, but only 39% of African-American children lived with both parents. High school completion rates have increased for all race/ethnic groups, although Hispanics, Blacks, and American Indians lag behind Whites. Overall, approximately 89% of 18–24 year olds have completed high school.

Crime

Juveniles as Victims

Much of the concern about crime in the USA revolves around violence, especially violence committed by and against young people. The National Crime

Victimization Survey (NCVS) indicates that, compared to adults, 12–17 year olds are twice as likely to be victims of serious assault and three times as likely to be victims of simple assault. Young males, racial and ethnic minorities, and residents of cities are most likely to be victims of these crimes. Consistent with a growing body of research about juvenile victimization,[4] it appears that juveniles who engage in delinquent offending put themselves at increased risk for victimization. This is particularly true for juvenile drug users, who are at a highly elevated risk for violent victimization.

Recent policy changes have occurred in response to perceptions of murder (the type of violence that receives disproportionate media attention). From 1987 to 1994, homicide rates increased dramatically, peaking in 1994 and declining since. The vast majority of homicide victims aged 12 to 17 are male (about 80%), Black (over 50%), and killed with a firearm (over 80%) by an acquaintance (about 90%). Juvenile homicides are also spatially concentrated. It is important to note in comparative context that homicide victimization rates in the USA (for both juveniles and adults) are consistently higher than those for other industrialized nations.

Juvenile Offenders

According to self-report data from the National Longitudinal Survey of Youth, a large proportion of juveniles have engaged in delinquent behaviors. Some of the more prevalent offenses include: using alcohol (39%), using marijuana (21%), engaging in property destruction (28%), carrying a gun (19%), belonging to a gang (5%), and stealing something valued at more than $50 (8%). In addition, 8% of juveniles report having been arrested in their lifetimes. Males report considerably more involvement in delinquency than females, and race/ethnic minorities report greater involvement in offenses such as assault and gang membership.

The majority of juveniles who enter the juvenile justice system make one appearance never to return again (54% of boys and 73% of girls). This has important implications for focused strategies of prevention and intervention, which we discuss later. Best estimates indicate that a juvenile who drops out of high school and engages in a lifetime of offending and drug use generates a cost to society between $1.7 and $2.3 million.

The major source of official data on juvenile offending is the Federal Bureau of Investigation's Uniform Crime Report (UCR). In 2009, an estimated 1.5 million juveniles were arrested. Nearly three quarters of these arrests were for Nonindex Offenses (i.e. 21 generally less serious offenses, including drug abuse violations,

Table 1.1 Juvenile Arrest Rates, 1980–2008 (per 100,000 persons aged 10–17)

Offense	1980	1985	1990	1995	2000	2005	2008
All offenses	7,414	7,425	8,031	9,286	7,299	6,343	6,318
Violent Index Crime	334	303	428	516	308	282	288
Property Index Crime	2,562	2,371	2,371	2,439	1,609	1,245	1,323

Source: Adapted from National Center for Juvenile Justice (2009).

simple assaults, and vandalism). Thus, although a substantial number of juveniles are arrested each year, the vast majority are arrested for minor offenses. Only 4% of juvenile arrests (68,000) were for Violent Index Crimes (i.e. murder/non-negligent manslaughter, forcible rape, robbery, and aggravated assault), of which 900 were for murder. Twenty-two percent of juvenile arrests were for Property Index Crimes (i.e. burglary, larceny-theft, motor vehicle theft, and arson), 76% of which involved larceny-theft.

Measured in terms of arrests, juvenile crime in the USA has undergone major shifts in the past 20 years (Table 1.1). Overall juvenile arrest rates and arrest rates for violence rose sharply from the early-1980s to the mid-1990s, while arrest rates for property crimes remained relatively flat during this period. From the mid-1990s to the present, substantial declines were observed in total arrests, and in both Violent Index and Property Index Crimes.

During the period 2005 to 2009 the only offenses as reported by the UCR that increased were robbery (up 8%) and larceny-theft (up 7%). The remaining 27 offenses reportedly had reduced rates of juvenile offending. This was in stark contrast to the period from 1991 to 2000 which saw dramatic increases in arrests for drug abuse violations (up 145%) and curfew and loitering (up 81%). Despite these seemingly positive changes, the Office of Juvenile Justice and Delinquency Prevention (OJJDP) cautions that "they should not provide a pretext for a misplaced sense of complacency."[5]

Juvenile crime is largely a male phenomenon. In 2009, females contributed 30% of all juvenile arrests, and only 18% of those in the Violent Index category. Recently, much has been made of the fact that while arrest rates for males declined (down 11%) over the past two decades, arrest rates for females increased (by 35%) (Table 1.2.). Such increases, especially for aggravated and simple assault, may be linked to increased nationwide enforcement of domestic violence (e.g. intrafamily disputes).

Table 1.2 Juvenile Arrest Rates by Gender, 1985–2000 (per 100,000 persons aged 10–17)

Offense	1985	1990	1995	2000	2005	2008
All offenses						
Male	10,987	12,090	13,524	10,263	8,725	8,642
Female	3,318	3,753	4,813	4,171	3,840	3,878
Violent Offense						
Male	528	736	856	490	450	465
Female	67	105	158	116	107	102
Property Offense						
Male	3,665	3,909	3,515	2,185	1,610	1,652
Female	1,013	1,152	1,302	1,001	861	979

Source: Adapted from National Center for Juvenile Justice (2009).

Juvenile arrests are also disproportionately concentrated among racial minorities (Table 1.3). Although rates of arrest for offenses overall and for Property Index offenses follow the same general trend for Blacks and Whites, arrest rates for Blacks are approximately double those for Whites. The gap between Whites and Blacks is much more pronounced for violent crimes. In 2000, there was a dramatic shift, as the arrest rate for violent crime among Blacks dropped to its lowest level in decades and the gap in arrest rates of Blacks and Whites narrowed. However, in subsequent years the rate of violent crime among Blacks increased as Whites arrest rates continued declining. In order to understand US juvenile justice policy and practice in recent decades, it is important that the reader be aware that the 15-year rise in violent crime depicted in Table 1.3, especially

Table 1.3 Juvenile Arrest Rates for Whites and Blacks, 1985–2000 (per 100,000 persons aged 10–17)

Offense	1985	1990	1995	2000	2005	2008
All offenses						
Whites	6,781	7,226	7,985	6,764	5,535	5,550
Blacks	12,155	14,063	17,496	11,541	11,444	12,161
Violent Offense						
Whites	172	254	308	220	176	178
Blacks	1,096	1,434	1,668	820	851	926
Property Offense						
Whites	2,149	2,339	2,122	1,442	1,083	1,131
Blacks	4,465	4,408	4,441	2,783	2,245	2,689

Source: Adapted from National Center for Juvenile Justice (2009).

among Blacks, has received a great deal of media attention. Violent crime has been "racialized," the young Black male has been demonized, and politicians have sought to assuage media-generated fears by advocating simplistic, punitive approaches to juvenile violence.

Youths in Juvenile Court

Juvenile courts process a large number of cases annually, but still only a fraction of all juvenile arrests. In 2008, over 1.6 million cases were handled by the juvenile courts of the USA. This figure represents more than four times as many cases as juvenile courts handled in 1960.

Once a case has been referred to juvenile court, it proceeds through a number of decision steps as shown in Fig. 1.1. During intake, a decision is made to close the case, handle it formally, or handle informally. In 2008, 56% of cases resulted in a formal petition. The detention decision determines whether the youth will be held in detention pending the outcome of the case, with about 21% of youths being held at this stage. If a petition was filed, the case then proceeds to the adjudicatory stage (equivalent to a criminal trial). If a youth is found or pleads guilty, he or she is adjudicated delinquent, representing 61% of cases. The case then proceeds to disposition (equivalent to sentencing in the criminal justice system). Disposition generally involves a hearing at which the judge determines the most appropriate sanction or service (e.g. probation, residential placement, fine).

Figure 1.1 Case flow diagram of the stages in delinquency case processing

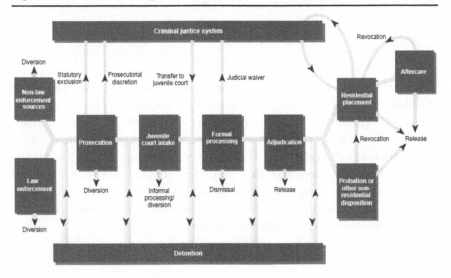

In 2007, the most recent year for which such data are available, nearly 90,000 juvenile offenders were held in residential placement facilities.[6] This was a 17% decrease from the 108,000 youths held in 2001. The majority of these juveniles were held for a delinquency offense (81%), though 4% were held on status offenses, and 16% were nonoffenders. Roughly 70% of these juveniles were held in public facilities, with the remainder in private facilities.

Similar to the arrest and petitioning stages of the juvenile justice system, minority youth are overrepresented in custody, while females account for only a small proportion of juveniles in custody. Forty-seven percent of offenders committed to public placement and 55% of offenders committed to private facilities were minority youths. On the other hand, females comprise only 13% of juveniles in custody, presenting challenges for management in residential facilities. They tend to be younger (31% under the age of 15) than males in custody (21% under the age of 15), and are more likely to have backgrounds of abuse, neglect, and family conflict.

KEY POLICY AREAS

Here we borrow from the framework identified by Klein just two decades ago.[7] At that time, Carter identified seven key policy areas that must be understood to fully appreciate juvenile justice systems in the United States: age, status offenses, discretion, other systems of control, diversion, demographic bias and trends. We deal with the first six here, policy trends are dealt with separately. It is important to observe that a report published by the U.S. Justice Department[8] concluded that, "… legislatures in 47 states and the District of Columbia enacted law that made their juvenile justice systems more punitive."

Age

There continues to be considerable variation across the states regarding the age of jurisdiction for the juvenile court. In the U.S. the states set these age limits. This variation occurs at both the minimum age of responsibility, the age at which waiver to the adult court is possible, the age at which a juvenile is eligible for a capital trial, as well as the upper age limit of jurisdiction. The trend across the states has been to lower each of these ages. The minimum age to consider a case for a delinquency hearing ranges from age 6 to age 10, while the maximum age for consideration ranges from 15 to 17. Some states even extend jurisdiction over juveniles into their twenties. Clearly, the age jurisdiction policies of American states have attempted to have it both ways, arguing that responsibility begins early (age 6 in North Carolina), but ends late (24 in California, Montana, Oregon and Wisconsin).

Status Offenses

Status offenses continue to be an important avenue for referral to the juvenile court. Status offenses are acts that if committed by an adult would not be considered violations of the law (e.g. curfew violation, incorrigibility, truancy). Some states have moved to handle status offenses in a manner similar to neglect or dependency cases as indicators of social problems rather than delinquency. Status offenders continue to be among the most difficult challenges for most juvenile court jurisdictions.

Discretion

Klein observed in 1984 that, with regard to discretion in the juvenile justice system, the United States was one of two nations that exercised the greatest amount of discretion. Little has changed to alter that perspective, except at the punitive end of discretion. Rather than move toward a system where judges and decision-makers consider the individual circumstances behind the actions of a juvenile, those decision-makers find their hands increasingly tied by punishment grids, mandatory minimums, and other forms of increased punishment. The exception to this is at the stage of intake.

Diversion

A trend in the 1970s and 1980s to divert large numbers of youth from formal processing has largely been sidetracked by the recent focus on formal, punitive responses. It is not an overstatement to observe that diversion was one of the key policy initiatives in the USA twenty years ago. However, diversion remains an important function in the American juvenile justice, particularly for prevention efforts and first-time or minor offenders.

Demographic Bias

There have been a number of policy initiatives that have attempted to address the reality of disproportionate minority confinement; to date none have been very successful. The federal government, several states, local juvenile court jurisdictions and private foundations have engaged in efforts to reduce disproportionate minority confinement, and found these to be tough policy and program choices.

POLICY TRENDS AND OUTCOMES

In the last 15 years, reforms have taken place at the local, state, and federal levels and have concentrated primarily on three fronts. The first, which has attracted a great deal of media attention both at home and abroad, involves a movement to "crack down" or "get tough" on serious and chronic offenders. For example, the Supreme Court decision in 1989 to uphold the constitutionality of the death penalty for crimes committed by persons as young as 16 was the most extreme reform.[9] Also representative of the "get tough" movement, are changing transfer policies nationwide. Second, governmental support for policies and programs of delinquency prevention and early intervention has grown. Although some prevention programs are delivered to the youth population at large, most are more selective, targeting those who exhibit empirically identified risk factors for delinquency. Finally, a transitory period is occurring with mid-range offenders, where punitive treatment is eclipsing the rehabilitative ideal the juvenile system was founded upon.

In the following section, we discuss each of these policy trends in greater detail. However, it is important to place each of these policy trends in a broader context, as none is unique to the recent generation of juvenile justice reform in the United States. Platt's[10] work on the origins of the juvenile court in the United States illustrates the conflicting orientations of the juvenile justice system. Notable among juvenile institutions was the New York House of Refuge, an early attempt to separate children from adults in confinement. In addition, the reformatory movement attempted to bring a more humane form of incarceration for offenders in the nineteenth century, albeit with questionable results.[11]

The history of juvenile justice and adult criminal justice in the US is replete with examples of interventions, policies and practices in which the rhetoric and reality differed considerably.[12,13,14,15,16,17] The two competing ideologies that seem to provide a foundation for much of the history of juvenile justice are "the welfare of the child" and "the safety of the community." These two extremes have led to "doing nothing" on the one hand, and intervening with harsh penalties on the other. As a result, there is a cycle of policy, which is driven by perceptions of high crime rates.[18] This produces an eventual call for increased leniency, in part because the court is faced with a "forced choice" between doing (little or) nothing and reacting harshly. Legal philosophers such as Allen[19] argue effectively that the lack of a coherent framework for intervention, policy and legislation leads to "irrationalities" that undermine the effectiveness of a system and create competing goals and in the end a somewhat chaotic system.

"Get Tough" Reforms for Serious Offenders

Since its inception at the end of the 19th century the juvenile court in the United States has always maintained a "trap door" through which young offenders could be removed to the criminal courts for prosecution and punishment as adults.[20] Prompted by dramatic increases in youth violence from 1987–1993 that received sensationalized media coverage, images of delinquent youth changed from the pot smoking kid (of any color) to the gun wielding minority drug dealer. As a result, nearly every state and the federal jurisdiction enacted laws that both expanded the pool of transfer-eligibles and expedited their removal from the juvenile system. During the past 15 years, these and other innovations that blur traditional lines of distinction between juvenile and criminal justice have generated questions of the need and rationale for juvenile courts, as well as who belongs in them. Change has proceeded in a theoretical void, and its end is very much uncertain.

To expedite transfer to criminal court, statutes were passed that circumvented the traditional mode of transfer–a waiver hearing in juvenile court by a judge. In *Kent v. United States*[21] waiver hearings were regularized and subject to a formal hearing and investigation of the youth's history. As a result, transfers were most often applied to repeat offenders who were nearing the age of majority and who had exhausted the court's treatment resources.

New "statutory exclusion" (i.e. legislature specifies criteria for transfer) and "prosecutorial waiver" (i.e. prosecutor makes transfer decision) statutes have shifted the responsibility for transfer from the judiciary to the legislative and executive branches. These new transfer methods accomplished three things: they expedited the transfer process, restricted the powers of a judiciary that was perceived as "too soft on crime," and removed the offender-focus that had the hallmark of the transfer decision. Unlike judicial waiver, the new transfer methods are purely offense-driven. Many states have also instituted blended sentencing, permitting (and sometimes requiring) judges to impose lengthy sentences–served initially in the juvenile system, then in the adult system–for specified offenses. These have been criticized for the irrationality of placement in two systems.

In some states, these reforms have greatly increased the numbers of youths entering the criminal courts. From 1985 to the mid-1990s, the number of transfers increased 90%, with over 13,000 transfers occurring in 1994.[22] However, their impact nationwide has been somewhat less consequential than predicted because prosecutors are not invoking the laws as frequently as they might have and criminal courts sentence transferred offenders more leniently than their adult counterparts.[23] In 2008 the number of juveniles transferred to adult court dropped to below 9,000.

Nevertheless transfer reforms had a tremendous impact on the kinds of juveniles who are entering adult corrections systems. Because legislative exclusion statutes most often target serious and violent offenders regardless of their age or offense histories, the proportions of young adolescents, racial minorities, and first-time offenders entering the adult system has increased. Finally, youth who enter the criminal justice system frequently have not had the opportunity to benefit from any sort of rehabilitative intervention they would have received in the juvenile system.[24,25]

Although we could point to numerous other examples of the "get tough" assault on serious juvenile offenders (e.g. subjecting them to sex offender registration laws; counting their prior juvenile convictions as "strikes" for purposes of invoking adult habitual offender statutes that carry capital and life sentences), those we have discussed represent the major punitive reforms. We turn now to a discussion of recent trends at the "front end" of the system.

Delinquency Prevention

At the same time that legislatures were passing punitive reforms for the worst offenders, Congress was authorizing funds for delinquency prevention programs. Some are early intervention initiatives, while others are aimed at youths who have already begun to engage in delinquent behavior.

Early Intervention

In the last decade, early intervention has taken on important new emphases and become increasingly research-based. Such programs were first seen in the 1960s with the development of Head Start, a well-funded pre-school program for young children in disadvantaged neighborhoods in the nation's inner cities. But, at that time, such programs for children were generally not implemented under the umbrella of "delinquency prevention." Influenced by important theoretical and research advances in developmental criminology,[26,27] policy makers have become more cognizant of the connections between the family, school, and neighborhood contexts in which young children live and their risk of later delinquency and crime.

We see this most clearly in the 1992 reauthorization of the federal Juvenile Justice and Delinquency Prevention Act of 1974, which created the Title V Community Prevention Grants Program.[28,29] Some of the most exciting aspects of this effort are its reliance on: 1) what we have learned from criminal careers research and epidemiological criminology about the individual, family, school, and community factors that put children at risk for serious delinquent involvement, 2) what we have learned from this same research regarding protective factors that buffer the exposure to risk, and 3) what we have learned from recent advances in evaluation research about intervention strategies that are most and least promising.[30,31]

The Communities That Care (CTC) program, which has been widely adopted, illustrates this new emphasis on risk-focused prevention.[32] Through CTC, entire communities receive funding and technical assistance to implement coordinated systems of delinquency prevention (*see* Caliber Associates for a review of the multi-step process).[33] The overall goal is to identify children at greatest risk, then to mobilize the community to reduce risk through well-coordinated interventions aimed at families, schools, peer groups, and neighborhoods. Although these are laudable goals, their attainment is hampered by a number of obstacles, including limited funding and fragmented community-level services (e.g. difficult to coordinate with multitude of agencies).

It remains to be seen whether programs funded under Title V, as well as other primary prevention programs, will endure and also whether they will be subject to rigorous evaluations to assess their long-term effectiveness. Prevention programs that focus on the long term, and whose effects are difficult to measure, have, at least until recently, been a "hard sell." Politicians responsible for funding anti-crime efforts have instead tended to focus on short-term programs that can demonstrate fairly immediate and quantifiable results.[34]

Secondary Prevention

Programs targeting youth who have already begun to exhibit problem behaviors are better funded. First time offenders are frequently diverted from formal juvenile justice processing because of the potentially damaging consequences outlined by labeling and societal reactions theories. Although that diversion movement was only a partial success,[35] a number of new diversion programs have emerged in the last decade. "Informal" teen courts (also called youth courts), where adolescents serve the roles of court actors, are one such innovation. The underlying premise of the program is that the judgment of a youth's peers may be more persuasive and beneficial than the judgment of adult officials.[36] Relative to comparison groups, teen court participants had significantly lower levels of recidivism over a 6-month follow-up period in two of the four sites.[37] Other secondary prevention efforts include the many variations on *Scared Straight,* a program grounded in deterrence theory where teens are exposed to the horrors of prison life by inmates.[38]

A discussion of recent trends in prevention would be incomplete without some mention of "zero tolerance policies." Recently, schools began introducing policies of automatic suspension or expulsion and arrest for bringing weapons of any type into schools. These policies have also expanded to include less serious offenses (e.g. cigarettes, fighting) and minimal violations (e.g. swearing, carrying a butter knife for lunch). These have been linked to increased rates of dropout and delinquency. Because zero tolerance policies have been implemented disproportionately in inner city schools, they have also had a differentially harsh impact on impoverished minority youths.

Other diversionary reforms flow out of the restorative justice movement, which was "virtually unknown to all but a small group of academics at the beginning of the 1990s."[39] Restorative justice programs take a variety of forms, including victim-offender mediation, community reparation boards, family group conferencing, and circle sentencing (Bazemore and Umbreit, 2001). The goals are to educate participants about the harms—especially the emotional harms and fracturing of relationships—caused by the offense; to repair the harms; and to rebuild relationships and strengthen systems of informal social control.

Juvenile Court: Processing, Sentencing, and Correctional Reforms for Middle-Range Offenders

The third front in American juvenile justice focuses on the very large group of offenders who are formally processed in the juvenile court. The number of youth formally processed in the juvenile courts rose significantly from 1990–1999, from about 650,000 in 1990 to nearly 1 million in 1999,[40] decreasing slightly by 2008 to over 900,000.[41] At the same time, arrest rates of juveniles decreased 16% from 1999 to 2008.[42] The reason for the discrepancy is twofold. First, there were changes in the way that police disposed of juvenile arrests. Over the last 25 years, law enforcement has been "cracking down" by referring a greater proportion of arrestees to the juvenile court. Second, the proportion of delinquency cases in which a petition was filed rose from 50% of all referrals in 1990 to 44% in 2008. The proportion of petitioned delinquency cases that resulted in formal adjudications of delinquency (i.e., convictions) also rose over the decade, from 60% of cases in 1990 to 66% in 2008. In terms of processing in the juvenile court, we see clear indications of much greater formal social control than was the case in decades past.

The juvenile court's orientation toward its youth clientele is far less clear. There are many indications that juvenile courts are beginning to converge with the criminal courts in their emphasis on punishment. In the past two decades, legislatures in many states have revised their juvenile codes to endorse "punishment," "accountability," and "public safety" as objectives of the juvenile court. However, legislatures have not abandoned the rehabilitative mission of juvenile courts. Currently all 50 jurisdictions still maintain provisions that distinguish juvenile courts from criminal courts in ways that are compatible with the juvenile court's traditional mission.[43] There are other indications that juvenile courts are beginning to resemble criminal courts. Recent changes have not expanded rights granted to juveniles in the 1960s and 70s (e.g. right to notice, right to counsel, right to remain silent, the requirement that the charges be proven beyond a reasonable doubt). Instead, the majority of states are making court proceedings public, allowing access to juvenile court records, and photographing and fingerprinting non-serious offenders.[44]

Juvenile courts' sentencing policies have also undergone change. State legislatures have passed determinate sentencing, guidelines-based sentencing, and mandatory minimum sentencing for some offenses. These "one size fits all" sanctions are contrary to the offender-focused dispositions that have long been a hallmark of the juvenile court. While most of these mandatory sentences do *not* involve incarceration, 26 states have adopted minimum mandatory periods of incarceration for certain violent crimes, weapons offenses, and repeat felony offenders.[45] Surveillance oriented sentences, including electronic monitoring and random drug testing, are also given out more frequently.

Nationally, the trend is toward sentencing youth based on notions of punishment and accountability, rather than rehabilitation. The federal government has endorsed a policy of "graduated sanctions" under which youth who have been adjudicated delinquent receive sanctions "proportionate to the offense" to hold them accountable for their actions and to prevent further law violations. OJJDP's Juvenile Accountability Incentive Block Grants program indicates that although participation in the graduated sanctions approach by individual courts is voluntary, states must encourage courts to participate. This clearly moves federal policy closer to a "pure punishment" approach.

Another recent development suggesting that a punishment agenda has taken hold was the establishment of boot camps in the 1980s. These short-term (90–120 day) residential programs where inmates are subjected to military-style basic training include physical labor, regimented activity, and intense verbal degradation. An evaluation of juvenile boot camps showed increased recidivism among participants.[46]

In the last 15 years, there have been major advances in evaluation research, and both private foundations and the federal government have invested significant funding in assessing the effectiveness of various forms of treatment.[47] This research has produced fairly consistent evidence that treatment-oriented programs, especially those that focus on interpersonal skill development and parent/family interventions, are considerably more effective than punishment-oriented ones.[48,49] Research has identified effective nonresidential treatment programs for minor and first-time offenders as well as effective residential interventions for serious and chronic offenders. In addition to Lipsey's research, the Center for the Study and Prevention of Violence has identified a number of "Blueprint Programs" that have produced reductions in recidivism (e.g. multisystemic therapy, life skills training, and multidimensional treatment foster care).

It is still too early to tell, but the punitive tide may be turning. Over the past ten years, fewer juveniles have been arrested, processed through the juvenile justice system, and transferred to the adult system. Opinion polls show that the public continues to support treatment for juvenile offenders. In addition, public officials have begun to express real worry about how they are going to manage the financial costs of America's "imprisonment binge."[50] In combination with the research evidence showing the substantial advantages of rehabilitative programs over punitive ones, these considerations may support a revival of interest in returning to traditional core principles of juvenile justice.

CONCLUDING THOUGHTS

In his seminal book on American street gangs Klein laments the fact that thirty years of gang intervention and programming have little to show for what works.[51] The situation is not quite that bad with regard to the impact of programs and policies in American Juvenile Justice, but almost. Lundman notes the American tendency to choose what he calls "cut-through" programs, programs that ignore root causes of delinquency and are seen as "quick fixes."[52] This predilection for such cut-through programs has led the United States to spend large amounts of money on programs such as DARE, Zero-tolerance programs, Scared Straight Programs, Boot Camps, large custodial programs, and curfew and truancy interventions. Evaluation results for these programs have been reviewed extensively by Howell and found wanting for positive results.[53]

Tremendous advances in program evaluation research have taken place in the last twenty years. We now know a great deal about ineffective policies and programs, as well as those that produce meaningful beneficial effects. However, many ineffective programs continue because the general public continues to believe that they are effective or because they serve retributive aims in an era that is highly punishment oriented. Effective programs may not be popular, or they may be implemented only sparsely among a few communities. Although the United States does not have national juvenile justice policy, there is much that could be done at the federal level to support the proliferation of effective strategies (e.g. by making funds available for communities that want to implement them). However, the current administration has been far more supportive of fairly simplistic and inexpensive punitive programs (that tend to be less effective) than of holistic and generally more costly strategies aimed at providing family intervention, education and training, social skills training, and social support. As important as it is to have good evaluation and research to use as a foundation for programs, it is equally important to have the political will and courage to use these results for effective programming. To date, the USA seldom shows that will. The last decade of policy, legislative and program changes have been overwhelmingly punitive, to the exclusion of considerations of the rights and welfare of juveniles. If Tom Bernard is right that juvenile justice moves from cycles of punitiveness to consideration of the welfare of children, the United States should be on the verge of a major change in the orientation of its juvenile justice system. We are not that optimistic.

NOTES

1. Robert Carter, "The United States," in *Western Systems of Juvenile Justice*, ed. Malcom Klein (Beverly Hills: Sage, 1984), 36.

2. U.S. Census Bureau. 2005–2009 American Community Survey. Washington, DC, U.S. Government Printing Office, 2009.

3. Office of Juvenile Justice and Delinquency Prevention, "OJJDP Statistical Briefing Book," 2011, http://www.ojjdp.gov/ojstatbb/population/qa01202.asp?qaDate=2010.

4. Janet Lauritsen, Robert Sampson, and John Laub, "The Link between Offending and Victimization among Adolescents," *Criminology*, 29 (1991): 265–292.

5. Office of Juvenile Justice and Delinquency Prevention, *Juvenile Arrests 2008* by Charles Puzzanchera (Washington, DC: U.S. Department of Justice, Office of Juvenile Justice and Delinquency Prevention, 2009).

6. Office of Juvenile Justice and Delinquency Prevention, *Easy Access to the Census of Juveniles in Residential Placement*, by Melissa Sickmund, Anthony Sladky, Wei Kang, and Charles Puzzanchera, (2011), http://www.ojjdp.gov/ojstatbb/ezacjrp.

7. Malcom Klein, "Introduction," in *Western Systems of Juvenile Justice*, ed. Malcom Klein (Beverly Hills: Sage, 1984), 1.

8. U.S. Department of Justice, Office of Juvenile Justice and Delinquency Prevention, *Juvenile Offenders and Victims: 1999 National Report*, by Howard Snyder and Melissa Sickmund (Washington, DC: U.S. Department of Justice, 1999).

9. *Stanford v. Kentucky*, 492 U.S. 361 (1989).

10. Anthony Platt, "The Triumph of Benevolence: The Origins of the Juvenile Justice System in the United States," in *Readings in Juvenile Justice Administration*, ed. Barry Feld (New York: Oxford, 1999), 20.

11. Alexander Pisciotta, *Benevolent Repression: Social Control and the American Reformatory-Prison Movement* (New York: New York University Press, 1996).

12. David Rothman, The *Discovery of the Asylum: Social Order and Disorder in the New Republic* (Boston: Little, Brown and Company, 1990).

13. Ibid.

14. Janet Ainsworth, "Re-Imagining Childhood and Reconstructing the Legal Order: The Case for Abolishing the Juvenile Court," in *Readings in Juvenile Justice Administration*, ed. Barry Feld (New York: Oxford, 1999), 8.

15. Alexander Pisciotta, "Parens Patriae, Treatment and Reform: The Case of the Western House of Refuge, 1849–1907," *New England Journal on Criminal and Civil Confinement* 10 (1984): 65.

16. Alexander Pisciotta, "A House Divided: Penal Reform at the Illinois State Reformatory, 1891–1915," *Crime and Delinquency*, 37 (1991), 165.

17. Alexander Pisciotta, *Child Saving or Child Brokerage?: The Theory and Practice of Indenture and Parole at the New York House of Refuge. 1825–1935*, ed. Albert Hess and Priscilla Clement (Aalen: Scientia Publishers, 1993), 533.

18. Thomas Bernard, *The Cycle of Juvenile Justice* (New York: Oxford, 1992).

19. Francis Allen, *The Rehabilitative Ideal* (New Haven: Yale, 1981).

20. David Tanenhaus, *Juvenile Justice in the Making* (New York: Oxford University Press, 2004).

21. *Kent v. United States*, 383 U.S. 541 (1966).

22. Ibid.

23. Sanjeev Sridharan, Lynette Greenfield, and Baron Blakley, "A Study of Prosecutorial Certification Practice in Virginia," *Criminology and Public Policy* 3, no. 4 (2004): 605.

24. Office of Juvenile Justice and Delinquency Prevention, *Juvenile Transfers to Criminal Court Study: Final Report*, by Lonn Lanza-Kaduce, Charles Frazier, Jodi Lane, and Donna Bishop, 2002, http://nicic.org/Library/017540.

25. Ibid.

26. Rolf Loeber and David Farrington, "Young Children Who Commit Crime: Epidemiology, Developmental Origins, Risk Factors, Early Interventions, and Policy Implications," *Development and Psychopathology* 12 (2000): 737.

27. Gerald Patterson and Karen Yoerger, *Developmental Models for Delinquent Behavior*, ed. Sheilagh Hodgins (Newbury Park: Sage, 1993), 140.

28. Office of Justice Programs, Office of Juvenile Justice and Delinquency Prevention, *2002 Report to Congress: Title V Community Prevention Grants Program*, NCJ 202019, by Caliber Associates (Washington, DC: U.S. Department of Justice, 2002).

29. Public Law 93–415: 42 U.S.C. Section 5601 et seq.

30. Office of Justice Programs, National Institute of Justice, *Preventing Crime: What Works, What Doesn't, What's Promising*, by Lawrence Sherman, Denise Gottfredson, Doris MacKenzie, John Eck, Peter Reuter, and Shawn Bushway (Washington, DC: U.S. Department of Justice, 1998).

31. Center for the Study and Prevention of Violence, *Blueprints for Violence Prevention* (2010), http://www.colorado.edu/cspv/blueprints/.

32. David Hawkins and Richard Catalano, *Communities that Care* (San Francisco: Jossey-Bass, 1992).

33. Ibid.

34. Steven Lab, "Crime Prevention, Politics, and the Art of Going Nowhere Fast," *Justice Quarterly* 21, no. 4 (2004): 681.

35. Its legacy includes "net widening," "bootstrapping" (relabeling status offenders as delinquents to render them eligible for formal intervention), and "transinstitutionalization" (displacement of offenders from juvenile correctional institutions to mental health facilities).

36. Office of Juvenile Justice Delinquency Prevention, *Teen Courts in the United States: A Profile of Current Programs*, by Jeffrey Butts, Dean Hoffman, and Janeen Buck (Washington, DC: U.S. Department of Justice, 1999).

37. Jeffrey Butts, Janeen Buck, and Mark Coggeshall, *The Impact of Teen Court on Young Offenders* (Washington, DC: The Urban Institute, 2002).

38. Ibid.

39. Gordon Bazemore and Lode Walgrave, *Introduction: Restorative Justice and the International Juvenile Justice Crisis*, ed. Gordon Bazemore and Lode Walgrave (Monsey: Criminal Justice Press, 1999), 1.

40. Charles Puzzanchera, Anne Stahl, Terrence Finnegan, Nancy Tierney, and Howard Snyder, *Juvenile Court Statistics 1999* (Pittsburgh, PA: National Center for Juvenile Justice, 2003).

41. Melissa Sickmund, Anthony Sladky, and Wei Kang, *Easy Access to Juvenile Court Statistics: 1985–2008*, http://www.ojjdp.gov/ojstatbb/ezajcs, 2011.

42. Ibid.

43. Joseph Sanborn and Anthony Salerno, *Juvenile Justice System* (Los Angeles: Roxbury, 2005).

44. Ibid.

45. Ibid.

46. Doris MacKenzie, "Evidence-Based Corrections: Identifying What Works," *Crime & Delinquency* 46 (2000): 457.

47. Interest in rehabilitation waned in the 1970s, following the release of the widely publicized "Martinson Report" (Martinson, Robert. (1974) What Works? Questions and Answers About Prison Reform. *Public Interest* 35: 22–54; Lipton, Douglas, Robert Martinson, and J. Wilks. (1975). *The Effectiveness of Correctional Treatment: A Survey of Treatment Evaluation Studies.* New York: Praeger. Critics of the report responded that the negative results could be explained by methodological problems and weak evaluations, rather than by the absence of effective treatments, but these responses—and even the subsequent retraction of the Martinson Report's conclusion by its authors—fell on deaf ears. Instead, the idea of rehabilitation was increasingly viewed with skepticism. Subsequent increases in juvenile crime, especially juvenile violence, contributed to the view that treatment was ineffective.

48. Mark Lipsey and David Wilson, "Effective Intervention for Serious Juvenile Offenders: A Synthesis of Research," in *Serious and Violent Juvenile Offenders: Risk Factors and Successful Interventions*, ed. Rolf Loeber and David Farrington (Thousand Oaks: Sage, 1998), 313.

49. Office of Juvenile Justice and Delinquency Prevention, *Effective Interventions for Serious Juvenile Offenders*, by Mark Lipsey, David Wilson, and Lynn Cothern (Washington, DC: U.S. Department of Justice).

50. John Irwin and James Austin, *It's About Time: America's Imprisonment Binge* (Belmont: Wadsworth Publishing, 1994).

51. Malcolm Klein, *The American Street Gang* (New York: Oxford, 1995).

52. Richard Lundman, *Prevention and Control of Juvenile Delinquency* (New York: Oxford, 2001).

53. James Howell *Preventing & Reducing Juvenile Delinquency: A Comprehensive Framework* (Thousand Oaks: Sage, 2003).

*Melanie Taylor** is currently a doctoral student in the School of Criminology and Criminal Justice at Arizona State University.

Donna Bishop is a professor at the College of Criminal Justice at Northeastern University.

Scott H. Decker is Foundation Professor and director of the School of Criminology and Criminal Justice at Arizona State University.

Donna M. Bishop and Scott H. Decker, "Punishment and Control: Juvenile Justice Reform in the U.S.," in *International Handbook of Juvenile Justice*, ed. Josine Junger-Tas and Scott H. Decker (New York: Springer 2006) (updated August 2011). Article updated and reprinted with kind permission from Springer Science+Business Media B.V.

DISCUSSION QUESTIONS

1. What is the proper function of the juvenile court? What is more important: for courts to offer youth rehabilitative or treatment services or for courts to be used for punishment and crime control?

2. Why were juvenile courts formed? Do the same principles that applied at the founding of the juvenile justice system hold true today?

3. Based on their history, how do you think juvenile courts will change in the future? What changes would be positive, what changes would be negative?

4. Is having a separate court for juveniles accused of committing crimes still important? Why or why not?

Chapter 2:

Understanding and Addressing
Disproportionate Minority Contact

One of the most troubling aspects of the administration of justice in America is that purportedly race-neutral laws target, or at the very least are unevenly applied to, youth of color. A disproportionate number of minority youth become trapped in the justice system every day. For example, in Chicago, as in other cities, youth of color are more likely to go to prison than to go to college.[1] This chapter gives readers a greater understanding of disproportionate minority contact (DMC) in the juvenile justice system and examines resulting problems, as well as some initiatives under way to reduce and prevent it.

The National Conference of State Legislatures' article "Disproportionate Minority Contact" lays out the framework of the issue. After providing troubling statistics, the article lists possible causes of DMC and then reviews some current efforts to address this problem. The next selection, "Decisions that Drive Disparity: Minority Overrepresentation in the Juvenile Justice System," by Dr. Ashley Nellis of The Sentencing Project, explores the causes and consequences of DMC in greater depth before moving on to policy recommendations and identifying community, evidence-based initiatives that can combat DMC. Finally, in "Dreams Denied: The Over-Incarceration of Youth of Color," James Bell of the W. Haywood Burns Institute discusses strategies for fighting disproportionate minority contact. Bell opens by providing the historical background surrounding the issue, then outlines four steps created by the Institute that juvenile justice communities can implement to reduce or prevent racial inequities.

NOTE

1. Michelle Alexander, *The New Jim Crow: Mass Incarceration in the Age of Colorblindness* (New York: The New Press, 2010).

Disproportionate Minority Contact

by the National Conference of State Legislatures*

INTRODUCTION

Youth of color are disproportionately overrepresented throughout juvenile justice systems in nearly every state. Disproportionality is recognized as a concerning problem by both states and the federal government. In response to the disconcerting numbers, state legislatures have taken measures to study the causes of disproportionality, identify strategies to reduce it and to create a fundamentally fair system.

Minority youth come into contact with the juvenile system at a higher rate than their white counterparts. Minority youth are overrepresented at every step

---

❑ Disparity

There are approximately 70.5 million youth aged 10–17; 59 percent are white, and 41 percent are racial minorities. In contrast, 31 percent of youth detained by law enforcement officials are white, while 69 percent are minorities.

The disparity is particularly stark for African American and Latino youth. African American youth represent 13 percent of the juvenile population; however, they are 31 percent of those arrested, 42 percent of those detained, 39 percent of those placed in a residential facility, 32 percent of those on probation, 35 percent of those adjudicated, 40 percent of those transferred to adult prison, and 58 percent of those sentenced to prison (2007). African American youth are four times more likely to be incarcerated than white youth.

In short-term juvenile detention facilities, 42 percent of inmates are African American, 25 percent are Latino and 30 percent are white. In long-term secure juvenile facilities, 40 percent of inmates are African American, 29 percent are Latino and 32 percent are white. In adult facilities, 36 percent of juvenile inmates are African American, 24 percent are Latino and 25 percent are white. From 2000 to 2008, the percentage of Latino youth in adult prisons increased from 12 percent to 20 percent.

---

of the process—they are more likely to be arrested, detained and confined. The proportion of minorities increases with each successive step into the system. Research by the National Council on Crime and Delinquency and the Center for Children's Law and Policy also indicates that minority youth receive harsher treatment than white youth. They are more likely to be confined and sentenced for longer periods of time and are less likely to receive alternative sentences or probation.

EXPLANATIONS FOR RACIAL AND ETHNIC DISPROPORTIONALITY

Overrepresentation cannot be explained by offending rates. Jurisdictional differences, various police practices, punitive juvenile crime legislation, and racial and ethnic-based biases all play a role in creating **race** disparities.

Jurisdiction

According to the Office of Juvenile Justice and Delinquency Prevention (OJJDP), the jurisdiction in which a juvenile is processed can influence the outcome of the case. Cases adjudicated in urban areas are more likely to result in harsher penalties than similar cases adjudicated in non-urban areas. On the other hand, some offenses like drug possession are not considered serious in urban areas, but are considered serious in rural and suburban areas. Because minority populations are concentrated in urban areas, a geographic effect may work to overrepresent minorities statewide.

Furthermore, minority youth crimes in urban areas tend to be more visible. For instance, white youth tend to use and sell drugs from their homes, while minority youth are more likely to do so on street corners or in public neighborhood gathering spots.

Law Enforcement

Police practices that target low-income, urban neighborhoods and the use of group arrest procedures contribute to racial and ethnic disparities in the juvenile justice system. Low-income neighborhoods, particularly in urban areas, are often majority minority.

Therefore, increased police presence in these areas leads to increased police contact with minorities and a greater opportunity for police officers to witness crimes committed by minority youth. OJJDP arrest rate statistics show that

African American youth are arrested at much higher rates than their white counterparts for drug, property and violent crimes.

Overrepresentation of minority youth at the initial contact with law enforcement carries over to each successive step in the juvenile justice process. The increased probability of arrest, partially due to increased police presence in disproportionately minority communities, makes it more likely that minority youth will have longer criminal histories. Due to this fact, minority youth are more likely to be charged harshly and given stricter sentences.

Adult Treatment of Juveniles

As a result of the increase in juvenile crimes in the early 1990s, many states enacted automatic transfer, direct file and judicial waiver laws.

- Automatic transfer laws categorically exempt prosecution of certain offenses from juvenile court jurisdiction, allowing juveniles to be adjudicated automatically in criminal courts. Twenty-nine states have automatic transfer laws, which are also referred to as statutory exclusion laws.

- Direct file laws grant prosecutors discretion to charge juveniles as adults. Fourteen states and the District of Columbia have such laws.

- Judicial waiver laws allow juvenile court judges to waive jurisdiction so juveniles can be adjudicated in criminal courts. Forty-four stares and the District of Columbia allow discretionary judicial waivers, 14 states and the District of Columbia allow presumptive judicial waivers, and 15 states have mandatory judicial waiver laws.

Research indicates that automatic transfer provisions have disproportionately affected minority youth. According to a 1997 survey on minority youth in secure facilities, these juveniles were transferred to criminal court around five times their proportion of the general population in Connecticut, Massachusetts, Pennsylvania, and Rhode Island.

Minority youth were overrepresented by four times their population in Montana and Tennessee, and by around three times in Maryland and New Jersey. In a 1996 evaluation of transfers of minority youth to criminal court in California, African American and Latino youth were six times more likely than whites to be transferred. In Los Angeles County alone, African American and Latino juveniles were 12 and 6 times, respectively, more likely to be adjudicated as adults than whites.

According to a 2007 study commissioned by the Campaign for Youth Justice, 83 percent of criminal court cases with juvenile defendants involved minority youth. For cases involving African American youth, 50 percent were transferred via statutory exclusion, 32 percent were transferred under direct file laws, and 19 percent were transferred by judicial waiver. A 2009 Campaign for Youth Justice report estimates that Latino youth are 43 percent more likely to be waived to adult court than white youth.

A 2007 National Council on Crime and Delinquency report estimated that, in 2002, minority youth accounted for 75 percent of the 4,100 juveniles admitted to adult state prisons nationwide. African American youth reportedly are 58 percent of total admissions to adult prisons. The same report found that nearly every state reported minority youth as overrepresented and white youth as underrepresented in admissions to adult state prisons.

Racial Bias

Overt and indirect racial biases contribute to creating the overrepresentation of minority youth in the system. OJJDP's analysis of various studies spanning 12 years reveals that, in approximately two-thirds of the studies, "negative racial and ethnic effects" were present at various stages of the juvenile justice process.

The complex explanations for the disproportionality, along with sensitive racial and ethnic issues, make it an important and difficult challenge for states.

INITIATIVES TO REDUCE THE RACIAL AND ETHNIC DISPARITIES

Federal Action

The federal Juvenile Justice and Delinquency Prevention Act (JJDPA), originally passed in 1974, sets standards for local and state juvenile justice systems and provides funding to encourage reform. To be eligible for funding, states must comply with the law's four core protections, one of which regards racial and ethnic disproportionality. This provision requires states to address the overrepresentation of minority youth at key stages of the juvenile justice process, from arrest to detention to confinement. The OJJDP, created by the JJDPA, is the central national office that facilitates coordination and provides leadership and resources to help states improve their systems.

States use various methods to address the disproportionality, including collecting data to determine the extent of the problem; establishing task forces and commissions to study policies to facilitate racially neutral decisions throughout the system; developing and expanding early intervention services for minority youth and their families; and creating alternatives to incarceration.

Models for Change

Models for Change is a national initiative funded by the John D. and Catherine T. MacArthur Foundation to accelerate reform of juvenile justice systems across the country. Focused on efforts in select states, the initiative aims to create replicable models for reform that effectively hold young people accountable for their actions, provide for their rehabilitation, protect them from harm, increase their life chances, and manage the risk they pose to themselves and to public safety. The Models for Change Research Initiative emphasizes evidence-based practices and provides support to the states in develop[ing], implement[ing], and sustain[ing] lasting reform. Targeted juvenile justice leverage points where success will stimulate systemwide reforms [include]:

- Aftercare
- Racial and ethnic fairness/Disproportionate minority contact
- Mental health
- Community-based alternatives
- Right-sizing jurisdiction
- Evidence-based practices
- Juvenile indigent defense

While all states involved in the Models for Change initiative are working to reduce racial and ethnic disparities in the juvenile justice system, the DMC Action Network was launched in 2007 to bring together teams from select local jurisdictions, expose them to the latest thinking of national experts, and give them an opportunity to learn from one another about effective ways to reduce the disproportionate contact of minority and ethnic youth with the juvenile justice system.

The DMC Action Network is active in the four core states and in four additional partner states—Kansas, Maryland, North Carolina, and Wisconsin. Twelve localities originally participated in the DMC Action Network. Each locality was required to implement at least two strategic innovations to help reduce disparities. Examples of strategic innovations include initiatives on collecting and reporting data, increasing cultural competency,[1] implementing detention alternatives, and reducing detention of post-disposition youth by using graduated sanctions or expediting post-disposition placements. Nine additional sites in Kansas, Maryland, North Carolina, Pennsylvania and Washington were added in 2009.

THE ORIGINAL 12 DMC ACTION NETWORK
LOCALITIES AND THEIR PROGRESS

- **Peoria, Illinois**
  In-school restorative justice programs, such as peer juries and peacemaking circles, helped reduce school referrals to secure detention by 35 percent, including a 43 percent decrease in referrals of African American students.

- **Sedgwick County, Kansas**
  Secure detention days were reduced by 45 percent, partially due to objective detention screening, alternatives to detention, and improved advocacy for diversion.

- **Jefferson Parish, Louisiana**
  Juvenile justice databases were updated for more accurate race and ethnic data collection. After full implementation of the detention screening tool, the detention population decreased by 25 percent.

- **Rapides Parish, Louisiana**
  A detention screening instrument was recently developed and tested. In July 1008, the instrument was used to guide decisions on whether a juvenile went to a secure facility, a detention alternative, or to a parent or guardian.

- **Baltimore City, Maryland**
  Following a detention utilization study that showed 60 percent of juveniles admitted to secure detention had a risk assessment score low enough to not warrant detention, the Pre-Adjudication Coordination and Training (PACT) Center, a community-based detention alternative, was created. Ninety-five percent of PACT participants were present for their court hearings, and 93 percent did not receive additional charges while in the program.

- **Union County, North Carolina**
  Plans developed to translate common forms into Spanish, provide cultural competency training, and conduct community forums. A graduated sanctions grid for probation violations reduced Union County's use of secure detention. A race and ethnic questionnaire was implemented at intake to better understand needs related to race, ethnicity and language.

- **Allegheny County, Pennsylvania**
  A failure to adjust study on post-disposition placements was conducted to identify and better understand disparities.

- **Berks County, Pennsylvania**
  A new detention screening instrument was implemented, and it reduced the average daily detention population by 50 percent. The Probation

Department has eliminated 24 beds in its secure detention facility—it removed locks from doors and now uses the space for several youth and family programs. Further, as a result of closely examining data used in decision making, Berks began using multi-systemic therapy instead of secure placements for post-disposition youth; it saved $4 million in the first year alone.

- Philadelphia, Pennsylvania
  A system of graduated sanctions was developed, along with a graduated sanctions court. The Youth-Law Enforcement curriculum in the Police Academy has also been expanded to include a module of cadet training involving direct contact with youth.

- Benton/Franklin Counties, Washington
  The Benton/Franklin Juvenile Court has made numerous community engagement attempts to better understand the needs, challenges and concerns of racial minority youth. The attempts included a needs assessment survey and a focus group process specifically for African American youth assigned to probation and their parents or guardians.

- Pierce County, Washington
  In an attempt to increase cultural competency in the evidence-based program functional family therapy, a number of actions have been taken, including the implementation of a specialized caseload for minority youth, cultural competency training, and increased staff diversity. A two-fold increase in completion in this program has occurred, which is expected to favorably affect African American youth.

- Rock County, Wisconsin
  An evidence-based, detention diversion program, aggression replacement training, was implemented, which has led to a 61 percent increase in minority youth diverted from detention. Due to policy reform, the site has also seen a 50 percent decline in African American youth being waived into adult criminal court since 2006.

Juvenile Detention Alternatives Initiative

The Juvenile Detention Alternative Initiative (JDAI) was founded by the Annie E. Casey Foundation to address the efficiency and effectiveness of juvenile detention. As one of JDAI's eight core strategies, JDAI gives priority to reducing racial disparities as an integral detention reform strategy.

Currently, there are 110 JDAI sites in 27 states and the District of Columbia. Within these sites, JDAI has made substantial progress in reducing the overrepresentation of minority youth in the system and in confinement, in particular. JDAI has worked to reduce the percentage of minority youth in secure detention and reduce the number of minority youth in detention generally.

JDAI has achieved this by implementing specific strategies that target racial disparities at the critical processing point of pretrial detention. JDAI developed risk assessment instruments for detention admissions screening; created new or enhanced alternative detention programs; expedited case processing to reduce time spent in secure detention; and promoted new policies and practices for responding to youth who have violated probation, have outstanding warrants or are awaiting placement, In addition, JDAI continues to promote collaboration between agencies and among stakeholders. JDAI also relies heavily on data to identify stages of disproportionate treatment, advocates for the use of objective decision-making and encourages cultural competency.

Recent JDAI Accomplishments

- **Multnomah County, Oregon**
  A detention intake team was created to evaluate youth in custody and help successfully implement risk assessment instruments and alternatives to detention. Between 1995 (when risk assessment instruments were first implemented) and 2000, the gap between detained white and minority youth—consisting of African Americans and Latinos—narrowed from around 11 percent to roughly 2 percent. Overall detention admissions were reduced by 65 percent. Also critical to the site's success was collaboration with law enforcement personnel and policymakers, sound data collection, and training to raise awareness about **race** disproportionality.

- **Cook County, Illinois**
  Between 1996 and 2000, the number of minority youth in detention dropped 31 percent. Detention alternatives were developed for youth who did not pose a serious threat. Alternatives include community-based evening reporting centers that offer constructive activities during afternoons and early evenings so youth can stay at home and in school.

- **Santa Cruz County, California**
  JDAI worked to reduce high rates of minority detention that emphasized streamlining case management and risk assessment screening tools. In Santa Cruz, a risk assessment instrument was used to detain only high-risk offenders; alternative programs and procedures were developed for low- and medium-risk youth. Partnerships with community organizations to provide

culturally responsive alternatives to detention were critical. This included recognizing the importance of having a bilingual staff and staff with close community ties and life experience that help them relate to youth.

STATE ACTION

During the 1990s, states began to enact policies prescribing methods to curb the overrepresentation of minority youth in the juvenile justice system. Washington was the first, passing legislation in 1993 to link county funding to programs that address overrepresentation, improve data collection, and implement cultural and ethnic training for judges and juvenile court personnel. Subsequent Washington laws required overrepresentation reporting by state agencies, the implementation of pilot programs to reduce inequality in juvenile prosecution, and the development of detention screening instruments.

Other states followed with similar efforts in the late 1990s and early 2000s. In response to the high rates of disproportionality, Connecticut formed a 20-member inter-branch Commission on Racial and Ethnic Disparity in the criminal justice system to explore ways to reduce the number of African Americans and Latinos in the system, including the juvenile justice system. In North Carolina, the

---

❑ Burns Institute

The W. Haywood Burns Institute (BI) has worked in more than 50 jurisdictions to reduce racial and ethnic disparities. The BI has created and implemented a data template that quickly allows disparities and various decision points to be identified. In nearly every jurisdiction, youth of color are overrepresented and detained for minor misbehaviors that do not result in detention for most white youth. The BI incorporates neighborhood involvement and stakeholder alliances to deconstruct the institutional culture and decision-making process that result in disparities. A key component of this work is surveying probation, law enforcement and judicial officers to determine their attitudes and perceptions about disparities and conducting department-wide trainings to highlight practices that result in disparities.

Changes in policies and practices that result in reducing disparities without jeopardizing public safety include creating detention alternatives for family disputes, instituting court notification systems, interventions prior to probation violations and behavior response grids.

Governor's Crime Commission created a Disproportionate Minority Contact Committee to evaluate overall disproportionality and make recommendations to reduce racial disparities. Missouri took steps to require the state court administrator to develop standards, training and assessment on racial disparities. Oregon established the Office of Minority Services as an independent state agency and formed pilot programs to initiate cultural competency training and detention alternatives. Oregon is also in its tenth year of conducting an annual governor's summit on minority overrepresentation in the juvenile justice system; attendees include judges, attorneys, among others.

In 2007, South Dakota established pilot programs in three cities to address the higher rates of contact with the juvenile system for minority youth. The arrest rate for Native American youth in South Dakota is almost 2.5 times greater than for white youth, and they also are overrepresented in other areas of the state juvenile justice system. Federal funding from the JJDPA is helping South Dakota implement the programs, which focus on Native American cultural awareness and agency cultural assessment training for juvenile justice practitioners and service providers.

In Iowa, a Youth Race and Detention Task Force established in 2007 is addressing racial and ethnic disproportionality—particularly for African American youth—in juvenile detention centers. Wisconsin's governor formed a Commission on Reducing Racial Disparities in 2007 that is to recommend strategies and solutions for decreasing minority youth overrepresentation within the state's criminal justice system. The commission, in its final report in 2008, listed numerous recommendations including better data collection, cultural awareness, stronger eligibility requirements for public defenders, and adequate interpreters throughout the judicial process.

Colorado's judicial and executive branches held a 2007 summit that was attended by more than 200 judges, judicial officers, prosecutors, child welfare administrators and others to discuss overrepresentation of minority youth in the state's juvenile court system. The Colorado Court Improvement Committee also sponsored cultural competency training for juvenile court personnel to address race disproportionality and raise awareness of culturally appropriate resources and approaches.

Iowa became the first state in 2008 to require a "minority impact statement," which is required for proposed legislation related to crimes, sentencing, parole and probation—as well as for any grant application to a state agency A statement for proposed criminal legislation must include the estimated number of criminal cases the bill will affect and the bill's impact on minorities, its fiscal impact, and its impact on existing correction facilities and resources. Connecticut soon followed, requiring racial and ethnic impact statements for bills and amendments that could, if passed, increase or decrease the pretrial or sentenced population of state correctional facilities. Similar to fiscal impact statements, the new requirements seek to provide greater understanding of the implications of a proposed law for minorities.

In Pennsylvania, a disproportionality subcommittee of a state advisory group has been working to improve the relationships between youth and law enforcement personnel in communities. Through a series of local forums, law enforcement officials and youth meet to learn from one another.

Indiana created a Board for the Coordination of Programs Serving Vulnerable Individuals. Vulnerable individuals are defined as youth of color who receive services or who are otherwise vulnerable. The board has numerous duties, including coordinating racial and ethnic-specific data collection; recommending early intervention and prevention programs; and monitoring, supporting and improving efforts to reduce disproportionate representation of youth of color in youth services. In 2008, Virginia adopted a law directing the Joint Commission on Health Care to continue its study of the mental health needs and treatment of young minorities.

Maryland enacted a 2010 law requiring cultural competency model training for all law enforcement officers assigned to public school buildings and grounds.

The training is to facilitate improved communication and understanding between the officers and school communities. The training requires personal exposure to the assigned community and learning about the available resources in order to prevent juvenile arrests.

According to OJJDP's 2007 formula grant calculations, 33 states have designated state-level coordinators to address race disproportionality; 37 states have subcommittees under their state advisory groups; and 34 states have invested financial support for local reduction sites that are working on the issue.

STRATEGIES FOR THE FUTURE

As states continue to study and formulate policies to reduce racial and ethnic disparities, some common problems and effective strategies are emerging. Reduction efforts are predominantly data driven; however, data collection is a common problem because race identification often is complex and personal. A standardized model for uniform data collection helps local data collectors accurately record and report information.

One important aspect of data collection is to recognize and record both race and ethnicity. Research suggests that, if ethnicity and race are not identified separately, Latino youth may be significantly undercounted. Guidelines from the National Center for Juvenile Justice and the Center for Children's Law and Policy suggest a series of questions—in addition to self-identification, observation and other sources such as court documents—to help obtain the most accurate and detailed documentation. Reliable data are important to effective analysis and development of appropriate solutions to reduce racial disparities. Awareness is a critical aspect of reducing institutional biases. The Models for Change initiative has raised awareness about racial and ethnic disproportionality among community representatives, leaders, parents and others. Some states have sponsored seminars and training sessions for prosecutors, judges, agency personnel and others involved in the juvenile justice process. According to OJJDP, 15 states have implemented cultural competency training and/or organization cultural competency assessments. Many counties, parishes and cities also have implemented awareness programs.

In line with JJDPA's system-wide effort to address racial and ethnic disproportionality, the Center for Children's Law and Policy and the Models for Change initiative suggest states analyze and address the problem at nine critical processing points. The Center for Children's Law and Policy encourages creation of an oversight body composed of stakeholders to identify where disparities exist, pinpoint unnecessary juvenile justice system involvement, and monitor implementation of reforms to address disproportionate minority representation. One specific suggestion is to use standardized screenings and protocols, which would remove subjectivity in decision-making.

Risk assessment that helps avoid overuse of secure detention also helps to reduce minority detention and overrepresentation. The Juvenile Detention Alternatives Initiative has used risk assessment instruments with measurable success in local programs, particularly in Multnomah County, Ore.

Appropriate use of alternatives to secure confinement of juveniles in correction facilities can be used to reduce disproportionality. These include community-based services and graduated parole violation sanctions. According to the Office of Juvenile Justice and Delinquency Prevention, 19 states currently use objective risk assessment instruments, and 25 fund alternatives to detention. Many counties, parishes and cities also have implemented such reforms.

CONCLUSION

The overrepresentation of minority youth in the juvenile system remains a complex issue for states. It also prompts questions about equality of treatment for youth by police, courts and other personnel in criminal and juvenile justice systems. How these juveniles are handled can significantly affect their development and future opportunities. State attention to the issue, along with the research and resources of various private organizations, can strengthen efforts to reduce the disproportionality and improve fairness for all youth in juvenile justice systems.

NOTE

1. In the fourth edition of OJJDP's *Disproportionate Minority Contact Technical Assistance Manual*, cultural competency is "defined as a set of congruent behaviors, attitudes, and policies that interface with each other in a system, an agency, or a network of professionals to work effectively in cross-cultural situations." The manual states that "[c]ultural competency training can engender a deeper awareness of cultural factors."

*The National Conference of State Legislatures (NCSL) is a bipartisan organization that serves the legislators and staffs of the nation's 50 states, its commonwealths and territories. NCSL provides research, technical assistance and opportunities for policymakers. This article originally appeared as a chapter in *Juvenile Justice Guidebook for Legislators*, the preparation of which was directed by Sarah Hammond in NCSL's Denver, Colorado, office. Chon-hwa Lee, a consultant to the project, was principal author of this article. Donna Lyons in NCSL's Criminal Justice Program provided review assistance; Vicky McPheron, also in the Criminal Justice Program, provided administrative assistance; and Leann Stelzer in the NCSL Communications Program edited and assisted in production. Special thanks to reviewers of the DMC chapter:

James Bell, Mark Soler and Candice Jones and to Laurie Garduque, Director of Juvenile Justice, MacArthur Foundation.

National Conference of State Legislatures, "Disproportionate Minority Contact," in *Juvenile Justice Guidebook for Legislators* (Washington, DC, and Denver, CO, 2011), http://www.ncsl.org/documents/cj/jjguidebook-DMC.pdf.

Used by Permission.

Decisions that Drive Disparity: Minority Overrepresentation in the Juvenile Justice System

by Ashley Nellis*

INTRODUCTION

Numerous studies now exist that try to explain the presence, cause, and severity of racial and ethnic disparity among youth in the juvenile justice system. A newer set of works explores reasons why disproportionate minority contact (DMC) reduction efforts fail. In recent years, generous investments from private foundations have led to a renewed sense of hope for success in the seemingly intractable problem of minority overrepresentation in the juvenile justice system, which is frequently the gateway to prison.

In 2007, official juvenile arrest statistics showed that while African Americans under 18 years old accounted for only 17% of the general population, they accounted for 51% of arrests for juvenile violent offenses and 32% of arrests for juvenile property crimes (Puzzanchera, 2009). In nearly all juvenile justice systems youth of color enter and stay in the system with much greater frequency than white youth. Regardless of the causes for DMC, our society should be alarmed by the fact that, if current trends continue, one in three black males born today will end up in prison (and one in 6 Latino males). Simply knowing the disparities exist for youth of color in the juvenile justice system does not absolve the responsibility to eliminate it.

The federal government has acknowledged the presence and severity of DMC and taken steps to assist states and localities in reducing it. For the past twenty years, it has mandated that federally-funded state juvenile justice systems abide by certain requirements under the Juvenile Justice Delinquency and Prevention Act (Pub. L. 93-415, 42 USC 5601 et seq.). Beginning in 1992, these requirements were tied to a potential loss of federal juvenile justice funds and expanded to address disproportionate minority confinement (DMC) in the juvenile justice system; in 2002, this requirement was refined to include racial and ethnic disparity at all points of contact. Thus "DMC" came to mean disproportionate minority contact with the juvenile justice system. Yet despite this federal mandate to address DMC, racial and ethnic disparities continue to permeate juvenile justice systems.

Many early DMC initiatives lacked guidance and oversight, were handicapped by political considerations and insufficient resources, and were poorly implemented. Not surprisingly, these early efforts, primarily focused only on assessing the problem, produced unsatisfactory results (Hamparian & Leiber, 1997; Leiber, 2002; Pope & Leiber, 2005). Since that time, methods for detecting minority overrepresentation and diagnosing its source(s) have made great improvements, yet states and localities are still stalled between the stages of identifying causes and moving toward remedying the problem.

In addition to the collection of studies examining where and why DMC is present, there is a range of opinions as to why youth of color continue to be overrepresented in the juvenile justice system despite the federal mandate and the numerous empirically-derived suggestions for reducing it. Some attribute this lack of progress to the fact that while state juvenile justice systems are federally mandated to study and address DMC, their ability to reduce it is impaired when the cause of DMC is determined to be outside the juvenile justice system (Piquero, 2008; Tracy, 2005).

Tracy (2005) suggests that progress on reducing DMC is greatly impeded by the politicized process inherent in the federal mandate. He further notes that the federal law and subsequent federal regulations assume that DMC is caused by system bias rather than differential offending patterns despite the lack of concrete evidence to demonstrate that this is the case (Tracy, 2005). He suggests that this assumption hampers the ability to reduce DMC. Others note that DMC could be the result of factors that originate from the system or the individual, but that attempts to remedy are sure to fail until jurisdictions determine the cause of DMC before launching into a solution (Nellis, 2005).

EXPLANATIONS

Research has identified several contributors to racial and ethnic disparity among those in the juvenile justice system. The most frequently identified causes of DMC include selective police enforcement (Feld, 1991; Huizinga et al., 2007), differential opportunities for treatment (U.S. Department of Health and Human Services, 2001), institutional racism (Bishop & Frazier, 1996; Trepaigner, 2007), indirect effects of socioeconomic factors (Hawkins, Laub, Lauritsen, & Cothern, 2000; Hsia, Bridges, & McHale, 2004; Pope and Snyder, 2003; Snyder and Sickmund, 1999), differential offending (Blumstein, 1995; Hawkins, Laub, & Lauritsen, 1998; Piquero & Brame, 2007; Pope & Snyder, 2003; Tracy, 2005), biased risk assessment instruments (Bridges & Steen, 1998; Chapman et al., 2003), differential administrative practices (Bridges & Steen, 1998), unequal access to effective legal counsel (Fagan, Forst, & Vivona, 1987), and legislative policies that disparately impact youth of color (Fabella et al., 2008; Richardson et. al, 2008). While any one of these contributors could lead to DMC on its own, it is more often the case that multiple contributors work simultaneously to increase representation of youth of color in the juvenile justice system.

These potential causes for minority overrepresentation have been studied extensively. More recently, two additional issues have been identified as reasons for the overrepresentation of youth of color: the use of detention to provide social services that would otherwise not be available to some youth, and school-based policies that drive youth of color into the system because of their disproportionate impact on this population.

Lack of Buy-In from Juvenile Justice Decisionmakers

Policies and practices to reduce DMC are only successful if the professionals tasked with carrying them out support them. Some research finds, however, that racially-biased perceptions about youth can lead to unwarranted disparity in treatment (Leiber, 1993, 2002). Unlike the adult criminal justice system, where courtroom outcomes are increasingly the result of mandatory sentences, the juvenile justice system still largely operates by discretionary decisionmaking. Some research has been completed on the perceptions of judges and other courtroom workgroup members to assess reasons behind their decisions to process or release youth who come into contact with the juvenile justice system.

A theme that emerges from this level of research is that some members of the courtroom workgroup do not fully accept DMC as a problem that they can and should address in their daily work. A recent study explored attitudes of probation officers in four Midwestern states and found that fewer than one half of the respondents agreed that minority overrepresentation was a serious problem. Moreover, this view is split along racial lines: White probation officers were significantly more likely than Black probation officers to disagree with the suggestion that DMC is a problem that the court must address and were significantly more likely to be ambivalent about the gravity of the DMC problem (Ward, Kupchik, Parker, & Starks, 2011).

Some explanation for the persistence of DMC has also been attributed to well-intentioned misuse of the juvenile justice system to meet the needs of youth who would otherwise not receive services such as mental health treatment (Bell et al., 2009; Cahn 2006; Kempf-Leonard, 2007). To this point, Cahn notes, "It is not so much the criminality of the behavior that brings juveniles into the justice system, but the lack of viable alternatives and diversion programs for children with severe [problems] expelled from school, and children whose families cannot provide adequate care. Incarceration of youth becomes the default response to any deviant behavior with which the justice system and other youth serving systems are unable to cope" (Cahn, 2006).

Detention for the purpose of accessing services is not the intended purpose of the juvenile justice system and leads to many long-lasting collateral consequences for youth, including associations with high-risk individuals (Lowencamp & Latessa, 2004) and deviant labeling (Thio, 1972). Staff education, program resources in high-need areas, and alternatives to detention aim to alleviate this misuse of the juvenile justice system as a social service agency.

School-Based Policies

Legislative and administrative policies such as school-related "zero tolerance" policies can create additional drivers for the racial and ethnic disparity in the juvenile justice system (Greene, Pranis, & Zeidenberg 2006; Hirschfield, 2008; Nellis, 2005; Sannah & Jacobs, 2008; Verdugo, 2002). A set of similar policies are said to have created the "school to prison pipeline" which emerged in a handful of states in the late 1980s, and gained federal endorsement in 1994 with President Clinton's signing of the Gun-Free Schools Act (20 U.S.C. Chapter 70, Section 8921), which mandated student expulsion for one year following referral to criminal or juvenile court for possession of a weapon. Following the passage of this Act, schools throughout the nation moved quickly to develop varieties of zero-tolerance policies not only for presence of weapons, but also drugs, alcohol, tobacco, and/or violence on school campuses (Hirschfield, 2008). These policies are more likely to exist in urban low-income school districts that include large numbers of youth of color (Verdugo, 2002).

The process of criminalizing school infractions through harsh school discipline policies has an especially negative impact on youth of color because of the predispositions of school systems to suspend minority youth despite a lack of behavioral differences compared to white students (Skiba & Rausch, 2006). A recent study that examined elementary school children in 990 different classrooms again demonstrated that, despite similarities in behavior, grades, and demeanor, young African American students are substantially more likely to be disciplined than white students. In this study, African American students were 30% more likely to be formally disciplined than white students (Rocque & Peternoster, 2011).

Policies and practices that have a disparate impact on youth of color, even though they may be unintentional, have long-standing consequences at the individual and community level. For instance, school push-out policies such as zero-tolerance and three strikes policies force young students to become disengaged from school, and the impact is more likely to be felt for youth of color. This sets up a series of consequences for youth's contact with other child-serving systems. Contact with the justice system reduces options for education, housing, and employment, and also weakens the stability of communities of color and results in a deepening of the divide between whites and nonwhites (Cahn, 2006; Clear, Rose, & Ryder, 2001).

WHAT WORKS? PROMISING INITIATIVES TO REDUCE DMC

Eliminating racial and ethnic disparities in the juvenile justice system is indeed a daunting task, but modest successes have been observed in recent years. Even though the causes of DMC derive from multiple sources and systems, the juvenile justice system can take steps to abate damage to youth of color through evidence-based actions.

Promising strategies to reduce DMC share a number of traits. The sharing of these successes has allowed for effective strategies that can be replicated in similarly situated environments. First, such strategies have community support; they tend to originate from local community concerns and include stakeholders from the community who have been affected by minority overrepresentation (Bell, et al., 2009; Soler & Garry, 2009).

Second, the strategies consistently rely on data from a variety of sources to identify where efforts should be undertaken and whether these need to be modified over time (Bell & Ridolfi, 2008; Bell et al., 2009). For example, if it is determined that referrals to the police from school-based incidents are racially disproportionate, this could mean that school-based law enforcement strategies are contributing to DMC. Third, effective strategies are transparent about their focus, their successes and their failures, and acknowledge that important lessons can be learned from both. And finally, they are committed to a long-term investment in lowering DMC that relies on evidence-based practices and follow-through with sustainable initiatives. DMC must remain a priority in order for communities to observe sustained drops in overrepresentation (Soler & Garry, 2009).

Over the years, private foundations have invested in juvenile justice reform in a number of states, and many of these investments aim to reduce DMC. For example, beginning in 2004 the MacArthur Foundation undertook a multiyear, $100 million investment in juvenile justice reforms nationwide, with a concentrated focus in four states (Illinois, Louisiana, Pennsylvania, and Washington).

In 2007, the foundation undertook a long-term investment in 12 county-level Action Network sites that work specifically on DMC initiatives in eight states: Illinois, Kansas, Louisiana, Maryland, North Carolina, Pennsylvania, Washington, and Wisconsin. The Action Network states work as a peer network of collaborations involving multiple state and local juvenile justice allies that address specific reform issues, including DMC. Specifically, the DMC Action Network states focus on making improvements in tracking and reporting data, enhanced cultural competency, community investment, diversion, and expanded alternatives to detention that are culturally diverse (Models for Change, 2009).

As a result of these investments at the county level, jurisdictions have begun to report improvements in DMC. In Berks County, PA, the DMC Action Network site committed to several steps: enhancing Spanish-language capability and cultural competence; reducing minority detentions through improved assessment screening and diversion; recruiting nontraditional service providers; and developing workforce opportunities.

In Peoria, IL, another DMC Action Network site, analysis of arrest data revealed a disproportionately high number of arrests for aggravated battery. Upon closer inspection it was found that many arrests resulted from fights at school. Once alternative conflict strategies were put into place, arrests for African American youth dropped 43% in one year (Griffin, 2008).

The W. Haywood Burns Institute (BI) has a mission to ensure equity and justice for all youth through providing technical assistance to certain eligible jurisdictions in facing and correcting their DMC problem. Some promising outcomes have been reported. For example, in Baltimore County, Maryland, the BI worked with local community stakeholders to develop DMC-reducing policies that resulted in a nearly 50% decline in the number of youth who were held in secure detention for failure to appear in court. In Pima County, Arizona, the Burns Institute staff worked with officials from probation, the courts, and members of the community to develop and rely on alternatives to detention. As a result, the county experienced a 50% drop in detention use among Black youth over the past 5 years (Bell et al., 2009).

RECOMMENDATIONS FOR REFORM

Reverse Disparity-Causing Policies

Efforts to provide youth, especially youth of color, with necessary programs and services will not show the desired results until disparity-causing policies are reversed. While some minority overrepresentation can be explained by differential offending patterns, and perhaps another portion can be explained by unequal services and opportunities available for youth of color, minority over-representation is also driven by policies and practices that disparately impact youth of color. Foremost among these are the various school exclusion policies that drive young people away from opportunities for success and toward involvement with the courts, juvenile justice systems, and prisons.

Strengthen Federal Policies on Reducing DMC

The Juvenile Justice and Delinquency Prevention Act (JJDPA) has not been reauthorized since 2002, and substantive changes have not been made to the Act in over a decade. National, state, and local child advocates have been urging the U.S. Congress to reauthorize the JJDPA since 2007, but have not succeeded as of this writing.

The JJDPA needs to be strengthened in its attention to the overrepresentation of youth of color. Based on recommendations submitted from policy analysts, practitioners, and advocates, the following recommendations are offered to improve the DMC focus within the JJDPA:

1. Establish coordinating bodies (i.e., DMC subcommittees or task forces) to oversee efforts to reduce disparities;

2. Identify key decision points in the system contributing to disparities;

3. Create systems to collect local data at every point of contact youth may have with the juvenile justice system (by race, ethnicity and offense) to identify where disparities exist and the causes of those disparities.

4. Develop and implement plans to address disparities that include measurable objectives for policy or practice change that are based on data; and

5. Publicly report findings and progress in efforts to reduce disparities on an annual basis.

Engage in Data-Driven Solutions

Systematic data collection is widely accepted as a key component for successful efforts to reduce DMC. States have come a long way in their ability to routinely collect data on race and ethnicity. When this area of study was first beginning, only a handful of states examined categories of race beyond "white" and "other/nonwhite" (Leiber, 2002). Today, most states differentiate several racial categories and a growing number of states distinguish race from ethnicity (i.e., Latino) as well. The distinction of ethnicity from race is critical to a complete understanding of which juveniles are in the system (Piquero, 2008).

States continue to be beset with problems associated with tracking youth through the system due to an inability of data systems to communicate with each other. Police data are often disconnected from court data, which are also disconnected from sentencing and corrections data. This makes it difficult to follow individual youth through the system; instead, individual systems provide a snapshot of the youth population in a particular domain. Ideally, one should be able to follow each youth through the system via datasets that are linked together (Nellis, 2005).

Community-level data collection is equally important to individual-level data for a complete understanding of DMC and may point out jurisdictional differences in the administration of juvenile justice that contribute to minority overrepresentation. As Kimberly Kempf-Leonard (2007) notes in her review of two decades of DMC research, jurisdictional differences in the treatment of youth, the availability of alternatives to detention, and "...the culture of the system" can serve to explain DMC (p.81). The nuances of a particular area in terms of service availability, administrative or legal policies, and day-to-day practices could account for some minority overrepresentation, but need to be operationalized and measured in order to know whether this is the case. This was recently accomplished in a study of 1,195 youth in Michigan. Examination of differences in the pretrial detention decision showed that black youth were three times more likely than white youth to be detained, and that suburban white youth were significantly less likely to be detained than urban white youth or black youth from the suburbs or the city (Shook & Goodkind, 2009).

Finally, multilevel research that takes macrolevel factors (e.g., residential mobility, school enrollment, child welfare and foster care patterns, poverty, and unemployment) into account allows a fuller understanding of the contextual issues that accompany DMC in a particular jurisdiction. For the reasons described above, a single lens focus on juvenile justice involvement is insufficient toward a sustained reduction in DMC.

Enact Racial Impact Statements

A 2007 study noted that Iowa topped the nation in racial disparity within its incarcerated population, and the state moved quickly to address this dubious distinction by requiring policymakers to prepare racial impact statements for proposed legislation that affects sentencing (Mauer & King, 2007). In 2008, Iowa's Governor Culver signed into law the Minority Impact Statement Bill (HF 2393), which requires legislators to have pending legislation reviewed to anticipate any disparate impact on race or ethnicity that might occur as a result of the legislation. Similar to environmental impact statements which require the inclusion of a social impact assessment, enacting laws requiring racial impact statements for pending legislation, as Mauer suggests (2008; 2009), is a legislative solution considered or adopted in a growing number of states. This approach shows promise; other states and municipalities should work to adapt similar impact statement structures to accompany crime policies that could have a negative impact on youth of color.

CONCLUSION

As the DMC reduction movement enters its second decade toward reform, some successes have been documented and many challenges remain. In the success side of the ledger, the establishment of professional statewide DMC coordinators, some of whom have been working within the movement for a decade or more, serves as a firm foundation upon which meaningful work can occur. In addition, whereas many states did not even have access to race and ethnicity data among their juvenile justice populations at multiple decision points, this is now standard in many jurisdictions. And, whereas states historically operated in silos, unaware of the successes and challenges of their neighboring states, there is now a community of state coordinators that has developed in which ideas are shared. Finally, in the early days of the movement, states were easily frustrated by the lack of leadership and guidance offered to them as they were charged with the formidable task of reducing racial disparity in juvenile justice systems. National experts have now emerged to guide and serve states and jurisdictions; areas with this guidance appear to be demonstrating the greatest improvements.

The relationship between race and justice has a long and toxic history. Though some modicum of success toward eliminating disparities has been observed, in many places disparities still seem reluctant to even budge. Recent considerations of multiple systems' contribution to DMC, such as the education system, help to explain the pervasiveness of the problem. More and more, evidence is showing that the decisions made in other systems contribute to the disparities we find in the juvenile justice system. Continued commitment to data-driven solutions, reversal of damaging policies, guidance from national experts, placement of the DMC issue as a local, state, and federal priority, and community investment have emerged as keystones for success in removing unwarranted disparities from the juvenile justice system.

References

Bell, James, and Laura Ridolfi. "Adoration of the Question: Reflections on the Failure to Reduce Racial and Ethnic Disparities in the Juvenile Justice System." San Francisco: W. Haywood Burns Institute, 2008.

Bell, James, Laura Ridolfi, C. Lacey, and M. Finley. "The Keeper and the Kept: Reflections on Local Obstacles to Disparities Reduction in Juvenile Justice Systems and a Path to Change." San Francisco, 2009.

Bishop, Donna M. "Contexts of Decision Making in the Juvenile Justice System: An Organizational Approach to Understanding Minority Overrepresentation." *Youth Violence and Juvenile Justice* 8, no. 3 (2010): 213–33.

Bishop, Donna M., and Charles E. Frazier. "The Influence of Race in Juvenile Justice Processing." *Journal of Research in Crime and Delinquency* 25, no. 3 (1988): 242–63.

Blumstein, Alfred. "Youth Violence, Guns, and the Illicit Drug Industry." *Journal of Criminal Law and Criminology* 86, no. 1 (1995): 10–36.

Bridges, George S., Darlene J. Conley, Rodney L. Engen, and Townsand Price-Spratlen. *Racial Disparities in the Confinement of Juveniles: Effects of Crime and Community Social Structure on Punishment.* Vol. 006, *Minorities in Juvenile Justice.*

Cahn, E. "How the Juvenile Justice System Reduces Life Options for Minority Youth." Washington, D.C.: The Joint Center Health Policy Institute, 2006.

Chapman, J. F., R. A. Desai, P. R. Falzer, and R. Borum. "Violence Risk and Race in a Sample of Youth in Juvenile Detention: The Potential to Reduce Disproportionate Minority Confinement." *Youth Violence and Juvenile Justice* 4, no. 2 (2001): 170–84.

Clear, Todd, D.R. Rose, and J.A. Ryder. "Incarceration and the Community: The Problem of Removing and Returning Offenders." *Crime and Delinquency* 47, no. 3 (2001): 335–51.

Derezotes, D., B. Richardson, C. Bear King, J. Rembert, and B. Pratt. "Evaluating Multi-Systemic Efforts to Impact Disproportionality through Key Decision Points." *Child Welfare Journal* 2 (2008): 241–45.

Fabella, D., S. Slappey, B. Richardson, A. Light, and S. Christie. "Disproportionality: Developing a Public Agency Strategy." Washington, D.C.: National Association of Public Child Welfare Administrators, 2007.

Fagan, Jeffrey, M. Forst, and T. S. Vivona. "Racial Determinants of the Juvenile Transfer Decision: Processing Violent Youth in Criminal Court." *Crime and Delinquency* 3, no. 2 (1987): 259–86.

Feld, Barry C. "Justice by Geography: Urban, Suburban, and Rural Variations in Juvenile Administration." *Journal of Criminal Law and Criminology* 82, no. 1 (1991): 156–210.

Greene, J., K. Pranis, and J. Zeidenberg. "Disparity by Design: How Drug-Free Zone Laws Impact Racial Disparity—and Fail to Protect Youth." Washington, D.C.: Justice Policy Institute, 2006.

Griffin, P. "Models for Change 2008 Update: Gathering Force." Pittsburgh: National Center for Juvenile Justice, 2008.

Hawkins, David, John Laub, Janet Lauritsen, and Lynn Cothern. "Race, Ethnicity, and Serious and Violent Offending." Washington, D.C.: Office of Juvenile Justice and Delinquency Prevention, 2000.

Hirschfield, P.J. "Preparing for Prison? The Criminalization of School Discipline in the USA." *Theoretical Criminology* 12, no. 1 (2008): 79–101.

Hsia, Heidi, George S. Bridges, and R. McHale. "Disproportionate Minority Confinement: 2002 Update." Washington, D.C.: Office of Juvenile Justice and Delinquency Prevention, 2004.

Huizinga, D., T. Thornberry, K. Knight, P. Lovegrove, R. Loeber, K. Hill, and D. Farrington. "Disproportionate Minority Contact in the Juvenile Justice System: A Study of Differential Minority Arrest/Referral to Court in Three Cities." Washington, D.C.: Office of Juvenile Justice and Delinquency Prevention, 2007.

Kempf-Leonard, Kimberly. "Minority Youths and Juvenile Justice: Disproportionate Minority Contact after Nearly 20 Years of Reform Efforts." *Youth Violence and Juvenile Justice* 5, no. 1 (2007): 71–87.

Leiber, Michael J. "Disproportionate Minority Confinement of Youth: An Analysis of Efforts to Address the Issue." *Crime and Delinquency* 48, no. 1 (2002): 3–45.

Leiber, Michael J., and Kristan Fox. "Race and the Impact of Detention on Juvenile Justice Decision Making." *Crime and Delinquency* 51, no. 4 (2005): 470–97.

Leiber, Michael J., and K. Jamieson. "Race and Decisionmaking within Juvenile Justice: The Importance of Context." *Journal of Quantitative Criminology* 11 (1995): 363–88.

Leiber, Michael J., and J. Mack. "The Individual and Joint Effects of Race, Gender, and Family Status on Juvenile Justice Decisionmaking." *Journal of Research in Crime and Delinquency* 40, no. 1 (2003): 34–70.

Lowencamp, C., and E. Latessa. "Understanding the Risk Principle: How and Why Correctional Interventions Can Harm Low-Risk Offenders." Washington, D.C.: National Institute of Corrections, 2004.

Mauer, Marc. "Racial Impact Statements: Changing Policies to Address Disparities." *Criminal Justice* 23, no. 4 (2009): 16–21.

Mauer, Marc, and Ryan King. "Uneven Justice: State Rates of Incarceration by Race and Ethnicity." Washington, D.C.: The Sentencing Project, 2007.

Mendel, R. "Two Decades of JDAI: A Progress Report." Baltimore: Annie E. Casey Foundation, 2009.

Nellis, Ashley. "Seven Steps to Develop and Evaluate Strategies to Reduce Disproportionate Minority Contact (DMC)." Washington, D.C.: Justice Research and Statistics Association, 2005.

Piquero, Alex R. "Disproportionate Minority Contact." *The Future of Children* 18, no. 2 (2008): 59–80.

Piquero, Alex R., and Robert W. Brame. "Assessing the Race-Crime and Ethnicity-Crime Relationship in a Sample of Serious Adolescent Delinquents." *Crime and Delinquency* 054, no. 003 (2008): 390–422.

Pope, Carl, and Michael J. Leiber. "Disproportionate Minority Confinement/Contact (Dmc): The Federal Initiative." In *Our Children, Their Children*, edited by David Hawkins and Kimberly Kempf-Leonard. Chicago: University of Chicago Press, 2005.

Pope, Carl, R. Lovell, and Heidi Hsia. "Disproportionate Minority Confinement: A Review of the Research Literature from 1989 through 2001." Washington, D.C.: Office of Juvenile Justice and Delinquency Prevention, 2002.

Pope, Carl, and Howard Snyder. "Race as a Factor in Juvenile Arrests." Washington, D.C.: Office of Juvenile Justice and Delinquency Prevention, 2003.

Puzzanchera, C. "Juvenile Arrests 2007." Washington, D.C.: Office of Juvenile Justice and Delinquency Prevention, 2009.

Rocque, M., and R. Paternoster. "Understanding the Antecedents of the School-to-Jail Link: The Relationship between Race and School Discipline." *Criminology* 101, no. 2 (2011): 633–65.

Sannah, S., and S. Jacobs. "Dignity Denied: The Effect of 'Zero Tolerance' Policies in Students' Human Rights." New Haven: American Civil Liberties Union, 2008.

Sickmund, Melissa, Todd Sladky, and W. Kang. "Census of Juveniles in Residential Placement Databook." Washington, D.C.: Office of Juvenile Justice and Delinquency Prevention, 2008.

Skiba, R., R.S. Michael, A.C. Nardo, and R.L. Peterson. "The Color of Discipline: Sources of Racial and Gender Disproportionality in School Punishment." *The Urban Review* 34, no. 4 (2002): 317–42.

Skiba, R., and R.L. Peterson. "The Dark Side of Zero Tolerance: Can Punishment Lead to Safe Schools?" *Phi Delta Kappan* 80, no. 5 (1999): 372–82.

Skiba, R., and M. K. Rausch. "Doing Discipline Differently: The Greenfield Middle School Story." Bloomington: Center for Evaluation and Education Policy, 2004.

———. "Zero Tolerance, Suspensions, and Expulsion: Questions of Equity and Effectiveness." In *Handbook of Classroom Management Research Practice and Contemporary Issues*, edited by Everston and Weinstein. Mahwah: Erlbaum Press, 2006.

Snyder, Howard, and Melissa Sickmund. "Juvenile Offenders and Their Victims: 2006 National Report." Washington, D.C.: Office of Juvenile Justice and Delinquency Prevention, 2006.

Soler, Mark, and Lisa Garry. "Reducing Disproportionate Minority Contact: Preparation at the Local Level." Washington, D.C.: Office of Juvenile Justice and Delinquency Prevention, 2009.

Thio, A. "The Poverty of the Sociology of Deviance: Nuts, Sluts, and Perverts." *Social Problems* 20, no. 1 (1972): 103–20.

Tracy, P. E. "Race, Ethnicity, and Juvenile Justice." In *Our Children, Their Children*, edited by David Hawkins and Kimberly Kempf-Leonard, 300–45. Chicago: University of Chicago, 2005.

U.S. Department of Health and Human Services. "Youth Violence: A Report of the Surgeon General." Washington, D.C. U.S. Department of Health and Human Services, 2001.

Verdugo, R. R. "Race-Ethnicity, Social Class, and Zero-Tolerance Policies: The Cultural and Structural Wars." *Education and Urban Society* 35, no. 1 (2002): 50–75.

Ward, G., A. Kupchick, A. Parker, and B. C. Starks. "Racial Politics of Juvenile Justice Policy Support: Juvenile Court Worker Orientations toward Disproportionate Minority Confinement." *Race and Justice* 1, no. 2 (2011): 154–84.

***Ashley Nellis**, PhD, is a research analyst at the Sentencing Project, where she leads research and legislative activities in juvenile justice reform. She specializes in analyzing criminal and juvenile justice policies and practices that contribute to disparities among youth of color and working with coalitions and policymakers on remedying these disparities.

Dreams Denied: The Over-Incarceration of Youth of Color

by James Bell*

INTRODUCTION

Racial and ethnic disparities represent one of the most intransigent and disturbing issues facing the youth justice apparatus in the United States. While comprising approximately 38% of the population eligible for detention, the overrepresentation of youth of color in secure confinement has increased to almost 70% over the last decade. These startling increases in disparities for youth of color occurred while arrest rates for serious and violent crimes declined by 45%.

Although current data collection could be significantly improved, we have enough reliable information to be sufficiently alarmed. According to the most recent data, African-American youth are treated more harshly at all stages of the juvenile justice system, resulting in a cumulative disadvantage. While only 16% of the African-American youth population are of sufficient age for detention, they represent 28% of juvenile arrests, 37% of detained youth and 58% of youth admitted to state adult prison.

Research reveals similar disparities for Latino youth. Although only 13 of 42 states consistently report data on Latino youth, once again, we have enough information to alert us to disquieting levels of overrepresentation. Latino youth were 4% more likely than white youth to be petitioned; 16% more likely than white youth to be adjudicated delinquent; 28% more likely than white youth to be detained; 41% more likely than white youth to receive an out-of-home placement; and 43% more likely than white youth to be waived to the adult system.

Although no two juvenile justice systems are exactly the same, there are several common decision points within the juvenile justice process at which overrepresentation can be measured. These include processes prior to judicial appearance such as cite and release, arrest, diversion after arrest, referral to a detention facility, and admission to detention. At each key decision point juvenile justice professionals exercise judgments about how the young person and their families should be handled.

Monitoring of these decision points reveals that youth of color are funneled deeper into the system for behaviors similar to their white counterparts when controlling for the offenses. For example, data reveal that white youth are more likely to be diverted from formal processing than are youth of color. Additionally, more youth of color are referred and admitted to detention than are their white counterparts for similar behaviors.

These data reflect a long history of disparate treatment for youth of color. In order to understand the complicated drivers that lead to the above mentioned disparities, an overview of the history of youth justice and its treatment of youth of color is important.

DISPARATE TREATMENT THEN AND NOW

From the earliest days of our nation, race conscious policies dictated that the detention of youth of color would be different than that of White youth coming into contact with the penal system for the same categories of offense. Throughout the 1800s, the exclusion of Black youth from White juvenile facilities often resulted in their placement in adult prisons. Black children were also incarcerated younger than White children, had fewer opportunities for advancement upon discharge, and suffered a disproportionately higher death rate.

Moreover, the overrepresentation of youth of color in the early penal system served as a convenient solution for labor needs in the post-Civil War South. A significant reason for opening the Baltimore House of Reformation for Black Children in Maryland was "the need for agricultural labor through [the] state, as well as the great want of competent house servants." The demand for cheap labor after the Civil War was quickly satisfied through widespread arrests of Blacks for minor violations under Jim Crow laws to fuel "convict leasing," which is described by Pulitzer Prize-winning historian David Oshinsky as "worse than slavery." This practice would continue through the 20th century.

As Black youth were experiencing disparate treatment within the burgeoning penal system, Native tribes not yet displaced by federal policies were attempting to maintain such restorative justice practices as family meetings and talking circles as discipline. But in 1885 Congress passed the Major Crimes Act, essentially obliterating centuries-old restorative justice approaches to youth misbehavior and replacing them with a punitive model that persists today on and around Indian reservations.

Ironically, as many juvenile justice professionals are now pushing for a return to restorative justice practices based on traditional tribal models, Native youth continue to suffer the fallout of centuries-long displacement and occupation.

They still have less access to services and are granted disproportionately harsher sanctions including secure confinement and transfers to the adult criminal system.

The problems that many juvenile advocates confront today were present even in the earliest days of the juvenile court. Just before the turn of the century, Jane Addams and other child advocates of the Hull House established the first juvenile court, in Chicago, IL. From its inception, Black children represented a greater percentage of the court case load than their overall population and were substantially underrepresented in the agencies and services contracted to assist them.

Judicial policies and practices that reflected the cultural norms of the day were first documented four decades after the establishment of the juvenile court by researcher Mary Huff Diggs. In her review of 53 courts across the country, Diggs reported, "It is found that Negro children are represented in a much larger proportion of the delinquency cases than they are in the general population. An appreciably larger percent of the Negro children came in contact with the courts at an earlier age than was true with the [W]hite children." Diggs continued, "Cases of Negro boys were less frequently dismissed than were [W]hite boys. Besides, they were committed to an institution or referred to an agency or individual much more frequently than were [W]hite boys."

It is important to recount this history to fully understand the entrenchment of racial and ethnic disparities in today's juvenile justice system. In its early history, the inequitable treatment of youth of color in the juvenile justice system was the result of intentional and blatant race-based policies. Today, our policies are race-neutral, but remain covertly steeped in the same legacy of structural racism.

When reviewing States' assessments of the current status of DMC, a survey showed that 32 of 44 states found evidence of ethnic or racial differences in juvenile justice system decision-making that was unaccounted for by differential criminal activity. Moreover, a recent review of studies on disproportionality found that the effects of race and ethnicity on juvenile justice decision-making do not reflect overt bias, but rather a subtle indirect impact. The review found that while the effects may not be as influential as legal factors, "[T]he cumulative effect across decision-making stages work to the disadvantage of minority youth."

Today, overrepresentation is rampant at all levels of juvenile justice systems across the country. But forward movement in the field is obstructed by the constant and misdirected citation of extrajudicial factors such as poverty and lack of fathers in the home as significant determinants of disparities.

Defaulting to these social determinants as rationales for disparate treatment of youth of color in the justice system does a disservice to us all. It allows decision-makers an escape route for race effects and establishes the elimination of racism and poverty as the only solution for equitable treatment—something we have been unable to eliminate in human history.

A Solvable Problem

Across the country, low-level offending youth of color who come into contact with youth justice systems are often placed in locked facilities even though they do not pose a public safety risk. This is because the decision to detain is often based on perception that youth of color are inherently more dangerous and there is a lack of trustworthy alternatives to detention.

There are a number of things we can do to ensure that all low-level offending youth are provided opportunities for rehabilitation rather than detention. First, we should use secure confinement facilities only as a last resort. It is expensive and does not reduce crime. Currently, we often use detention as a first resort resulting in an extremely expensive and largely ineffective system for adjusting youth behavior. Reducing disparities is possible if jurisdictions have political will, determination, leadership, accurate and reliable data and technical assistance.

Evidence Based Components of Success

The W. Haywood Burns Institute ("BI") is a leading national organization working to reduce the overrepresentation of youth of color in the juvenile justice system. The BI model requires the active commitment and participation of the key traditional and nontraditional stakeholders in the juvenile justice system in each site—including judges, prosecutors, public defenders, police, probation, political leaders, service providers and community groups. The BI leads these stakeholders through a data-driven, consensus-based process that focuses specifically and intentionally on reducing disproportionate minority confinement. The BI has learned from its work in multiple sites that jurisdictions must be intentional, focused and strategic in order to measurably reduce disproportionality.

Participating jurisdictions begin the BI process by forming a representative governing body (Board). The Board should include high-level representation from the key agencies in the juvenile justice system—judges, prosecutors, public defenders, police, probation and political leaders—as well as representation from community groups, parents and youth. The Board is the key decision-making body in the BI process and responsible for ensuring that all of the process steps are completed.

The jurisdiction should then hire a full-time, local site coordinator to lead the process locally. Our experience has shown that trying to reduce DMC without local staff capacity is a huge mistake. The local site coordinator leads all aspects of the strategic efforts and is responsible for the planning and implementation of all of the procedural steps enumerated below.

A. Targeted Data Collection

Jurisdictions will be required to analyze local juvenile crime data by race, gender, offense, time and location by using police data on juvenile arrests and/or probation data on youth in detention. This data collection is important because it informs participating jurisdictions of certain groups of youth committing specific types of offenses at precise times, so that appropriate interventions and services can be tailored for such youth. For example, it is important to know if a 14-year-old Black male who lives in zip code 94026 and is arrested for minor behaviors in his neighborhood at 3:00 pm on a Sunday can be released to an alternative to detention that provides adequate supervision during the times and in the location most relevant to that youth.

This analysis is important by giving us the ability to learn what the crimes are by ethnicity so that we can establish programs which meet the needs of that community. It gives us the time of day to target interventions and services and we learn if juvenile justice system interventions are available in the communities that need them the most.

B. RAI—The Front Door

The Annie E. Casey's Juvenile Detention Alternatives Initiative (JDAI) is the state of the art regarding technologies to reduce unnecessary detention and rational detention policies. JDAI carefully scrutinizes front door admissions by implementing a Risk Assessment Instrument which structures decision-making. Young people are given points based upon offense, prior history and other factors[1] which categorize them into low, medium and high risk. Low risk youth should be immediately released without supervision. Medium risk youth should be released with some supervision to assure they get to court and do not re-offend.

C. Create Equity as a Departmental Value

An important goal is ensuring that staff in key positions are culturally competent and have bilingual capacity in jurisdictions where appropriate. It is necessary to establish guidelines to ensure that staff has the skills and abilities to provide services to a diverse client population. An inventory of caseloads and clients should be conducted to determine cultural and language profiles.

It is useful to conduct surveys to help identify barriers to services and family involvement. For example, if parents do not understand the role of the intake officer and the importance of their ability to supervise their child, they may appear to be less than cooperative, thereby increasing the likelihood of a detention recommendation for their child. This dynamic can be particularly acute when ethnic, cultural, socioeconomic, and language differences create communication challenges. Programs and services may exclude families or may not address their needs and, thus, result in high failure rates. Ensuring that barriers to family involvement and court or program access are eliminated can have a positive impact on reducing racial and ethnic disparities.

D. Develop Alternatives to Formal Handling and Incarceration

In addition to applying risk-based detention criteria, jurisdictions must create two or three tiers of community-based alternatives to detention. Involving community-based organizations and the children's parents in the operation of these supervision programs can help ensure cultural competence and parental support. Programs that provide crisis response and multi-agency (wraparound) services are particularly successful.

A lack of postdispositional options, particularly culturally sensitive programs, can result in overreliance on secure detention by the courts. Stakeholders must carefully define and develop the local continuum of services and ensure that youth of color have equal access at each level. Once again, it is important to review each program for cultural competence.

CONCLUSION

Over two centuries ago, German philosopher Johann Christoph Friedrich von Schiller introduced his immutable law of events, stating that "into today already walks tomorrow." As professionals, scholars, practitioners and community members vested in the future of the next generation, we cannot allow the over-incarceration of youth of color to go unchecked. Our mandate must be to create fair, equitable and humane approaches for children in trouble with the law, which have positive, service-oriented interventions and consequences, and maintain public safety.

Civil rights leader Cesar Chavez once said that "the love for justice that is in us is not only the best part of our being but it is also the most true to our nature." Justice demands that we be ever vigilant about who suffers and who is shielded from harm. All young people deserve to be treated equally and fairly by the systems that mean to serve and protect them. It is everyone's job to work tirelessly to achieve this goal.

*James Bell, JD, is the founder and executive director of the W. Haywood Burns Institute, which uses a data-based approach to unite communities and justice officials in the fight against policies that unfairly affect a high number of youth of color. Mr. Bell has been recognized by numerous groups for his work on disproportionate minority contact.

DISCUSSION QUESTIONS

1. What do you think are the root causes of disproportionate minority contact?

2. Do you agree that socioeconomic factors (such as poverty and chaotic families) are "excuses" used to explain away and avoid correcting the problem of DMC? What, if any, role do socioeconomic factors play in youth crime?

3. Do you believe DMC is a serious enough problem that the federal government should take further action against it? If so, what actions would you recommend?

4. Who bears the responsibility for addressing or preventing DMC?

5. Which strategies used to reduce DMC appear to be most effective or promising? Why?

Chapter 3:
Effective Juvenile Defense

A young person who stands accused in juvenile delinquency court has a constitutional right to a lawyer. In the vast majority of cases, the lawyers who represent juveniles do not practice in prestigious law firms where a team of lawyers devotes time to a single case. Instead, most youth rely on the lawyers provided by the state. If a youth (or, in some instances, his parent) is deemed to be indigent—meaning he cannot afford a lawyer—the government is required to provide counsel. There are three primary systems of indigent defense: (1) full-time public defender offices, where lawyers exclusively represent indigent defendants; (2) part-time public defender offices, where lawyers are given a flat fee to accept appointments, while also maintaining a private caseload; and (3) court appointment systems, where judges appoint private attorneys to represent children for a flat or hourly fee. Unfortunately, each of these systems often fails to provide every youth with a competent or adequately resourced attorney.

The articles in this section discuss the challenges to providing a quality and zealous defense. First, in "The Importance and Role of the Juvenile Defender," Sam Goldberg discusses the critical part a juvenile defender plays in a delinquency proceeding. He identifies legislation and projects aimed at recognizing and addressing problems in indigent defense systems. He also outlines the most common barriers to providing an effective defense. Next, in "The Challenges of Defending Juveniles in Delinquency Court," Tamar R. Birckhead delves more deeply into the culture of the juvenile court and discusses why, even when defense lawyers want to be strong and effective advocates, the system often does not allow them to be. Finally, in "Whose Side Are You on Anyway?", Jacqueline Bullard summarizes how the genesis and development of the juvenile court has led to confusion about the role of lawyers as zealous advocates.

The Importance and Role of the Juvenile Defender

by Samuel Goldberg*

INTRODUCTION TO JUVENILE INDIGENT DEFENSE

Many people as teenagers (maybe even you) made prank calls or participated in some type of silly, adolescent behavior. Some of those calls may have even included rude or "vulgar" language. But it is unlikely that for doing so you faced criminal charges. If you did face criminal charges you were probably represented by a lawyer, and if represented by a lawyer you were most likely not sentenced to six years in a secure, brutal juvenile correctional facility far away from home. However, in 1964, fifteen-year-old Gerald Gault stood before a juvenile court judge, accused of the crime of making a prank phone call, and he had no one to defend him. For that single misdeed Gerald received a sentence of six years at a juvenile correctional facility.

Based on a woman's complaint that she received a prank phone call, Gerald was taken from his home without notice or warning to his parents. He was detained for four days and then released without explanation as to the reason for either detention or release. Gerald was forced to testify against himself at multiple hearings. The woman he allegedly prank called did not testify against him. The judge sentenced Gerald to six years in detention because Gerald had "habitually [been] involved in immoral matters" despite no evidence or stated reason for believing that to be the case. And throughout the entire ordeal Gerald did not have the benefit of a lawyer.

Gerald appealed the decision all the way to the United States Supreme Court, arguing that a child facing criminal charges and incarceration should have the same constitutional protections as adults, including being represented by a lawyer. In 1967, applying the Due Process clause of the 14th Amendment of the United States Constitution, the U.S. Supreme Court determined that children have the right, when accused of a crime, to legal representation during delinquency proceedings. Ever since that decision lawyers have played a critical role in protecting the rights of children during delinquency proceedings.

Juvenile defense remains a developing field: it combines a rich history of reform (e.g. *Gault*) with both the great need and equally ample opportunity for change. In the *Gault* case, the Court ruled that children facing "the awesome prospect of incarceration" have the right to counsel under the Due Process Clause of the 14th Amendment of the United States Constitution.[1] The Court recognized that "a juvenile needs the assistance of counsel to cope with problems of law, to make skilled inquiry into the facts, to insist upon regularity of the proceedings, and to ascertain whether he has a defense and to prepare and submit it."[2] Since the *Gault* decision, juvenile defense attorneys for youth have played an important role in zealously defending children against the charges leveled at them and protecting their due process rights. This article is about the increasingly substantial effect juvenile defenders have had and can continue to have on the juvenile justice system's treatment of children. Most notably, there has been a mobilization of the juvenile defense community, leading to the creation of a larger network of specialized juvenile defenders who train and support each other and, through collective efforts, are able to make substantive changes to the juvenile justice system. One result of the efforts of the juvenile defense community is that the United States Supreme Court and policy makers are beginning to recognize the value of social science that clearly demonstrates the developmental differences between adults and children, allowing for new arguments regarding the limited culpability of children (i.e. children are less responsible for their actions because as children they are more susceptible to peer pressure, more impulsive, and less able to calculate long-term risks) and the increased amenability for reform of children (i.e. children are still developing and therefore more capable of growing out of negative behaviors).

A. Juvenile Justice and Delinquency Prevention Act and *A Call for Justice*

With the Supreme Court's decisions in *Gault* and other cases, and the President's 1967 Commission on Law Enforcement and the Administration of Justice, the treatment of youth in the juvenile justice system attained national prominence. On the heels of *Gault's* spotlight on the dismal state of the nation's juvenile justice system—a system whose informality and profound absence of fundamental fairness emboldened the Supreme Court to call it a "kangaroo court"[3]—Congress continued to sound the drum for protection of youths' due process rights. In 1974 Congress enacted the Juvenile Justice and Delinquency Prevention Act (JJDPA), which still stands as the most important piece of federal juvenile justice legislation in the country's history.[4] The Act includes four core mandates for state authorities: deinstitutionalization of status offenders (status offenders are children convicted of violations for which adults could not be guilty, such as truancy or smoking tobacco); prohibition of the detention of juveniles in adult correctional facilities for more than 6 hours, with a few exceptions; sight and sound separation in the event that a juvenile is held in the same facility as adults; and taking steps to address disproportionate minority contact (DMC).

The JJDPA also established the Office of Juvenile Justice and Delinquency Prevention (OJJDP), a federal agency under the aegis of the Department of Justice, which supports and funds juvenile justice work nationwide. In 1992 Congress, via the JJDPA, charged the OJJDP with devising a program in response to the inadequate legal representation of juveniles in delinquency court. The OJJDP responded to Congress' request by funding the Due Process Advocacy Project led by the ABA Juvenile Justice Center, together with the Youth Law Center and Juvenile Law Center. The goal of the project was to evaluate and understand juvenile indigent defense systems and identify strategies that would strengthen those systems. Two years later the culmination of the project, a review of the legal representation of children in delinquency proceedings entitled *A Call for Justice: An Assessment of Access to Counsel and Quality of Representation in Delinquency Proceedings,* was released.[5]

A Call for Justice documented the findings of a national assessment of the state of juvenile indigent defense based on a representative sample of the country's juvenile defense delivery systems. The assessment examined all stages of representation, from the point of arrest through the point of discharge from the juvenile justice system. The assessment sought to reveal both deficiencies and promising approaches in the representation of youth in delinquency proceedings. Spanning ten states, it covered all regions of the country, including urban, suburban, and rural areas, to allow development of appropriate strategies for improving representation in a range of community settings.

A Call for Justice revealed that, with far too few exceptions, youth facing delinquency proceedings, if they were represented at all, were not receiving the competent, diligent, individualized representation contemplated in *Gault*. The report examined the causes of this widespread inadequate representation and made recommendations to juvenile defenders, state and local bar associations, state legislatures, law schools, juvenile courts, and others to improve the quality of legal services rendered to children charged in delinquency proceedings.

B. Context of the Last Fifteen Years

In juvenile defense over the last fifteen years there has been increased membership in, and activity by, the specialized juvenile defense community, expanding the role that lawyers play in representing children accused of crimes. The increased activity of the growing juvenile defense community arose because of the findings of *A Call for Justice,* which prompted an outpouring of concern from judges and lawyers across the country. In the last fifteen years this has led to: (i) a recognition of the need for specialization in juvenile defense; (ii) a national summit of juvenile defense lawyers that provides training, networking, organizing and strategic planning; (iii) the creation of a juvenile defender community with shared expertise; (iv) additional resources for juvenile indigent defense; and (v) state-specific assessments to inform decision-making and reform.

Motivated by the success of A Call for Justice, and in an effort to maintain momentum, the ABA Juvenile Justice Center (now the National Juvenile Defender Center) held the first annual Juvenile Defender Leadership Summit in 1997. This Summit brought together, for the first time, hundreds of juvenile defense attorneys from every state and the District of Columbia. The purpose of the Summit was to energize and inspire attorneys who are often faced with staggering caseloads, extremely limited resources, and a juvenile justice system that is fraught with racial and ethnic bias. The only national gathering of juvenile defenders, the Summit has enabled defenders to come together to take part in cutting-edge workshops, develop and share strategies to better represent the legal interests of children, learn from experts, and draw strength from their community. Defenders leave the Summit with the renewed courage to keep fighting, with the knowledge they have a juvenile defense community standing firmly behind them, and with a deeper understanding of how incredibly important their work is in the lives of so many children.

A Call for Justice not only led to the Summit, but also created a juvenile defender community with a shared expertise. Prior to A Call for Justice, defenders around the country often worked in bubbles, wholly separate from defenders in other locations. By operating without a community, defenders were less informed on changes to the law, were not empowered to challenge judges or prosecutors, and were unable to consult with more experienced attorneys. That, however, all changed after A Call for Justice led to the creation of a juvenile defender community. Juvenile defenders came together not only at the Summit, but regionally and locally to both learn from, and provide support to, one another. For example, rural defenders in Ohio now have an annual training; juvenile defenders in Florida and Louisiana began working together to end the practice of sentencing juveniles to life without the possibility of parole; and defenders all over the country participate in national, regional and/or state based listservs. Learning and working together has empowered lawyers to be more aggressive and effective in their advocacy efforts on behalf of youth.

A Call for Justice also raised awareness about the failings of the juvenile indigent defense system, which led to large, although still inadequate, increases in funding for juvenile indigent defense. Most prevalent among the many increases

❑ The Importance of Advocacy

The increased activity of the juvenile defense community has created significant changes in the representation of juveniles over the last fifteen years, including convincing courts to accept research on adolescent development. The most prominent example of courts' recognition of the science of adolescent development occurred in two U.S. Supreme Court cases: *Roper v. Simmons* and *Graham v. Florida*. Relying on scientific understandings of adolescent development presented to the court by juvenile defense lawyers, juvenile defense organizations and experts on adolescent development, the U.S. Supreme Court in *Roper* held the death penalty cruel and unusual punishment when applied to individuals who committed crimes when under eighteen years of age. The Court wrote: "From a moral standpoint it would be misguided to equate the failings of a minor with those of an adult, for a greater possibility exists that a minor's character deficiencies will be reformed." *Roper v. Simmons*, 543 U.S. 551, 570 (2005). In *Graham*, similarly relying on evidence presented by experts from the juvenile defense community, the Court held that a sentence of life without the possibility of parole for a juvenile convicted of a non-homicide offense also constituted cruel and unusual punishment in violation of the U.S. Constitution. The Court in *Graham* wrote that, "developments in psychology and brain science continue to show fundamental differences between juvenile and adult minds." *Graham v. Florida*, 130 S.Ct. 2011, 2025 (2010). These two cases are extremely important to juvenile indigent defense. They have provided an opportunity for defenders to creatively advocate for juveniles, particularly regarding services for developing youth; they underscore the importance of counsel for the still-developing adolescents; and the cases have rallied the juvenile indigent defense community because these issues are again getting recognition from the United States Supreme Court.

in funding, on local, state and national levels, from governments and foundations, has been the support of the MacArthur Foundation. In 1996, the year after *A Call for Justice*, the Foundation entered the juvenile justice field, launching the *MacArthur Research Network on Adolescent Development and Juvenile Justice*. This led to *Models for Change*, a long-term investment of over $100 million aimed at developing fair, rational and effective approaches to juvenile justice, including indigent juvenile defense. As part of *Models for Change*, MacArthur funded the *Juvenile Indigent Defense Action Network*, whose goal has been to "engage leadership in targeted strategies to improve juvenile indigent defense policy and practice." The *Juvenile Indigent Defense Action Network* has been hugely success-ful, leading to numerous reforms, including ending the practice of shackling of juveniles in Florida and increasing the availability of post-dispositional represen-tation of juveniles in New Jersey and a number of other states (post-dispositional representation includes all representation of clients after they have been found guilty and sentenced, such as correcting legal errors on appeal or monitoring children's progress in placement facilities).

Juvenile defense advocates' response to *A Call for Justice* led to comprehensive assessments of access to counsel and quality of representation in individual states. Since 1995, state-specific juvenile defense assessments have been conducted in: Florida, Georgia, Indiana, Illinois, Kentucky, Louisiana, Maine, Maryland, Mis-sissippi, Montana, Nebraska, North Carolina, Ohio, Pennsylvania, South Caro-lina, Texas, Virginia, Washington and West Virginia. Re-assessments have been conducted in Kentucky and Louisiana. County-based assessments were conducted in Cook County, Illinois, Marion County, Indiana and Caddo Parish, Louisiana. New assessments are currently under consideration in Missouri and Colorado. The state assessments have led to numerous changes across topics ranging from waiver of counsel to post-dispositional advocacy. National Juvenile Defender Center, which has facilitated all of the state assessments, has a goal of undertak-ing at least one assessment of the juvenile defense delivery systems of every state, Washington, D.C., and Puerto Rico.

C. Challenges Confronting the Juvenile Defense Community

Based on the 19 statewide assessments, there are ten major issues still facing most juvenile indigent defense systems and court involved indigent youth. In each area there remain serious deficiencies in nearly every jurisdiction. The ten areas are outlined below.

1. *Timing and Appointment of Counsel*: When and how a child gets an attor-ney is crucial. Often counsel is appointed far too late in the process to make a meaningful difference in the case. For example, many children do not get an attorney until after the critical detention decision has already been made. Important questions to ask about timing and appointment of counsel are: When is counsel actually appointed? What does the appoint-ment process look like? Is the appointment process judge-driven? Do judges appoint only those defenders who suit their needs (e.g., those who will not take up too much court time or advocate too vigorously)? The answers to these questions can have a tremendous effect on the outcome of the case.

2. *Waiver of Counsel*: Thousands of youth in the juvenile justice system waive their right to counsel (i.e., decide to proceed without a lawyer, usually at the behest of parents and judges). An alarmingly high percentage of children waive their right to defense counsel before they have even seen a lawyer to discuss the long- and short-term consequences of the waiver decision. Waivers can happen at the initial hearing (first court appearance), or even earlier, so that the child navigates the entire court process alone. This often leads to children pleading guilty without ever having someone advise them on whether the State would be able to win the case or on the long-term consequences of pleading guilty.

3. *Plea Bargains*: The vast majority of juvenile court cases are resolved by plea bargains, often at the initial hearing. Most plea bargains are entered into without previous, independent investigation, or pre-trial advocacy to test the strengths and weaknesses of the government's case. In this way, plea bargains foreclose zealous legal advocacy. Aggravating the problem, judges fail to properly explain to youth what rights they are forfeiting by pleading guilty, so that young people do not understand the terms of the plea agreement or the life-long consequences of having a juvenile adjudication on their record—including potential disqualification from military service, ineligibility for student loans and public housing, and, for some children, required registration as sex offenders.

4. *Caseloads*: Juvenile defenders' caseloads are far too high. Some juvenile defenders handle up to 500 or even 1,000 cases each year. This high number of cases impacts every facet of defense. There is evidence that waiver of counsel and plea bargains are being used as case reduction tools, despite their long-term consequences and finality. Although a handful of public defender offices have been able to successfully argue that they must be allowed to stop taking cases because their staggering caseloads render them ineffective, victories like these are few and far between.

5. *Inadequate Resources*: Juvenile defenders routinely operate without adequate resources. Many juvenile defenders do not even have the bare minimum tools necessary to mount a vigorous defense—computers, office file cabinets, access to online legal research—let alone access to paralegals, investigators, social workers, and experts. Assessment observers have seen juvenile defenders who do not even have client files. Juvenile defense offices have to use creative means to maintain and increase their funding, and, more often than not, face budget shortfalls that interfere with providing quality representation.

6. *Inadequate Training and Supervision*: Many children who cannot afford to hire an attorney are appointed contract attorneys, not public defenders. Contract attorneys are often solo practitioners who are disconnected from trends and developments in juvenile law generally and are not specifically trained in areas of juvenile trial advocacy. Even in public defender offices, juvenile defenders often do not have access to specialized juvenile court training. In fact, in many public defender offices, juvenile defenders are sent to juvenile court as if juvenile court were Siberia—a place where defenders work alone, removed from any training or supervision.

7. *Inadequate Oversight and Monitoring*: Juvenile indigent defense systems are extremely varied and *ad hoc*. Many states do not have juvenile-specific practice standards or guidelines, and some need to amend their juvenile court rules. Other issues to consider when evaluating a state's oversight and monitoring of its juvenile indigent defense system include the role of a formal system of oversight, whether there is a commission with such responsibilities, and what leadership role, if any, the state Supreme Court has played.

8. *Juvenile Court Culture*: The culture in many juvenile courts reflects society's persistent ambivalence about what juvenile courts should look like. The choices are: (1) a juvenile court that simply copies the adult model; (2) a forum in which a benevolent judge shines wisdom upon wayward youth with little regard to due process or fundamental fairness; or (3) a hybrid of the two. Forty years after the *Gault* decision, many, if not most, juvenile courts still operate in a pre-*Gault* mode, as if the defense attorney is irrelevant and unnecessary. In some states, juvenile court suffers from a kiddie-court mentality where stakeholders do not believe that juvenile court is important. Many other states allow juvenile defenders to use juvenile court as a training ground, where inexperienced attorneys can hone their advocacy skills at the expense of children. As a result of the juvenile court culture, real lawyering often does not, and cannot, occur and the fair administration of justice is impeded.

9. *Parity*: There is an overall lack of fairness and equality in the juvenile defense system, for both juvenile defenders and their clients. Often, juvenile defenders are not paid the same salary as adult criminal defenders, even in the same public defender office. Salary increases are attached to moving "up" from juvenile court into adult criminal court. Some offices also have forced rotations, so that juvenile defenders who want to devote their careers to representing youth are forced to represent adults if they

want promotions or raises. Outside of their offices, juvenile defenders do not have pay parity with juvenile prosecutors. Besides the obvious inequities, the overarching problem with this very common situation is that these practices undermine the critical goal of having specialization in juvenile defense (which is necessary to develop a core of excellence). Juvenile respondents are also treated unfairly. Thousands of dollars in fees and surcharges are assessed against juvenile respondents and their families—to pay for detention, for restitution fees, and for victim funds. The impact of fees and surcharges on juvenile respondents is significant. In one case that assessment investigators observed, a 19-year-old was brought into court in handcuffs because she had not paid fees that had been assessed against her when she was a child. That 19-year-old, now a college student, was detained until she made a payment and agreed to a payment plan.

10. *Lack of Leadership:* The juvenile defense bar is lacking in leadership and capacity. Juvenile defenders need to be included as not just important, but necessary players in all juvenile justice initiatives. Chief defenders are key players for defining the values that we as a society wish to protect in juvenile court. They are also key to the distribution of resources, and to creating professional opportunities for juvenile defenders. Chief defenders are essential to linking frontline defenders with judges, so that there is an open dialogue between the stakeholders. Chief Judges are also crucial to the juvenile defense reform process and can help ensure that juvenile defenders are at the table designing reforms that can take hold.

The United States Constitution, state statutes, prevailing academic scholarship, and model rules all require that youth involved in delinquency proceedings have meaningful access to quality representation. The *Gault* decision announced that, "[t]he child requires the guiding hand of counsel at every step in the proceedings against him." That "guiding hand" must be available from the beginning of the case, so that the timing and appointment of counsel should provide a meaningful opportunity to advocate for a fair and balanced outcome. It must continue through the early stages of the case, with online legal research, investigation and pre-trial motions practice. Counsel should proceed through the resolution of the case with a well-bargained plea agreement or an adjudication, and through disposition, with social workers and experts who can generate an individualized disposition plan that meets the needs of the child and addresses the concerns of the court. If needed, this "guiding hand" will persist through post-disposition, where legal errors can be corrected on appeal and children's progress in placement facilities can be monitored.

CONCLUSION

Juvenile defense is a field in which great strides have been made over the past 45 years, especially the last fifteen, but much remains to be done. Children are guaranteed the right to counsel, but in many jurisdictions they have that right in name only. Courts and legislatures are beginning to recognize that children are categorically developmentally less mature than adults. But at the same time numerous states continue to punish children as adults, locking them up for the rest of their lives for crimes they committed at age sixteen or even younger. The juvenile defense community has grown immensely in the past fifteen years, yet some offices still use juvenile court as the training ground for juvenile defenders, and funding remains an issue. Juvenile defense continues to be an area of legal practice where compassionate individuals are desperately needed, and where dedicated defenders are capable of making great strides in the protection of our most vulnerable youth.

NOTES

1. *In re Gault*, 387 U.S. 1, 36 (1967).
2. Ibid.
3. Ibid. at 28.
4. Pub. L. 93-415 (1974).
5. ABA Juvenile Justice Center, Juvenile Law Center & Youth Law Center, *A Call for Justice: An Assessment of Access to Counsel and Quality of Representation in Delinquency Proceedings* (1995), available at http://www.njdc.info/pdf/cfjfull/pdf.

*Sam Goldberg, JD, is the Gault Fellow at the National Juvenile Defender Center (NJDC). NJDC promotes excellence in juvenile defense and justice for all children by providing juvenile defense attorneys a more permanent capacity to address important practice and policy issues, to improve advocacy skills, to build partnerships, to exchange information, and to participate in the national debate about juvenile justice.

The Challenges of Defending Juveniles in Delinquency Court

*by Tamar R. Birckhead**

Juvenile defendants are at special risk for being wrongfully convicted.[1] Because of developmental differences, juveniles are less competent during pretrial and trial proceedings than adults, and they are more compliant and suggestible during police interrogations.[2] The constitutional due process protections in place for criminal defendants are in many cases of little use to juveniles in delinquency court because of the nature of juvenile court culture.[3] Trials, for instance, are not true tests of whether the state can prove the case because few states grant juveniles the jury trial right.[4] Judges for the most part are not objective fact-finders when they preside over bench trials in juvenile court.[5] Likewise, the right to counsel means little when children can readily waive that right, which they can do in the juvenile courts of many states.[6]

Professional guidelines direct attorneys who represent youth in juvenile delinquency court to advocate based on their young client's "expressed interest" (what the youth says she wants), rather than relying on what the attorney believes is "best" for the child.[7] Yet, this basic premise is often more challenging to follow than is commonly acknowledged. The standards of effective criminal defense practice emphasize rigorous oral and written advocacy with little mention of whether the client has learned a lesson from the experience. This is in direct conflict with the informal culture that exists in most juvenile courtrooms in the United States, where delinquency court judges fail to apply the beyond-a-reasonable-doubt standard of proof, prosecutors neglect to respond meaningfully to discovery motions[8] filed by the defense, and probation officers recommend punitive sentences regardless of the child's actual needs.[9] In such instances, defense attorneys are confronted with hurdles that are difficult to overcome.[10] Furthermore, the parents of juvenile clients may have priorities that differ greatly from those of the attorney, a serious problem that is compounded when the parent is a co-defendant, witness, or alleged victim of the offense.[11] Likewise, even defense attorneys who are firmly committed to their role and to rigorous representation may feel conflicted, as their young clients can be impulsive, unreliable, and incapable of mature decision-making.

Because the role of the defense attorney can be easily overlooked and its significance underestimated, this Article examines the impact of substandard or ineffective lawyering in juvenile court. It emphasizes the importance of acknowledging the challenging nature of the problem and taking proactive steps to change the culture of juvenile court.

I. Indigent Defense Standards

The adversary criminal trial, in which the prosecutor presents evidence and proof, the defendant is represented by counsel, and the judge is a neutral and passive decision maker, is of fairly recent historical origin.[12] Prior to the seventeenth century, prisoners were denied many basic rights even when charged with capital crimes of treason and felony, including the right to counsel, to summon witnesses, to know the details of the charges against them, and to have access to the statements of prosecution witnesses.[13] It was not until the nineteenth century that prisoners were routinely allowed legal representation, which signaled a shift away from the inquisitorial system, in which the judge conducts the trial and determines what questions to ask, and toward the adversarial model, which better protected the lives and liberty of imperiled defendants.[14] Some of the tensions that exist between adversarial representation and inquisitorial practice are found in today's juvenile court system, resulting in a clash between the advocacy standards of the criminal defense bar and the informal procedures found in juvenile delinquency court.

A. Rigorous Advocacy

The contemporary best practice standards of criminal defense are perhaps best reflected by the Model Rules of Professional Conduct, which emphasize the lawyer's dual role as advisor and advocate. The Rules state that the defense attorney must provide the client with "an informed understanding of the client's legal rights and obligations" and must also "zealously assert the client's position under the rules of the adversary system."[15] In addition, the Rules assert that "a lawyer can be a zealous advocate on behalf of a client and *at the same time assume* that justice is being done."[16] In other words, as long as the defense attorney provides rigorous representation within the bounds of the law, her ethical obligations are complete; she need not take any additional actions to ensure that justice is achieved. Similarly, the American Bar Association standards for defense attorneys explicitly state that defense counsel's basic duty is to serve as the "accused's counselor and advocate with courage and devotion and to render effective, quality representation."[17]

The importance of the defense lawyer's role as advocate is also emphasized by the training and practice models at premier public defender offices such as the

Public Defender Service ("PDS") for the District of Columbia, the Neighborhood Defender Service of Harlem ("NDS"), and Bronx Defenders.[18] PDS is regarded as one of the best public defender offices in the United States and is often the benchmark by which other public defender systems are measured.[19] In addition to providing its indigent clients with excellent legal advocacy, PDS is committed to holistic representation in which the defense lawyer works closely with social workers and criminal investigators.[20] Further, the organization expends significant effort toward coordinating education programs for the communities they serve and taking on broad public policy issues that affect those communities.[21] In New York City, NDS has taken the concept of holistic or whole-client lawyering even further by handling not only the client's criminal matter and social service needs but also corollary legal matters such as eviction and forfeiture. In addition, NDS continues to work with the client and her family long after the criminal case is closed, linking them to housing, medical, and employment resources in the community and offering educational outreach programs that have received national recognition.[22] Bronx Defenders also models itself on client or community-centered representation in which defenders and social workers work together to provide clients and their families with housing, employment, and educational opportunities that extend far beyond the boundaries of the criminal case.[23] In a profession in which public interest practice and poverty law are often considered unappealing and carry little prestige, all three offices actively recruit and consistently retain top Ivy League law school graduates.[24]

Likewise, non-profits that are specifically dedicated to trial practice training of defense counsel also work hard to reinforce these comprehensive advocacy standards. For instance, the National Criminal Defense College ("NCDC") in Macon, Georgia, offers extensive training programs for criminal defense attorneys through its Trial Practice Institute that are designed to sharpen skills in such specialty areas as jury selection, cross examination, impeachment, and closing arguments.[25] Similarly, the National Legal Aid and Defender Association ("NLADA") conducts the National Defender Leadership Institute, which provides rigorous training, education, and assistance to defense lawyers.[26] Both of these organizations emphasize the essential role of rigorous client-centered representation.

B. Expressed Interest Not Best Interest

Only in recent years has zealous representation been considered an essential part of the defense attorney's duty to her *juvenile* client. In fact, for many decades young offenders regularly appeared without counsel.[27] It was not until 1967 that the United States Supreme Court held in the landmark case of *In re Gault* that youth have a right to counsel in delinquency adjudications.[28] The decision triggered a debate among academics and juvenile justice advocates regarding the specific role and responsibilities that the child's lawyer would assume.[29] *Gault* left open a number of critical questions: should the attorney adopt a best-interest approach or an adversarial one when advocating on behalf of her young client? Does the juvenile have a right to representation at the sentencing phase in addition to the trial of the case? What role should the youth's parents have in regard to their child's representation in juvenile court?[30] Consensus over the role of the defense attorney in juvenile cases was not reached until the early 1980s when the American Bar Association published Juvenile Justice Standards that explicitly called for client-directed, zealous advocacy at *all phases* of the delinquency case.[31]

Since that time, those who train and set advocacy standards for juvenile defenders have emphasized the duty of counsel to represent the client's "expressed interest" or what she says she wants to accomplish in the case, rather than her "best interest" as determined by her lawyer, parents, probation officer, prosecutor, or judge.[32] Endorsed by scholars and policy makers,[33] this model has become the standard by which delinquency lawyers are judged.[34]

II. JUVENILE COURT CULTURE

Contrasting the standards of indigent defense practice with the culture that exists in many juvenile courts in the United States is instructive. Such a comparison helps reveal the process by which rigorous advocacy and accurate fact-finding can become compromised in the name of consensus-building and helping the child. This Part details the role played by each of the principal players in the juvenile courtroom—from the judge and prosecutor to the probation officer and parent. It illustrates the ways in which their attitudes and perspectives can collectively undermine the defense lawyer's duty to provide juveniles with zealous, holistic, and client-centered advocacy.[35]

A. Judges

Juvenile courts were originally designed over a century ago to be forums for the rehabilitation of youth, rather than the vehicle by which young offenders would be punished.[36] Prior to *Gault*, youth rarely had legal representation in juvenile delinquency court, justified by the system's focus on treatment and reform.[37] Juvenile court sessions typically consisted of casual dialogues between the judge and the child, often across a desk in chambers rather than in a courtroom, which were a combination of instruction, lecture, and counseling session.[38] By the 1950s and '6os, the informal tone of the proceeding had not changed, but delinquency dispositions had become increasingly severe. Young offenders were sentenced to lengthy terms in juvenile penitentiaries without benefit of counsel or basic due process protections. Others were transferred to adult criminal court without regard to objective standards or constitutionally sanctioned criteria.[39] In fact, one of the catalysts for the *Gault* decision was the recognition that juveniles were being denied *both* basic due process protections as well as meaningful rehabilitative services, leaving them with the "worst of both worlds."[40]

Given this background, it is not surprising that some judges persist in focusing on the needs of the juvenile without first determining whether a criminal offense has been committed.[41] Furthermore, most jurisdictions do not provide juveniles with the right to a jury trial,[42] and the bench trial model typically employed in juvenile court, in which the judge alone hears the evidence, has problematic features that perpetuate unfairness.[43] It has been found, for example, that juvenile court judges are inclined to evaluate evidence in a manner that favors the prosecution. This may follow from the judge's desire to protect the community by erring on the side of conviction, to avoid being perceived as soft on crime, or to ensure that troubled youth receive services as mandatory conditions of probation.[44] It may also arise from instances of individual bias on the part of the trial judge.[45] As a result, although the United States Supreme Court held in 1970 that the high standard of proof used in criminal cases ("beyond a reasonable doubt") also applies to juvenile delinquency cases,[46] this is inconsistently reflected in practice.[47]

In addition, juvenile court judges managing heavy dockets[48] or operating in jurisdictions in which all pending matters must be handled within a single court session face systemic pressures to resolve cases. This can give rise to judges' impatience and distain for defense attorneys who file motions[49] or request adjudicatory hearings/trials rather than advise their young clients to admit to the charges.[50] Defense attorneys who fail to cooperate may face both subtle and direct forms of retaliation, including reduction in fees and removal from court-appointed lists.[51] Such an attitude on the part of judges can be exacerbated by the prevailing view that the youth charged as a delinquent may not have committed the offense charged, but she must have done *something*.[52] In jurisdictions in which juvenile court judges are elected and therefore compelled to campaign on their record in order to win the popular vote, such views are even more likely to predominate.[53]

Further, juvenile court is frequently used as a training ground or brief rotation for judges, many of whom are unfamiliar with the state juvenile code or the ways in which adolescent development, mental health, and special education needs can impact a child's behavior.[54] These judges may have distorted views of the delinquency court system and the young people who are in it.[55] When a juvenile's lawyer is also untrained and inexperienced—a not-uncommon occurrence—a power imbalance can develop in the courtroom that results in an overreliance by all parties on the probation officer.[56] This, too, compromises the system's commitment to justice and contributes to the risk of wrongful convictions.

B. Prosecutors

Prosecutors who are assigned to juvenile delinquency court are a second contributing factor in the calculus. They commonly receive minimal supervision and training. They are saddled with unwieldy caseloads, and they—like judges—are under pressure to resolve matters quickly and efficiently.[57] As a result, many juvenile court prosecutors have little understanding or tolerance for defense attorneys who practice with more than the barest amount of diligence. They are annoyed when expected to provide discovery[58] in advance of a hearing.[59] They are perplexed and sometimes resentful when juvenile defenders file written motions,[60] although the practice is, of course, allowable under the rules of criminal procedure and juvenile code of every state.[61] They are offended when the defense interviews prosecution witnesses prior to the trial ("adjudicatory hearing") and have suggested that such a practice is unethical and burdens the alleged victim.[62]

Likewise, juvenile court prosecutors benefit from the structural realities of the system. They typically have access to investigative resources that the defense lacks.[63] They have the discretion to file certain cases in adult court, and they use the threat of transfer to adult court to extract admissions from juveniles who otherwise would have requested a hearing.[64] In addition, prosecutors often share the mistaken view of the judge that juvenile court is not an adversarial forum and that no negative consequences to the child will result.[65] Thus, given the distain with which prosecutors treat those few attorneys who are committed to rigorous, client-directed representation, it is not surprising when defenders assume the posture of one who is seen and not heard.

C. Probation Officers

Probation officers who work with juveniles in delinquency court often face a dilemma when making sentencing ("dispositional") recommendations on behalf of juveniles. In theory, they can recommend a comprehensive package of services that includes psychological treatment, anger-management counseling, and academic tutoring. However, because of the resource-strapped budgets of many juvenile courts, mental health agencies, and school systems, often the only real choice is some form of incarceration.[66] Even in jurisdictions in which funding is not at issue, probation officers make harsh recommendations because of a fear of appearing soft and losing credibility with the judge and prosecutor.[67] Likewise, it is not uncommon for probation officers to become burned out after years in the trenches with heavy caseloads and little support. Some become tired of fighting the more punitive aspects of the system, while others internalize the clichés and stereotypes perpetuated about juveniles and buy into the warehousing of "bad kids."[68] The result is that a juvenile probation officer may privately acknowledge to a defender that her client's family is dysfunctional and that the child has serious psychological, developmental or learning issues that have never been properly addressed. Yet, in the courtroom the officer will recommend the most punitive sanction:[69] the child's commitment to what is euphemistically known as a "detention home," "training school" or "youth development center."[70]

The problematic role of juvenile probation officers is compounded by the fact that they are often the best informed people in the courtroom and have the most sustained contact with the child.[71] This results in an overreliance on their judgments by the judge and prosecutor that can make the facts of the case and the applicable law only minimally relevant to the ultimate disposition.[72] In jurisdictions in which juveniles commonly waive their right to counsel, probation officers often provide procedural as well as substantive legal advice to juveniles. In such instances, they arguably cross the line into the unlicensed practice of law.[73] The failure of defense counsel to question the nearly unfettered discretion of the probation officer or to challenge the accuracy of the facts contained within probation reports serves to further the department's influence in juvenile court.[74] This phenomenon is particularly troublesome in complex cases in which the juvenile has serious mental health or drug treatment needs or has been found delinquent of a sex offense, the potential consequences of which can be particularly severe.[75]

D. Defenders

Before the *Gault* decision in 1967, fewer than 10 percent of children in juvenile court received *any* legal assistance.[76] Traditionally, the lack of counsel for juveniles was justified by the view that attorneys serve neither the interests of the child nor the interests of justice, and that the judge is "the defender as well as corrector of the child."[77] In fact, pre-*Gault* judges were encouraged to discuss the special nature of juvenile court with counsel and to instruct them that they had a professional obligation to *assist in* the child's supervision, rehabilitation, and treatment.[78]

Forty years later, state assessments of juvenile court practice have established that the model of client-directed robust defense is infrequently put into practice.[79] Some juvenile defenders are experienced and have received high-quality training and supervision, but many are new to the practice of law and have been placed there by under-staffed public defender offices. Others accept assignments in juvenile court out of their own misguided belief that it is an appropriate learning ground because the stakes are low.[80] Meanwhile, there are some who are crossovers from family court or abuse, neglect, and dependency court (also known as "DSS" or Department of Social Services court). They have no criminal defense training but have developed delinquency caseloads as a result of being regulars in these corollary courts—or sometimes merely because they happen to be warm bodies who practice in the local district or even traffic court.[81]

Systemic barriers also contribute to the challenges faced by today's defenders. It is not unusual, for instance, when courthouses lack adequate space and resources for the defense bar. This means that lawyers and their young clients must forego private discussion or attempt to consult in whispers in order to speak in confidence before, during, or after court hearings.[82] In addition to these types of physical limitations, the complacent attitude of the local defense bar can serve as a deterrent to effective representation.[83] If most of the lawyers in an office put little effort into their juvenile cases, it is likely that the diligent few will gradually lower their standards. Likewise, the fact that most juvenile cases are resolved by guilty plea ("admission") further supports the misconception that preparation is unnecessary and an impediment to judicial economy. In fact, it is not uncommon for a lawyer to negotiate a plea agreement without first speaking to her juvenile client. She may briefly discuss it with the youth in the moments before the hearing and then immediately proceed into the courtroom with the client to enter the plea.[84] It is also not unusual for salary disparities to exist between those attorneys who represent juveniles in delinquency court and their higher paid counterparts who represent defendants in adult criminal court, further reinforcing the message that juvenile defenders are worth less than "real lawyers." The same discrepancies in compensation, however, are not typically found between juvenile court and adult criminal court prosecutors.[85]

Therefore, lawyers defending children are particularly susceptible to the negative message conveyed by others in the juvenile court system: don't investigate, don't talk to state's witnesses, don't file motions, don't make the state meet its burden, and—in short—don't be zealous, hard-working advocates. As a result, many assume that their only role is to work in partnership with the judge and prosecutor in order to get "help" for the child.[86]

E. Parents

Juvenile courts have jurisdiction over the parents or guardians of children in the system, establishing a formal role for them in delinquency cases.[87] The defense attorney, therefore, often has little choice but to interact with and gain the cooperation and trust of her client's parents.[88] As a result, the interests and attitudes of the parents can conflict and interfere with the defender's role in relation to her juvenile client.

While many parents of children charged with criminal offenses in juvenile delinquency court have constructive—even amicable—working relationships with their child's attorney, others stand in direct opposition to the defense lawyer's goals and objectives.[89] Some parents pressure their child to "do the right thing," which usually translates to admitting to the crime and taking responsibility for what they did, regardless of the consequences.[90] They believe that in this way their son or daughter will emerge from the experience a better person. They insist that the youth make amends and show remorse, despite a lack of evidence.[91] Others, however, do not accept that their child could have been capable of committing the act alleged. They insist upon an adjudicatory hearing and refuse even to consider allowing the youth to admit to the charge—again, regardless of the consequences for the juvenile.[92]

In general, most parents of juveniles are, at best, conflicted. Parenting involves conveying positive values, providing support and encouragement, and utilizing constructive forms of discipline. It can be difficult to helplessly stand by as one's child is labeled a juvenile delinquent or taken to detention in shackles and leg irons.[93] To further complicate matters, the parent may be the alleged victim in the case, a witness to the offense, a co-defendant, or in danger of being held in contempt because of her failure to abide by a court order.[94] Further, many parents are unable to escape the lingering question that inevitably arises when a youth is accused of violating the law: how does my child's case reflect upon me as a parent and as an individual?

Because of the parent's established role in delinquency matters, in many ways the juvenile court pits the child's lawyer against the parent, as the goals and objectives of each group may not only differ but may be diametrically opposed.[95] The parent is determined either to keep her child out of the system (which may be rational but unrealistic) or to get her child into the system (as a result of the parent's frustration or lack of resources). Meanwhile, the child's lawyer stands at the other end of the spectrum working, at least in theory, for the least punitive result for her client—nothing more and nothing less.[96]

Further, even defense lawyers who are committed to their role and to the most rigorous form of advocacy are not immune from feeling conflicted themselves. They are adults, but their clients are children or adolescents whose brains are not fully formed. Juvenile clients can be impulsive, unpredictable, and incapable even of providing a clear account of what happened.[97] Further, the role of the adult in relation to the child is intended to be that of mentor, counselor, and protector—one who offers direction and guidance for children to live by as they mature. Yet any defender who is worth her salt will admit that this familial function can be in direct opposition to the blunt legal counseling that may be needed by a juvenile defendant.[98]

The result is that the child's lawyer is caught in the middle and gradually worn down by all sides. Accurate fact-finding stops being a priority. Advocacy, both oral and written, falters. The quality of representation suffers, and wrongful convictions, among other harms, occur. Further, while this Article's focus is on juvenile delinquency court, this same dynamic can also develop and predominate among attorneys who represent youth in adult criminal court. Young people transferred to that forum for prosecution may face longer terms of imprisonment, but the fact of their immaturity and developmental incompetence remains.[99]

III. PROPOSALS

Given the dynamic established in the preceding sections, what strategies might be used to lessen the competing pressures faced by juvenile defenders? This Part sets forth proposals directed at confronting the challenges that can negatively impact the ability of lawyers to represent juveniles effectively in delinquency court.

A. Acknowledge the Problem

In a variety of forums both formal and informal, juvenile defenders are repeatedly told to rely on their client's expressed interest and not their best interest. Yet, it is rarely acknowledged that this is often easier said than done, even for the most defense-minded advocates.[100] Whether the client is nine, thirteen, or seventeen, it can be a struggle for the attorney to put aside the impulse to act based on what would be "best" for the youth. This is particularly the case given that the defense lawyer is the only party in the system who does *not* operate under this mandate, according to the profession's Model Rules. In any attorney-client relationship, assumptions, biases, and feelings of resignation may arise. When the client is a child, this dynamic is magnified as such factors as paternalism, role confusion, and culture clash enter into the mix.[101]

As social science research has demonstrated, the act of describing and naming a condition or set of symptoms can provide great comfort and solace to those who experience it.[102] Upon learning that one's experiences are typical of others who are similarly-situated and that the phenomenon has standard traits, most people are better able to address its underlying causes.[103] Rather than engage in self-blame under the mistaken belief that their feelings are aberrant and, thus, fraudulent, they can more objectively analyze the situation. Rather than deny that the dynamic persists and perpetuate self-delusion, they can directly confront it.[104] This sort of positive development has been seen with clinical conditions, such as chronic fatigue syndrome,[105] lupus,[106] and Alzheimer disease,[107] as well as with laws that are directed towards specific conduct, such as sexual harassment and hate crimes.[108]

Without suggesting that the conflict experienced by juvenile defenders is comparable to the diagnoses mentioned above, much can be learned from the beneficial effect of giving *voice* to a common set of behaviors and experiences.[109] By recognizing the challenges that defenders face in the juvenile court system, and by acknowledging the difficulty of negotiating among competing interests, constructive steps may be taken toward remediation.

B. Change the Culture

Lastly, advocates should not settle for the status quo in juvenile court but should take proactive steps to challenge the prevailing attitude that it is *only* "kiddie" court. In this way, they can convince the legal community, as well as policy makers and legislators, that juvenile court is important in terms of human resources, prestige, and outcomes.[110] Following are several modest but essential reforms to help accomplish this objective. To emphasize the importance and specialized nature of the practice, advocates can organize with state or local bar associations to make juvenile defense a formal sub-specialty of criminal law that is recognized and certified by the state bar.[111] They can lobby for funding for in-house investigators, social workers, and clinicians to work alongside juvenile defenders, with the goal of developing holistic representation models for youth.[112] They can educate judges on the importance of accurate fact-finding by explaining that the juvenile's need for services—whether social, educational, medical, therapeutic, or rehabilitative—does not justify *wrongfully* adjudicating her delinquent.[113] They can bolster the juvenile appeals bar[114] and encourage young clients to file ineffective assistance of counsel[115] claims to establish meaningful remedies for children harmed by substandard legal representation.[116] Lastly, they can challenge the notion that delinquency adjudications do not have a negative impact upon a child's future by calling attention to the stigma associated with appearing in juvenile court as well as other types of harmful ("collateral") consequences.[117]

CONCLUSION

Even the best juvenile defense attorney will acknowledge that she has occasionally been caught between acting as an aggressive, win-at-all-costs trial lawyer and serving as a counselor who gives advice based only on what she believes would be best for her young clients. Unfortunately, there is no magic bullet for resolving this dilemma. Defenders must try to build meaningful relationships with juveniles and help them make decisions that are both legally savvy and beneficial for their personal growth.[118] However, it is not always easy. When heavy caseloads, court pressure, and concerns regarding expedience take over, lawyers operate on autopilot. Facts are overlooked, laws are misconstrued, and mistakes inevitably are made. Perhaps by recognizing the challenges faced by juvenile defenders, we can take proactive steps to change the culture of juvenile court and, as a result, lower the risk of wrongful convictions of youth.

NOTES

1. Although the formal terminology for a conviction in juvenile court is "adjudication," for purposes of both clarity and emphasis the term "conviction" is used here.

2. Steven A. Drizin and Greg Luloff, "Are Juvenile Courts a Breeding Ground for Wrongful Convictions?," *N. KY. L. Rev.* 34 (2007): 260.

3. Ibid., 260, 266–83. "Culture" as used in this piece refers both to objective culture or that which we observe, including artifacts, food, clothing, names, as well as subjective culture, which refers to the invisible, less tangible aspects of behavior, including one's values, beliefs, and attitudes. Cross-cultural misunderstandings typically occur at the level of subjective culture. See Sue Bryant & Jean Koh Peters, "Five Habits for Cross-Cultural Lawyering," in *Race, Culture, Psychology, & Law*, ed. Kimberly Holt Barrett & William H. George, (Thousand Oaks, CA: Sage Publications, 2005), 47, 48 & 60 n.3.

4. Drizin and Luloff, "Breeding Ground for Wrongful Convictions?," 260, 303.

5. See Martin Guggenheim and Randy Hertz, "Reflections on Judges, Juries, and Justice: Ensuring the Fairness of Juvenile Delinquency Trials," *Wake Forest L. Rev.* 33 (1998): 564–71.

6. Drizin and Luloff, "Breeding Ground for Wrongful Convictions?," 285; Tamar R. Birckhead, "Toward a Theory of Procedural Justice for Juveniles," *Buff. L. Rev.* 57 (2009): 1448–95.

7. Robin Walker Sterling, *Role of Juvenile Defense Counsel in Delinquency Court*, (Nat'l Juv. Defender Ctr., 2009), 3, 7–9, http://www.njdc.info/pdf/njdc_role_of_counsel_book.pdf.; see also "Model Rules Of Professional Conduct" (American Bar Association, 2010): Rule 1.2, comment 1.

8. A motion is a written or oral request that a court make a specified ruling or order. "Discovery" refers to disclosure, at a party's request, of information that relates to the litigation. When a discovery motion is granted by the court, the opposing side must provide the requested information to the other party.

9. Sterling, *Role of Juvenile Defense Counsel*, 6.

10. Ibid., 5–7; Kristin Henning, "Loyalty, Paternalism, and Rights: Client Counseling Theory and the Role of Child's Counsel in Delinquency Cases," *Notre Dame L. Rev.* 81 (2005): 247.

11. Birckhead, "Toward a Theory," 1502–04; Hillary B. Farber, "The Role of the Parent/Guardian in Juvenile Custodial Interrogations: Friend or Foe?," *Am. Crim. L. Rev.* 41 (2004): 1293–94; Kristin Henning, "It Takes a Lawyer to Raise a Child?: Allocating Responsibilities among Parents, Children, and Lawyers in Delinquency Cases," *Nev. L.J.* 6 (2006): 849–52.

12. John Hostettler, *Fighting for Justice: The History and Origins of Adversary Trial*, (Winchester, UK: Waterside Press, 2006), 11.

13. Ibid., 11–13.

14. Ibid., 17; Stephan A. Landsman, "A Brief Survey of the Development of the Adversary System," *Ohio St. L.J.* 44 (1983): 732–33.

15. "Model Rules of Prof'l Conduct," preamble §2.

16. "Model Rules of Prof'l Conduct," preamble §§ 5, 8 (emphasis added).

17. ABA Standards for Criminal Justice: Prosecution Function and Def. Function Standard 4-1.2(b) (1993).

18. Cait Clarke, "Problem-Solving Defenders in the Community: Expanding the Conceptual and Institutional Boundaries of Providing Counsel to the Poor," *Geo. J. Legal Ethics* 14 (2001): 448; Criminal Practice, Legal Aid Soc'y, last visited Aug. 11, 2010, http://www.legal-aid.org/en/criminal/criminalpractice.aspx; Philadelphia Public Defender, City of Philadelphia, last visited Aug. 11, 2010, http://www.phila.gov/defender/.

19. Barbara A. Babcock, "How Can You Defend Those People?: The Making of a Criminal Lawyer," *Geo. Wash. L. Rev.* 53 (1984–85): 312 (book review); Clarke, "Problem-Solving Defenders," 453–54.

20. Clarke, "Problem-Solving Defenders," 453.

21. Ibid.

22. Ibid., 449–51; Kim Taylor-Thompson, "Taking it to the Streets," *N.Y.U. Rev. L. & Soc. Change* 29 (2004): 198.

23. Clarke, "Problem-Solving Defenders," 452–53.

24. Babcock, "How Can You Defend?" 312.

25. Trial Practice Institute, Nat'l Criminal Def. College, last visited Aug. 11, 2010, http:www.ncdc.net/tpi/index.html.

26. National Defender Leadership Institute, Nat'l Legal Aid and Defender Ass'n, last visited Aug. 11, 2010, http://www.nlada.net/ndli.

27. Barry C. Feld, "The Right to Counsel in Juvenile Court: An Empirical Study of When Lawyers Appear and the Difference They Make," *J. Crim. L. & Criminology* 79 (1989): 1199–1200.

28. *In re Gault*, 387 U.S. 1, 41–42 (1967).

29. Henning, "It Takes a Lawyer," 250.

30. Ibid., 250–54.

31. Ibid., 255–56; Standards Relating to Counsel For Private Parties §§3.1(a), 9.4(a) (IJA-ABA Joint Comm'n on Juv. Justice Standards, 1996).

32. Sterling, *Role of Juvenile Defense Counsel*, 7.

33. Martin Guggenheim, "The Right to be Represented but Not Heard: Reflections on Legal Representation for Children," *N.Y.U. L. Rev.* 59 (1984); Ellen Marrus, "Best Interests Equals Zealous Advocacy: A Not So Radical View of Holistic Representation for Children Accused of Crime," *Md. L. Rev.* 62 (2003).

34. Henning, "It Takes a Lawyer," 257.

35. Sterling, *Role of Juvenile Defense Counsel*, 5.

36. Christopher Slobogin and Mark R. Fondacaro, *Juveniles at Risk: A Plea for Preventative Justice* (New York: Oxford University Press, forthcoming).

37. Katayoon Majd and Patricia Puritz, "The Cost of Injustice: How Low-Income Youth Continue to Pay the Price of Failing Indigent Defense Systems," *Geo. J. On Poverty L. & Pol'y* 16 (2009): 544.

38. Julian Mack, "The Juvenile Court," *Harvard L. Rev.* 23 (1909): 120.

39. Slobogin and Fondacaro, *Juveniles at Risk*; Jeffrey Fagan, "Juvenile Crime and Criminal Justice: Resolving Border Disputes," *The Future of Children* 18, no. 2 (Fall 2008): 81–82, http://www.princeton.edu/futureofchildren/publications/docs/18_02_05.pdf.

40. *In re Gault*, 387 U.S. 1, 19 n.23 (1967) (citing *Kent v. United States*, 383 U.S. 541, 556 (1966)).

41. Guggenheim and Hertz, "Reflections on Judges," 564–70.

42. Birckhead, "Toward a Theory," 1451 (stating that only twenty states "either provide jury trials to juveniles by right or allow them under limited circumstances"); Linda A. Szymanski, "Juvenile Delinquents' Right to a Jury Trial (2007 Update)," *NCJJ Snapshot* (Pittsburgh, PA: Nat'l Ctr. for Juvenile Justice, Feb. 2008).

43. See Guggenheim and Hertz, "Reflections on Judges," 564–82.

44. Ibid., 569–70.

45. Ibid.

46. *In re Winship*, 397 U.S. 358, 368 (1970).

47. See Guggenheim and Hertz, "Reflections on Judges," 564–65.

48. "Docket" refers to the schedule of cases pending before a court.

49. See note 9.

50. See Sterling, *Role of Juvenile Defense Counsel*, 5.

51. Ibid., 27. Courts keep lists of private attorneys whom they may appoint to represent indigent defendants when public defenders are unavailable.

52. ABA Juvenile Justice Ctr. & S. Ctr. For Human Rights, *Georgia: an Assessment of Access to Counsel and Quality of Representation in Delinquency Proceedings* (2004): 24, http://www.njdc.info/dpf/georgia.pdf.

53. Texas Appleseed Fair Def. Project on Indigent Def. Practices in Tex. - Juvenile Chapter, *Selling Justice Short: Juvenile Indigent Defense in Texas* (2000), 16–17 [hereinafter *Texas Assessment*], http://www.njdc.info/pdf/TexasAssess.pdf.

54. Patricia Puritz and Cathryn Crawford, *Florida: An Assessment of Access to Counsel & Quality of Representation in Delinquency Proceedings* (Nat'l Juvenile Defender Ctr, 2006), 54–55, http://www.njdc.info/pdf/Florida%20Assessment.pdf.

55. Ibid., 55.

56. Ibid.

57. Caren Harp, *Bringing Balance to Juvenile Justice* (Am. Prosecutors Research Inst., 2002), 5; Tamar R. Birckhead, "North Carolina, Juvenile Court Jurisdiction, and the Resistance to Reform," *N.C. L. Rev.* 86 (2008): 1498.

58. See note 9.

59. *Texas Assessment*, 22–23.

60. *Georgia Assessment*, 24; Elizabeth M Calvin, et al., ABA Juvenile Justice Ctr. et al., *Washington: An Assessment of Access to Counsel and Quality of Representation in Juvenile Offender Matters* (2003), 30.

61. Standards Relating to Counsel for Private Parties, § 7.2.

62. *Georgia Assessment*, 23.

63. ABA Juvenile Justice Ctr. and Mid-Atlantic Juvenile Defender Ctr., *Maryland: An Assessment of Access to Counsel and Quality of Representation in Delinquency Proceedings* (2003), 31, http://www.njdc.info/pdf/mdreport.pdf.

64. Ibid., 62; Jessie Beck, Patricia Puritz, and Robin Walker Sterling, Nat'l Juvenile Defender Ctr., *Nebraska: Juvenile Legal Defense: A Report on Access to Counsel and Quality of Representation for Children in Nebraska* (2009), vi [hereinafter *Nebraska Assessment*], http://www.njdc.info/pdf/nebraska_assessment.pdf.

65. *Georgia Assessment*, 30–31.

66. *Georgia Assessment*, 37; *Washington Assessment*, 38.

67. ABA Juvenile Justice Ctr. & Mid-Atlantic Juvenile Defender Ctr., *Virginia: An Assessment of Access to Counsel and Quality of Representation in Delinquency Proceedings* (2002), 27, http://www.njdc.info/pdf/Virginia%20Assessment.pdf.

68. Patricia McFall Torbet, "Juvenile Probation: The Workhorse of the Juvenile Justice System," *Juv. Just. Bull* (Washington, D.C.: Office of Juvenile Justice & Delinquency Prevention, Mar. 1996): 1.

69. *Washington Assessment*, 38; *Georgia Assessment*, 35.

70. N.C. Gen. Stat. § 7B-1501(9), (29) (2009).

71. Elizabeth Gladden Kehoe, Nat'l Juvenile Defender Ctr. & Kim Brooks Tandy, Cent. Juvenile Defender Ctr., *Indiana: An Assessment of Access to Counsel and Quality of Representation in Delinquency Proceedings* (2006), 37, http://www.njdc.info/pdf/Indiana%20Assessment.pdf ; Laval S. Miller-Wilson, Juvenile Law Ctr. and Patricia Puritz, ABA Juvenile Justice Ctr., *Pennsylvania: An Assessment of Access to Counsel and Quality of Representation in Delinquency Proceedings* (2003), 7, http://www.njdc.info/pdf/pareport.pdf.

72. *Pennsylvania Assessment*, 7; *Florida Assessment*, 45; ABA Juvenile Justice Ctr. & S. Juvenile Defender Ctr., *North Carolina: An Assessment of Access to Counsel and Quality of Representation in Delinquency Proceedings* (2003), 4, http://www.njdc.info/pdf/ncreport.pdf.

73. *Georgia Assessment*, 35.

74. *Pennsylvania Assessment*, 6.

75. Ibid.; *Washington Assessment*, 37.

76. President's Comm'n on Law Enforcement and the Admin. of Justice, *Task Force Report: Juvenile Delinquency & Youth Crime* (1967), 82.

77. Herbert H. Lou, *Juvenile Courts in the United States* (Chapel Hill: UNC Press, 1927), 138.

78. William B. McKesson, "Right to Counsel in Juvenile Proceedings," *Minn L. Rev.* 45 (1961): 845–46.

79. Barbara Fedders, "Losing Hold of the Guiding Hand: Ineffective Assistance of Counsel in Juvenile Delinquency Representation," *Lewis & Clark L. Rev.* 14 (2010): 791–92.

80. Patricia Puritz and Robin Walker, Nat'l Juvenile Defender Ctr., *Mississippi: An Assessment of Access to Counsel and Quality of Representation in Youth Court Proceedings* (2007), 45, http://www.njdc.info/pdf/mississippi_assessment.pdf.

81. *Virginia Assessment*, 3.

82. *Mississippi Assessment*, 45; *Nebraska Assessment*, 36.

83. *Nebraska Assessment*, 36.

84. *Nebraska Assessment*, 36–37.

85. *Florida Assessment*, 53; *Mississippi Assessment*, 45; H. Ted Rubin, "The Legal Defense of Juveniles: Struggling but Pushing Forward," *Juv. Just. Update*, June-July 2010, 1–2.

86. *Georgia Assessment*, 24; *Texas Assessment*, 24; *Washington Assessment*, 24.

87. Mich. Comp. Laws Serv. § 712A.18(1)(g) (LexisNexis 2005); Mont. Code Ann. § 41-5-1412(3) (2007); N.C. gen. Stat. § 7B-2703(b) (2009).

88. Henning, "It Takes a Lawyer," 845–47.

89. *North Carolina Assessment*, 39.

90. Henning, "It Takes a Lawyer," 300–01.

91. Ibid.

92. Ibid., 851.

93. Ibid., 849–51.

94. Birckhead, "Toward a Theory," 1502–03.

95. Henning, "It Takes a Lawyer," 853–66.

96. *Florida Assessment*, 52; Henning, "It Takes a Lawyer," 853; Marrus, "Best Interests Equals Zealous Advocacy," 315.

97. Henning, "It Takes a Lawyer," 271–73.

98. Marrus, "Best Interests Equals Zealous Advocacy," 321–22.

99. Elizabeth S. Scott and Thomas Grisso, "Developmental Incompetence, Due Process, and Juvenile Justice Policy," *N.C. L. Rev.* 83 (2005): 843–44.

100. Henning, "It Takes a Lawyer," 256–57.

101. Richard J. Bonnie and Thomas Grisso, "Adjudicative Competence and Youthful Offenders," in *Youth on Trial*, ed. Thomas Grisso & Robert Schwartz (Chicago: University of Chicago Press, 2000), 73, 91–92; Ellen Marrus, "Can I Talk Now?: Why Miranda Does Not Offer Adolescents Adequate Protections," *Temp. L. Rev.* 79 (2006): 517.

102. Marcus J. H. Huibers and Simon Wessely, "The Act of Diagnosis: Pros and Cons of Labeling Chronic Fatigue Syndrome," *Psychol. Med.* 36 (2006): 897.

103. Ibid., 898; Phyllis Solomon, "Peer Support/Peer Provided Services Underlying Processes, Benefits, and Critical Ingredients," *Psychiatric Rehabilitation J.* 27 (2004): 395.

104. Huibers and Wessely, "The Act of Diagnosis," 898.

105. Ibid.

106. Andrea Stockl, "Complex Syndromes, Ambivalent Diagnosis, and Existential Uncertainty: The Case of Systemic Lupus Erythematosus (SLE)," *Soc. Sci. & Med.* 65 (2007): 1552.

107. Anna M. Byszewski et al., "Dementia Diagnosis Disclosure: A Study of Patient and Caregiver Perspectives," *Alzheimer Disease Ass'n Disorder* 21 (2007): 112.

108. Catharine A. MacKinnon, *Feminism Unmodified: Discourses on Life and Law*, (Cambridge, MA: Harvard University Press, 1987), 103–04.

109. Leslie Bender, "A Lawyer's Primer on Feminist Theory and Tort," *in Feminist Legal Theory: Foundations*, ed. D. Kelly Weisberg (Philadelphia: Temple University Press, 1993), 58, 61; Virginia Woolf, *A Room of One's Own* (1929, repr. New York: Harcourt, Brace & World, 1957), 31–38.

110. Sterling, *Role of Juvenile Defense Counsel*, 5; *Florida Assessment*, 53. But see Rubin, "Legal Defense of Juveniles," 2, 12.

111. N.C. Advocates for Justice & Juvenile Def. Section, IDS Office of the Juvenile Defender, Electronic Newsletter, (N.C. Admin. Office of the Courts, Feb. 2010), http://www.aoc.state.nc.us/www/ids/Juvenile%20Defender/Newsletters/Feb_2010.htm; Specialty Areas, Tex. Bd. of Legal Specialization, http://www.tbls.org/SpecialtyAreas.aspx (last visited Aug. 12, 2010).

112. Clarke, "Problem-Solving Defenders," 426.

113. Guggenheim and Hertz, "Reflections on Judges," 583–85; Barry C. Feld, "Criminalizing Juvenile Justice: Rules of Procedure for the Juvenile Court," *Minn. L. Rev.* 69 (1984): 234.

114. The juvenile appeals bar is the group of lawyers qualified to represent juveniles who seek to have decisions of the delinquency court reconsidered by a higher court.

115. "Ineffective assistance of counsel" occurs when a defendant is deprived of a fair trial because of the lawyer's incompetence, lack of effort, or because of a conflict of interest.

116. Fedders, "Losing Hold," 771–819.

117. Ibid., 773–74; Michael Pinard, "The Logistical and Ethical Difficulties of Informing Juveniles About the Collateral Consequences of Adjudications," *Nev. L.J.* 6 (2006): 1114–18; Michael Pinard, "An Integrated Perspective on the Collateral Consequences of Criminal Convictions and Reentry Issues Faced by Formerly Incarcerated Individuals," *B.U. L. Rev.* 86 (2006): 634–35.

118. Emily Buss, "The Role of Lawyers in Promoting Juveniles' Competence as Defendants," in *Youth on Trial*, ed. Thomas Grisso & Robert Schwartz, (Chicago: University of Chicago Press, 2000), 253–62.

*Tamar R. Birckhead** is an assistant professor of law, University of North Carolina at Chapel Hill School of Law. She has written extensively on criminal procedure and juvenile justice policy and reform.

"Whose Side Are You On Anyway?": Best Interest Versus Expressed Interest Representation of Minors In Delinquency Court

by Jacqueline L. Bullard*

"Whether it is a minor or an adult who stands accused, the lawyer is the one person to whom society as a whole looks as the protector of the legal rights of that person in his dealings with police and the courts."[1]

The problem of youth in conflict with the law is hardly a new phenomenon. In the fourth century B.C., the philosopher Plato complained, "What is happening to our young people? They disrespect their elders, they disobey their parents. They ignore the law. They riot in the streets inflamed with wild notions. Their morals are decaying. What is to become of them?"[2] Yet more than two millennia after Plato uttered his famous lament, adults in large measure remain befuddled as to a solution. Prior to the creation of a separate juvenile court system in 1899, criminal courts drew few distinctions between children and adults.[3] Youth were tried as adults and, depending on the nature of the offense, could be executed, imprisoned with adults, or placed in euphemistically-named "Houses of Refuge" where they frequently suffered maltreatment and abuse.[4]

Appalled by the conditions faced by youth ensnared in the criminal justice system, social reformers created the first juvenile court in Chicago in 1899, and by 1925 the entire nation had followed suit.[5] While the age at which youth fell under the jurisdiction of juvenile courts varied from state to state, most included youth up to 16 or 17 years of age. Grounded in the doctrine of *parens patriae*, these new delinquency courts rested on the notion that youth were less culpable for their actions and more amenable to rehabilitation than their adult counterparts, and that treatment rather than punishment was the appropriate response to juvenile crime.[6] Even the nomenclature of the courts changed. "Convictions" became "adjudications" in juvenile court; "sentences" became "dispositions." Hearings and records were confidential to protect youth from stigma, and judges were granted broad discretion over minors and their families when crafting dispositions.[7]

Perhaps the most significant distinction between delinquency and criminal court rested on the substantive and procedural rules which applied. Fairness in state and federal criminal courts was constitutionally guaranteed through the right to adequate notice, the right against compelled self-incrimination, the right to subpoena witnesses, the right to confront and cross-examine the government's witnesses, the right to a jury trial, the right to be proven guilty beyond a reasonable doubt, and the right to counsel.[8] Each of these rights was deemed fundamental to a fair trial, but few were more important than the right to counsel, for without the assistance of a skilled attorney, most defendants were incapable of vindicating any of their remaining constitutional rights.[9] Thus, by 1963 all indigent criminal defendants facing felony charges were guaranteed the right to appointed counsel to assist in their defense.[10]

These same constitutional protections, however, were dispensed with in delinquency court, under the theory that the rules which governed criminal proceedings had no place in a non-adversarial system which had discarded notions of crime and punishment in favor of treatment and rehabilitation.[11] Because all children were considered to be in a perpetual state of custody by virtue of being cared for by responsible adults,[12] it was assumed that normal rules governing the state's ability to restrict individual freedom did not to apply to minors in delinquency court.[13] As a result, when 15-year-old Gerald Gault was arrested for making a telephone call "of the irritatingly offensive, adolescent, sex variety" to a neighbor in 1964, he was arrested without notice to his parents, held in detention, adjudicated delinquent based on hearsay evidence, and committed to a juvenile institution until his 21st birthday—all without the assistance of counsel.[14] Had Gerald been an adult in criminal court, he would have faced a maximum penalty of two months in jail and a $50 fine.[15] Gerald appealed, and his case eventually found its way to the United States Supreme Court, where, in a watershed decision, the Court held that minors in delinquency hearings were constitutionally guaranteed the right to counsel under the due process clause of the 14th amendment.[16]

The *Gault* decision was rooted in both a realistic assessment of the nature of juvenile court and principles of fundamental fairness. Although the rehabilitative aims and compassionate treatment which characterized the first juvenile courts remained prevalent in most delinquency courtrooms, the shift from punishment to rehabilitation had, as the Supreme Court charitably observed, "not been entirely satisfactory."[17] Many juvenile court judges lacked the qualifications to rule on matters of law or evaluate the unique needs of the youth before them, and funding for rehabilitative services often was woefully insufficient.[18] By the 1960s, the term "delinquent" "ha[d] come to involve only slightly less stigma than the term 'criminal,'"[19] and the confidentiality of juvenile court records had become "more rhetoric than reality."[20] Even in the most beneficent of courtrooms, delinquency proceedings were "comparable in seriousness to a felony prosecution."[21]

The State's goal was the enforcement of its criminal laws, and youth who were found guilty could be taken from their families and incarcerated for years.[22]

Based largely on the lack of constitutionally-based standards and procedures, some of these youth found themselves adjudicated delinquent based on inadequate evidence or facing well-intentioned but nonetheless inappropriate dispositions.[23] The unluckiest faced outright abuses, with some local authorities invoking juvenile court proceedings against minors in order to chill or punish their participation in the burgeoning civil rights movement.[24] Ironically, the confidentiality provisions of juvenile court designed to protect minors made these abuses extraordinarily difficult to detect.[25] "[H]istory ha[d] again demonstrated that unbridled discretion, however benevolently motivated, is frequently a poor substitute for principle and procedure."[26]

Given the serious consequences which flowed from delinquency adjudications and the complexity of the proceedings themselves, the Supreme Court in *Gault* concluded that there was no distinction between criminal and juvenile proceedings with respect to the necessity of counsel.[27] "The juvenile needs the assistance of counsel to cope with problems of law, to make skilled inquiry into the facts, to insist upon regularity of the proceedings, and to ascertain whether he has a defense and to prepare and submit it. The child 'requires the guiding hand of counsel at every step in the proceedings against him.'"[28] Accordingly, the Court held that minors were entitled to counsel at delinquency hearings, and that they and their parents must be advised of this right.[29]

In addition to the right to counsel, *Gault* held that minors had the constitutional right to adequate notice of the charges, the right against compelled self-incrimination, and the right to confront and cross-examination the witnesses against them.[30] Three years later, the Court held that the reasonable doubt burden of proof was constitutionally required in delinquency proceedings.[31] As a result, youth in delinquency court now enjoyed most of the same basic constitutional protections applicable in criminal court. With advocates by their side, youth became "participants rather than spectators" in the proceedings against them.[32]

Before long, the right to counsel gained added significance, as the stakes grew higher for youth who found themselves in conflict with the law. In a shift which coincided with the advent of the 24-hour news cycle,[33] a temporary spike in juvenile crime gave rise to public fears that pint-sized "superpredators" soon would be lurking around every corner.[34] Although this predicted crime wave failed to materialize, and juvenile crime rates actually fell in the ensuing years, public fear drove public policy, and by the end of the 1990s most state legislatures had made radical changes to their juvenile court acts.[35] The primary focus of the delinquency system shifted from rehabilitation to protecting public safety and punishing offenders. Confidentiality provisions were substantially eroded,[36] minors became subject to harsher sanctions, and cases previously handled as delinquency matters were now routinely or automatically transferred to criminal court.[37]

In the midst of this changing landscape, the role of counsel was the subject of widely inconsistent practice. Legal scholars and judicial and bar associations largely agreed that the *Gault* right to counsel guaranteed minors zealous advocates who were guided by their clients' expressed interests.[38] Yet attorneys in many courtrooms acted as guardians *ad litem* (GALs) while representing what they perceive to be their clients' best interests, or they attempted to fulfill the role of both defense attorney and GAL by providing "hybrid" representation.[39]

The role of zealous advocate and that of GAL differ in three critical respects regarding the client's power to direct the objectives of representation, the attorney's duty to maintain client confidences, and the attorney's duty of loyalty. In the traditional attorney-client relationship, the client is the ultimate arbiter on such major decisions as to whether to plead guilty or elect a trial and what type of disposition to seek—even when the attorney believes that the client's decisions are foolish.[40] In contrast, a GAL may override a client's expressed wishes on major decisions based on what the GAL deems is in the client's best interest.[41]

Substantial differences between the two models of representation also exist in relation to client confidentiality. For while client confidences in the traditional attorney-client relationship are held inviolate under nearly all circumstances,[42] a GAL, as an agent of the court, is free to reveal otherwise confidential information if such disclosures are deemed to be in the client's best interests.[43] In addition, zealous advocates have an undivided duty of loyalty to their clients,[44] while GALs have an obligation to serve the best interests of society as well.[45] As a result, GALs are authorized to act in ways which would constitute serious ethical breaches for defense attorneys, such as soft-pedaling a client's defense, revealing client confidences, or overriding a client's wishes, so long as the GAL believes that an adjudication or disposition would be in the best interests of the client and the community.

THE BEST INTEREST MODEL OF REPRESENTATION

The practice of best-interest representation in delinquency court arose for several reasons. First, and perhaps foremost, *Gault* itself was not clear about the precise role of counsel in delinquency proceedings. Rather than grounding its analysis in the sixth amendment right to counsel applicable in criminal proceedings, the Court found that a minor's right to counsel arose from the fundamental fairness guarantees of the 14th amendment due process clause.[46] The Court failed to address, however, if, or how, this distinction affected counsel's representation.[47]

Given the lack of adequate direction from the Court, a model of representation grounded in the original rehabilitative aims of the juvenile court was bound to emerge. Post-*Gault* attorneys often encountered a courtroom culture where the participants were expected to cooperate in providing minors with whatever services or consequences the adults deemed appropriate, and attorneys who attempted to provide traditional, adversarial representation on behalf of their clients frequently met with resistance.[48]

Practitioners of GAL and hybrid representation believe that a legal foundation exists for best interest representation. Best-interest attorneys note that the *Gault* right to counsel is found in due process guarantees alone, rather than in the sixth amendment right to counsel applicable in criminal proceedings.[49] As a result, these advocates reason, a minor's right to counsel does not guarantee the traditional defense attorney envisioned by the sixth amendment. Best-interest attorneys note that the law is replete with examples of minors being granted fewer rights or facing greater restrictions by virtue of their immaturity, including decisions relating to marriage, driving, alcohol consumption, and entering into contracts.[50]

The proponents of best-interest representation also stress that juvenile court has as one of its express aims the rehabilitation of the minor. Attorneys who spend time in juvenile court frequently empathize with their clients and recognize that the behavior of these minors is too frequently rooted in factors outside their control. These youth often live in violent neighborhoods, attend failing schools, and have suffered physical and sexual abuse.[51] Given that it was poor decision-making which landed many of these youth in delinquency court in the first place, it seems reasonable for attorneys to either influence or override their clients' decisions if doing so (in the attorney's opinion) might benefit the minor.

Some proponents of GAL and hybrid representation believe that their clients often are not capable of acting in their own best interests. Adolescent brain research reveals that those portions of the human brain associated with reasoning, the passage of time, abstract thought, impulse control, and the weighing of alternatives are underdeveloped in teenagers, and, as a result, adolescents are more focused on immediate rewards, are hampered in their ability to weigh risks, are more impulsive, are particularly vulnerable to pressure, and have extraordinary difficulty engaging in counterfactual thinking (the ability to imagine alternate courses of action and determine which would lead to a desirable outcome).[52] As a result of these cognitive deficits, best-interest attorneys may feel justified in substituting their judgment for that of their clients.[53]

The Expressed Interest, Zealous Advocacy
Model of Representation

Advocates of the zealous advocacy model also find a legal basis for their position. These attorneys note that, in addition to the right to counsel, minors have been granted a variety of other constitutional rights, including the right against compelled self-incrimination, and the rights to notice, confrontation, cross-examination, and a reasonable doubt burden of proof—rights which would have little meaning in the absence of a zealous advocate to vindicate them.[54] They note that the need for zealous advocacy when challenging the admissibility of confessions is particularly critical when representing juvenile clients, given their susceptibility to coercion[55] and their consistent over-represented in studies of false confessions.[56]

The GAL or hybrid attorney's ability to disclose client confidences jeopardizes the minor's constitutional rights even further. Minors who believe that they are being represented by a defense attorney can be misled into making self-incriminating statements to counsel, only to have those statements used against them either directly through express disclosure or indirectly through less than vigorous representation.[57] Minors who do understand the GAL's ability to reveal client confidences will be deprived of the effective assistance of counsel, because they will be disinclined to turn to their lawyers for advice and will withhold pertinent facts for fear that the information will be used against them.[58] As a result, their attorneys will be less able to provide sound legal advice and advocacy.[59] "Lawyers who assume the GAL model may be forced, therefore to choose between honesty [in describing their roles to their clients] and effectiveness."[60]

Expressed-interest advocates argue that hybrid representation poses a particularly insidious threat to the minor's constitutional rights, given that attorneys acting in this dual capacity have both a duty to the minor to provide zealous, client-directed representation and an obligation to serve the interests of the court and society. Minors will always have an interest in being acquitted of the charges against them, regardless of their guilt or innocence. In her capacity as defense attorney, counsel will have a duty to pursue "the single aim of acquittal by all means fair and honorable."[61] In her capacity as GAL, however, the attorney may believe that an adjudication of delinquency is in the best interest of the minor or society.[62] When faced with such a dilemma, hybrid attorneys may not follow their clients' expressed wishes, but may instead "fail to adequately research and investigate a case, believing that an adjudication that will lead to probation, and services, is what the child needs most."[63] The subliminal effects of such conflicts are especially difficult to detect and demonstrate in the delinquency context, given that minors, by virtue of their age, development, and experience, are less likely than adults to recognize and raise issues of attorney incompetence, and the attorneys themselves are less sensitive to potential conflicts in light of the historical view of juvenile court as less adversarial and more focused on rehabilitation.[64]

In addition, hybrid representation can undermine the rehabilitative aims of juvenile court. No other cohort feels the sting of injustice or hypocrisy quite as deeply as adolescents. When these minors discover that their "defense" attorneys are betraying their confidences, failing to vigorously seek acquittal, and/or ignoring their wishes regarding the outcome of the proceedings, the attorney will be viewed as just another paternalistic authority figure who cannot be trusted.[65] Under these circumstances, "even the juvenile who has violated the law may not feel that he is being fairly treated and may therefore resist the rehabilitative effort of court personnel."[66]

Advocates of the zealous advocacy model also argue that the consequences which arise from delinquency adjudications are so serious that an adjudication can never be in a minor's best interest, and that lawyers accordingly must act as true defense attorneys.[67] In recent decades, delinquency proceedings have become more punitive, the court's traditional focus on rehabilitation and confidentiality has eroded, and the consequences which flow from an adjudication have become more serious. Delinquent minors can be transferred to adult court, imprisoned for years in institutions where they may be subject to abuse, required to submit DNA samples for inclusion in statewide and national databases, and required to register as sex offenders for the same period as adults.[68] Delinquency adjudications can disqualify minors and their families from living in public housing, can interfere with their employment and educational opportunities, can serve as future sentence enhancements, can render minors ineligible for future military service, and can result in the deportation of immigrant youth.[69]

Expressed-interest advocates argue that hybrid representation also undermines the interests of society, because it undermines the truth-seeking function of trials and thus strikes at the core of the legal system. The law has long recognized that the discovery of truth, the conviction of the guilty, and the acquittal of the innocent is best accomplished through vigorous advocacy on both sides, and that the chances of achieving a correct result are increased when the defense forces the State to present strong evidence in support of its position.[70] That balance, however, is skewed when an attorney who believes that a delinquency adjudication would serve the best interest of his client or society renders less than zealous advocacy in the role of GAL. In no other context is an attorney placed in the position of determining the guilt or innocence of a client and adjusting the vigorousness of the defense based on what the attorney believes is a desirable outcome for the client and/or society.

Finally, expressed-interest advocates argue that developmental immaturity does not warrant the usurpation of a client's will regarding the objectives of representation. GAL representation traditionally has been associated with clients who are so incompetent to make decisions about their own welfare that a traditional attorney-client relationship cannot be maintained. The immaturity and developmental delays associated with adolescence do not ordinarily rise to this level of legal incompetence. Attorneys who specialize in juvenile representation stress that lawyers who have been properly trained in how to communicate with adolescents, who familiarize themselves with class and cultural factors which might adversely affect their interaction with their clients, and who value client autonomy are able to provide the type of legal advice which allows their clients to make informed decisions about their cases.[71] Only those clients who satisfy the legal standard for incompetence should be represented by a GAL, but even these clients should also be represented by a defense attorney. Simply put, minors who are competent enough to be held accountable for their actions should be granted the autonomy to determine the objective of representation which will so profoundly affect their lives.[72]

HOLISTIC, SPECIALIZED JUVENILE REPRESENTATION

In recent years, many juvenile advocates have called for an alternate model of representation which fully encompasses the zealous advocacy model, but which also recognizes the unique needs of juvenile clients and honors the rehabilitative aims of delinquency court.[73] Advocates of this holistic model argue that by rooting a minor's right to counsel in the broad fundamental fairness principles of due process rather than the sixth amendment right to counsel in criminal proceedings, *Gault* guarantees more than a traditional defense attorney, and may well encompass holistic representation.[74] Under the holistic model, counsel would always act as a zealous defense attorney in vindicating the minor's constitutional rights and expressed wishes, but "would also attempt to identify and assess the deficits and needs of the child, such as learning disabilities or developmental disabilities, as well as positive attributes that might be nurtured or supported."[75] In an ideal world with sufficient resources, the holistic advocate would have access to a team of experts who could provide input and assistance.[76]

In addition to possessing expertise in criminal and juvenile law, holistic attorneys must be familiar with adolescent development, special education and mental law, the collateral consequences of an adjudication, and the appropriate services, schools, and placements which are available should their clients be adjudicated delinquent.[77] Holistic practitioners must be able to communicate in a manner which the client can understand, recognize when their clients may be incompetent, effectively engage parents as allies, and be willing to engage experts when necessary.[78] In short, attorneys in delinquency court must be highly-skilled specialists.[79]

Because the attorney who provides holistic representation both acts as a zealous advocate at the adjudicatory stage of the proceedings and actively participates in presenting a rehabilitative disposition consistent with the client's expressed interests, proponents of this model see the purported conflict between best interest and expressed interest representation as a false dichotomy.[80] Holistic representation provides all of the benefits and protections of the expressed interest mode, by fostering honest and complete communication between attorney and client, and by zealously safeguarding the minor's right against compelled self-incrimination, and the rights to notice, confrontation, cross-examination, and a reasonable doubt burden of proof. In addition, however, holistic representation accounts for the unique needs of the minor, respects client autonomy, and more actively fosters the rehabilitative aims of the juvenile court.[81] In so doing, holistic representation zealously serves the best and expressed interests of the client.[82]

NOTES

1. Fare v. Michael C., 442 U.S. 707, 719 (1979).
2. Tanya Byron, "We see children as pestilent," *The Guardian: Education Guardian*, March 17, 2009, http://www.guardian.co.uk/theguardian/2009/mar/17/educationguardian.
3. Andrew M. Carter, "Age Matters: The Case for a Constitutionalized Infancy Defense," *University of Kansas Law Review* 54 (2006): 708–10. (In the centuries preceding the creation of juvenile courts, children below the age of seven were immune from criminal prosecution based on an inability to form a criminal intent, and children between the ages of seven and thirteen were presumed incapable of forming a criminal intent, a presumption which could only be rebutted by strong evidence.)
4. Joanna Markman, "*In re Gault*: A Retrospective in 2007: Is It Working? Can It Work?" *Barry Law Review* 9 (2007): 125; *In re Gault*, 387 U.S. 1, 15 (1967).
5. *Gault*, 387 U.S. at 14–15.
6. Markman, "*In re Gault*: A Retrospective," 125–26.
7. Ibid., 127.
8. *In re Oliver*, 333 U.S. 257, 273 (1948) (right to notice applies to the states); *Gideon v. Wainwright*, 372 U.S. 335, 344–45 (1963) (6th amendment right to counsel applies to the states); *Malloy v. Hogan*, 378 U.S. 1, 6 (1964) (5th amendment guarantee against self-incrimination applies to the states); *Pointer v. Texas*, 380 U.S. 400, 403 (1965) (6th amendment confrontation clause applies to the states); *Washington v. Texas*, 388 U.S. 14, 18 (1967) (6th amendment compulsory process clause applied to the states); *Duncan v. Louisiana*, 391 U.S. 145, 149 (1968) (6th amendment right to jury trial applies to the states; *In re Winship*, 397 U.S. 358, 364 (1970) (14th amendment guarantees that all criminal defendants be proven guilty beyond a reasonable doubt).
9. *Gideon*, 372 U.S. at 341, 345.
10. Ibid., 344–45.

11. *Gault,* 387 U.S. at 15–16.

12. Ellen Marrus, "Best Interests Equals Zealous Advocacy: A Not So Radical View of Holistic Representation for Children Accused of Crime," *Maryland Law Review* 62 (2003): 299.

13. *Gault,* 387 U.S. at 17.

14. Ibid., 5–8.

15. Ibid., 29.

16. Ibid., 30–31, 41; *McKeiver v. Pennsylvania,* 403 U.S. 528, 541 (1971) (Most likely because the Sixth Amendment by its express terms is limited to "criminal prosecutions" [U. S. Const., amend. VI], *Gault* found that a minor's right to counsel arose wholly from the due process protections of the Fourteenth Amendment).

17. *Gault,* 387 U.S. at 17–18.

18. Ibid., 14 fn. 20, 22 fn. 30.

19. Ibid., 24–25.

20. Ibid.

21. Ibid., 36.

22. Ibid., 36–37.

23. Ibid., 18–20.

24. Ibid., 18 fn. 24.

25. For a modern-day example of similar abuses, see "Luzerne County Kids-For-Cash Juvenile Court Scandal," Juvenile Law Center, accessed July 20, 2011, http://www.jlc.org/luzerne/.

26. *Gault,* 387 U.S. at 18.

27. Ibid., 36–37.

28. Ibid.

29. Ibid., 36, 41.

30. Ibid., 30–31, 33, 55, 57.

31. *Winship,* 397 U.S. at 368.

32. Robin Walker Sterling, *Role of Juvenile Defense Counsel in Delinquency Court,* (National Juvenile Defender Center, 2009), 2.

33. Markman, "*In re Gault*: A Retrospective," 123–24, 129.

34. Elizabeth Becker, "As Ex-Theorist on Young 'Superpredators,' Bush Aide Has Regrets," *The New York Times,* February 9, 2001, http://www.nytimes.com/2001/02/09/us/as-ex-theorist-on-young-superpredators-bush-aide-has-regrets.html?src=pm.

35. Markman, "*In re Gault*: A Retrospective," 130 fn. 54; Becker, "Bush Aide Has Regrets."

36. Markman, "*In re Gault*: A Retrospective," 127–28.

37. Patricia Puritz and Katayoon Majd, "Ensuring Authentic Youth Participation in Delinquency Cases: Creating a Paradigm for Specialized Juvenile Defense Practice," *Family Court Review* 45 (2007): 471.

38. National Council of Juvenile and Family Court Judges, *Juvenile Delinquency Guidelines: Improving Court Practice in Juvenile Delinquency Cases,* (2005), 30–31; Institute of Judicial Administration/American Bar Association Joint Comm'n on Juvenile Justice Standards, "Standards Relating to Counsel for Private Parties," § 3.1(a) (1996); National Advisory Committee for Juvenile Justice and Delinquency Prevention, "Standards for the Administration of Juvenile Justice," Commentary to §3.134, 278–29 (1979); "Recommendations of the UNLV Conference on Representing Children in Families: Child Advocacy and Justice Ten Years after Fordham," *Nevada Law Journal.* 6 (2006): 592, 609; "Recommendations of the Conference on Ethical Issues in the Legal Representation of Children," *Fordham Law Review* 64 (1996): 1301–02; "Recommendations of the Conference on Ethical Issues in the Legal Representation of Children in

Illinois," *Loyola University Chicago Law Journal* 29 (1998): 382; Sterling, *Role of Juvenile Defense Counsel*, 7; Kristin Henning, "It Takes a Lawyer to Raise a Child?: Allocating Responsibilities Among Parents, Children, and Lawyers in Delinquency Cases," *Nevada Law Journal* 6 (2006): 868–69; see also American Council of Chief Defenders & National Juvenile Defender Center, *Ten Core Principles for Providing Quality Delinquency Representation Through Indigent Defense Delivery Systems* (2005).

39. Barbara Fedders, "Losing Hold of the Guiding Hand: Ineffective Assistance of Counsel in Juvenile Delinquency Representation," *Lewis & Clark Law Review* 14 (2010): 786.

40. Diane Geraghty, "Ethical Issues in the Legal Representation of Children in Illinois: Roles, Rules, and Reforms," *Loyola University Chicago Law Journal* 29 (1998): 291–92.

41. Ibid., 292.

42. For examples of when an attorney may disclose client confidence, see *People v. Kidd*, 178 Ill.2d 92, 134 (1997) (when client gives informed consent); *People v. Calhoun*, 351 Ill.App.3d 1072, 1085–86 (2004) (when client clearly expresses intent to commit perjury); *People v. Childs*, 305 Ill.App.3d 128, 136–37 (1999) (when necessary for counsel to defend against client claim of wrongdoing).

43. Geraghty, "Ethical Issues," 293.

44. People v. Flores, 128 Ill.2d 66, 83 (1989).

45. In re B.K., 358 Ill.App.3d 1166, 1171 (2005); In the Interest of R.D., 148 Ill.App.3d 381, 387 (1986).

46. Fedders, "Losing Hold," 783–84.

47. Ibid.

48. Katherine Hunt Federle, "The Ethics of Empowerment: Rethinking the Role of Lawyers in Interviewing and Counseling the Child Client," *Fordham Law Review* 64 (1996): 1678–79.

49. Ellen Marrus, "Best Interests Equals Zealous Advocacy: A Not So Radical View of Holistic Representation for Children Accused of Crime," *Maryland Law Review* 62 (2003): 299.

50. See Fedders, "Losing Hold," 786.

51. For a discussion on the pitfalls of an empathy-driven practice, see Abbe Smith, "Too Much Heart and Not Enough Heat: The Short Life and Fractured Ego of the Empathic, Heroic Public Defender," *University of California Davis Law Review* 37 (2004): 1203–1265.

52. Kenneth J. King, "Waiving Childhood Goodbye: How Juvenile Courts Fail to Protect Children from Unknowing, Unintelligent, and Involuntary Waivers of Miranda Rights," *Wisconsin Law Review* (2006): 434–42.

53. Fedders, "Losing Hold," 785–86.

54. *Gault*, 387 U.S. at 39 n.65.

55. Steven A. Drizin and Greg Luloff, "Are Juvenile Courts a Breeding Ground for Wrongful Convictions?," *Northern Kentucky Law Review* 34 (2007): 260, 269, 274–75.

56. Steven A. Drizin and Richard A. Leo, "The Problem of False Confessions in the Post-DNA World," *North Carolina Law Review* 82 (2004): 944.

57. See *State v. Joanna V.*, 136 N.M. 40, 43–44 (2004) (unlikely that minor will be able to distinguish when the attorney is acting as defense counsel and when counsel is acting as GAL).

58. Emily Buss, " 'You're my What?' The Problem of Children's Misperceptions of Their Lawyers' Roles," *Fordham Law Review* 64 (1996): 1713–16; see *Upjohn Co. v. U.S.*, 449 U.S. 383, 389 (1981) (confidentiality in the attorney-client relationship serves broad public interests in the observance of law and the administration of justice by maximizing the ability of attorneys to render sound legal advice and advocate for their clients based on full disclosure).

59. See *Swidler & Berlin v. U.S.*, 524 U.S. 399, 403 (1998) (attorney is best able to render sound advice and advocacy after full disclosure by the client).

60. Buss, " 'You're my What?,' " 1717.

61. *People v. Hernandez*, 231 Ill.2d 134, 143 (2008).

62. See *People v. Daly*, 341 Ill.App.3d 372, 376 (2003) (GAL has duty to society).

63. Fedders, "Losing Hold," 794.

64. See Children and Family Justice Center et al., *Illinois: An Assessment of Access to Counsel & Quality of Representation*, http://www.modelsforchange.net/publications/171.

65. Henning, "It Takes a Lawyer," 873.

66. *Gault*, 387 U.S. at 26; see also Kristin Henning, "Loyalty, Paternalism, and Rights: Client Counseling Theory and the Role of Child's Counsel in Delinquency Cases," *Notre Dame Law Review* 81 (2005): 285–86.

67. See Marrus, "Best Interests Equals Zealous Advocacy," 331–32.

68. Puritz and Majd, "Ensuring Authentic Youth Participation," 471; Marrus, "Best Interests Equals Zealous Advocacy," 331–32 (noting that instances of abuse in juvenile correctional centers remain a problem).

69. Puritz and Majd, "Ensuring Authentic Youth Participation," 471.

70. *United States v. Cronic*, 466 U.S. 648, 655–56 (1984).

71. Federle 1690–92.

72. Ibid., 1676.

73. Puritz and Majd, "Ensuring Authentic Youth Participation," 471.

74. Marrus, "Best Interests Equals Zealous Advocacy," 299.

75. Maureen Pacheco, "The Defense of Children—A Call to Arms," *Champion*, August 2010, 51.

76. Ibid.

77. Sterling, *Role of Juvenile Defense Counsel*, 4–5.

78. Ibid., 5.

79. Puritz and Majd, "Ensuring Authentic Youth Participation," 471.

80. Marrus, "Best Interests Equals Zealous Advocacy," 326.

81. Puritz and Majd, "Ensuring Authentic Youth Participation," 472–76.

82. Marrus, "Best Interests Equals Zealous Advocacy," 334–47.

*Jacqueline Bullard is an assistant appellate defender with the Illinois Office of the State Appellate Defender, where she represents the expressed interests of her juvenile and adult clients before the Illinois Appellate and Supreme Courts. She is active in juvenile justice reform efforts and regularly leads sessions on juvenile law at the local, state, and national level.

DISCUSSION QUESTIONS

1. Should a lawyer be a zealous advocate even when she does not think it would be in the best interest of her client?

2. How much say should the youth have in deciding how to proceed with his or her case?

3. Should a juvenile be allowed to waive his/her right to counsel? Why or why not?

4. What should the government do to ensure that all children receive competent counsel?

5. What are the most difficult challenges facing juvenile defense attorneys?

Chapter 4:
Prosecuting and Sentencing Children as Adults

Although children are clearly developmentally different from adults, every state allows for the criminal prosecution of children in adult courts. Research on adolescent brain development and behavior indicates that juveniles are less biologically and psychosocially mature than adults, which leads them to be more impulsive and to engage in more risk taking. Their lack of maturity also compromises their ability to engage in long-term planning and to assess and consider consequences. Research has also shown that juveniles are more capable of being rehabilitated than adults. Further, studies have demonstrated that youth who are prosecuted in juvenile rather than adult court are less likely to reoffend and have better overall outcomes. Nevertheless, children accused of committing certain types of offenses, or children who are deemed to be repeat offenders, continue to be prosecuted in adult courts. Treating children in the justice system as if they were adults is both expensive and counterproductive. Alternatives to prosecuting and sentencing youth as adults can help reduce spending on prisons and allow youth the opportunity to become productive members of society.

"State Trends: Legislative Victories from 2005 to 2010—Removing Youth from the Adult Criminal Justice System," by Neelum Arya, examines the costs and consequences of treating youth in the justice system as adults. From misperceptions on youth crime to the role of brain development in behavior, "State Trends" explores a variety of issues that should be considered by those grappling with the question of whether to prosecute youth as adults. The article also reviews positive trends in removing children from the adult system across the country. In "Extreme Sentencing of Youth in the United States," by Allison Conyers, Shobha Mahadev, Caitlin Shay, and Sarah Silins, readers are asked to consider the harshest punishment adolescents can receive: juvenile life without the possibility of parole (JLWOP), essentially a sentence to die in prison. The four authors tackle numerous issues surrounding this punishment, including international human rights treaties and two key U.S. Supreme Court decisions (*Roper v. Simmons* and *Graham v. Florida*). The article ends with the stories of two individuals currently serving a JLWOP sentence and one family whose son is serving such sentence.

State Trends: Legislative Victories from 2005 to 2010—Removing Youth from the Adult Criminal Justice System

by Neelum Arya*

OVERVIEW

In the rush to crack down on youth crime in the 1980s and 1990s, many states enacted harsh laws making it easier for youth to be prosecuted in adult criminal courts. Every state allows youth to be prosecuted as adults by one of several mechanisms such that an estimated 250,000 children are prosecuted, sentenced, or incarcerated as adults each year in the United States.[1] In more than half of the states, there is no lower age limit on who can be prosecuted as an adult. This means that in these states very young children, even a 7-year-old, can be prosecuted as adults.[2]

When youth are tried in adult courts, they often face the same sentencing guidelines as adult offenders. In the majority of cases a juvenile court judge has not had an opportunity to evaluate the circumstances of the case before a youth is prosecuted as an adult, and adult criminal court judges often have very little discretion in the type of sentence they can impose on a youth convicted in the adult system. Incarcerating children in the adult system puts them at higher risk of abuse, injury, and death while they are in the system, and makes it more likely that they will reoffend once they get out.

At the time the laws were passed, few policymakers understood these consequences. Now they do. Politics has caught up with public opinion and now seems to reflect what 90% of Americans believe—that rehabilitative services and treatment for incarcerated youth can prevent future crimes.[3]

State Trends: Legislative Changes from 2005 to 2010—Removing Youth from the Adult Criminal Justice System provides state policymakers, the media, the public, and advocates for reform with the latest information about youth in the adult criminal justice system. The first half of this article explains the dangers to youth, public safety, and the overall prosperity of our economy and future generations. The second half of the article looks at legislative reforms aimed at removing youth from the criminal justice system by examining state juvenile justice legislation compiled by the National Juvenile Defender Center and the National Conference of State Legislatures.[4] The legislative scan identified 15 states that have changed their state laws, in four categories.

How a Youth Ends Up in the Adult Justice System

Age of Juvenile Court Jurisdiction	These laws determine the age of adulthood for criminal justice purposes. They effectively remove certain age groups from the juvenile court control for all infractions, whether violent or nonviolent, and place them within the adult court jurisdiction. Thirteen states have defined the age of juvenile court jurisdiction as below the generally accepted age of 18 years old.
Transfer and Waiver Provisions	These laws allow young people to be prosecuted in adult courts if they are accused of committing certain crimes. A variety of mechanisms exist by which a youth can be transferred to adult court. Most states have transfer provisions, but they vary in how much authority they allow judges and prosecutors to exercise.
Judicial Waiver	Almost all states have judicial waiver provisions which is the most traditional and common transfer and waiver provision. Under judicial waiver laws, the case originates in juvenile court. Under certain circumstances, the juvenile court judge has the authority to waive juvenile court jurisdiction and transfer the case to criminal court. State statutes vary in how much guidance they provide judges on the criteria used in determining if a youth's case should be transferred. Some states call the process "certification," "remand," or "bind over for criminal prosecution." Others "transfer" or "decline jurisdiction."
Prosecutorial Waiver	These laws grant prosecutors discretion to file cases against young people in either juvenile or adult court. Such provisions are also known as "concurrent jurisdiction," "prosecutorial discretion," or "direct file." Fifteen states have concurrent jurisdiction provisions.
Reverse Waiver	This is a mechanism to allow youth whose cases are being prosecuted in adult court to be transferred back down to the juvenile court system under certain circumstances. Half of the states have reverse waiver provisions.
Statutory or Legislative Exclusion	These laws exclude certain youth from juvenile court jurisdiction entirely by requiring particular types of cases to originate in criminal rather than juvenile court. More than half of the states have statutory exclusion laws on the books.
"Once an Adult, Always an Adult"	These laws require youth who have been tried as adults to be prosecuted automatically in adult courts for any subsequent offenses. Two-thirds of the states have such provisions, but most require the youth to have been convicted in the initial criminal prosecution.
Blended Sentencing	These laws allow juvenile or adult courts to choose between juvenile and adult correctional sanctions in sentencing certain youth. Courts often will combine a juvenile sentence with a suspended adult sentence, which allows the youth to remain in the juvenile justice system as long as he or she is well-behaved. Half of the states have laws allowing blended sentencing in some cases.

Source: Campaign for Youth Justice, National Center for Juvenile Justice

Trend 1: Four states (Colorado, Maine, Virginia and Pennsylvania) have passed laws limiting the ability to house youth in adult jails and prisons.

Trend 2: Three states (Connecticut, Illinois, and Mississippi) have expanded their juvenile court jurisdiction so that older youth who previously would be automatically tried as adults are not prosecuted in adult criminal court.

Trend 3: Ten states (Arizona, Colorado, Connecticut, Delaware, Illinois, Indiana, Nevada, Utah, Virginia and Washington) have changed their transfer laws making it more likely that youth will stay in the juvenile justice system.

Trend 4: Four states (Colorado, Georgia, Texas, and Washington) have all changed their mandatory minimum sentencing laws to take into account the developmental differences between youth and adults.

UNDERSTANDING THE CONSEQUENCES OF TRYING YOUTH AS ADULTS

Teen Brains Are Not Fully Developed

As any parent knows, teenagers are works in progress. They do not have the same abilities as adults to make sound judgments in complex situations, to control their impulses, or to plan effectively for the long term. Recent brain science has been able to demonstrate why it is that adolescents act the way they do.

What science tells us is that the brain architecture is constructed through a process that starts before birth and continues into adulthood. During adolescence, the brain undergoes dramatic changes to the structure and function of the brain impacting the way youth process and react to information. The region of the brain that is the last to develop is the one that controls many of the abilities that govern goal-oriented, "rational" decision-making, such as long-term planning, impulse control, insight, and judgment.

The downside to these brain changes is that this means that youth are particularly vulnerable to making the kinds of poor decisions that get them involved in the justice system. By examining age-specific arrest rates we can see that youth is a time characterized by delinquency that then sharply drops off. In fact, engaging in delinquent activities is a normal part of the adolescent experience. Almost all of the readers of this report will likely be able to recall participating in an activity during their adolescence that violates at least one criminal law today. It is also true that for the vast majority of readers, these activities were temporary and did not indicate that they would become lifelong offenders.

The upside of this brain research is that the rapid growth and development happening in adolescent brains make them highly elastic and malleable to change. The relationships made and behaviors learned during this crucial developmental stage are hard-wired into the brain architecture and help determine long-term life outcomes. When young people hit a rough patch, guidance from responsible adults and developmentally appropriate programs, services, and punishment can get them back on track.

The juvenile justice system is based on this science and provides troubled adolescents with mentors, education, and the guidance to help most of them mature into responsible adults. In contrast, warehousing minors in the adult system ensures that they will *not* have guidance from responsible adults or have access to age-appropriate programs, services and punishment to help build positive change into their brains during this crucial developmental period. Instead, they will face the reality of having a permanent criminal record and the increased likelihood of becoming career criminals. This is not the outcome we want for America's children.

Moving Youth into the Adult System Costs States Millions: Lessons from Rhode Island

With the current financial crisis, states across the country are exploring ways to decrease the costs of the justice system. According to the Pew Center on the States, state correctional costs quadrupled over the past two decades and now top $50 billion a year, consuming one in every 15 general fund dollars.[5] When state policymakers have conversations about reforms to either the juvenile or adult criminal justice system, an issue that often gets forgotten is youth in the adult system. Some states see the juvenile and adult systems as interchangeable and seek to consolidate the two systems in an effort to save money. This is a very costly mistake for states as each high-risk youth diverted from a life of crime saves society nearly $5.7 million in costs over a lifetime.[6]

Children are not little adults, and a criminal justice system that is designed for adults does not work for youth.

Rhode Island is a state that recently experimented with moving 17-year-olds into their adult system as a way to close a budget shortfall in 2007.[7] It took only a couple of months for the state to realize that it would cost much more to keep youth safe in the adult system, and the legislature quickly repealed the law.[8] Rhode Island now stands as a powerful example to other states that consolidating or otherwise moving more youth into the adult system is a bad idea.

The Juvenile Justice System Demands More than the Adult Justice System

The adult system is typically thought to be more punishment-oriented than the juvenile system, but the minor crimes that youth commit mean that the majority of youth are only given an adult probation sentence as well as a lifelong adult criminal record that makes it hard for them to get jobs in the future. In contrast, the juvenile justice system holds youth accountable for their crimes by placing more requirements on youth and their families. The juvenile justice system often requires that youth attend school, pay community and victim restitution, and receive the counseling, mentoring, and training they need to turn their lives around. The adult justice system completely fails those youth who would benefit from the services of the juvenile system by letting them "slip through the cracks."

[...]

Most Youth in the Adult System Are Convicted of Minor Crimes

Any mention of juvenile crime tends to evoke images that perpetuate three specific myths about youth. First, newspaper and television coverage of youth crime tends to involve stories focused on gangs or murder leading to a distorted view of the nature of juvenile crime. Youth who have been arrested for violent crimes are rare and only account for about 5% of all juveniles arrested each year.[9] Drugs, burglary, theft, and other property crimes are among the more common reasons teens are prosecuted in adult courts.

Second, there is a perception that juvenile crime is on the rise. In reality, youth crime has been going down for many years and is now at historic lows. The number of adults arrested between 1999 and 2008 increased 3.4%, whereas the number of juveniles arrested dropped a staggering 15.7% during that same time frame.[10]

Third, there is a perception that youth commit the majority of crime in the nation. The truth is that adults commit the majority of crime in America. In 2008, only 12% of violent crime and 18% of property crime nationwide were attributed to youth.[11] According to the FBI, youth under age 18 accounted for 15% of all arrests.[12]

These three misperceptions apply equally to youth in the adult justice system. The overwhelming majority of youth who enter the adult court are not there for serious, violent crimes. Despite the fact that many of the state laws were intended to prosecute the most serious offenders, most youth who are tried in adult courts are there for nonviolent offenses.[13] A significant proportion of youth, in some states the majority, only receive a sentence of probation. However, even youth

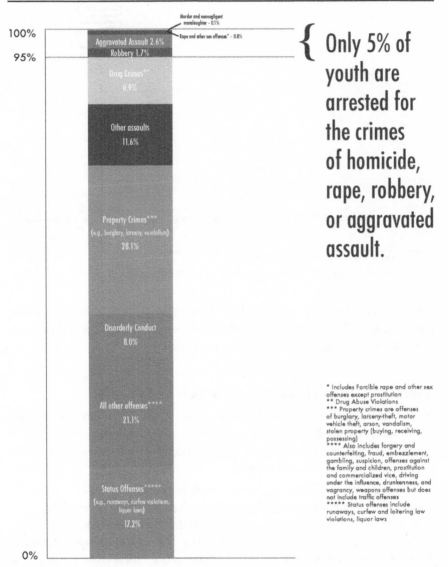

Source: Federal Bureau of Investigation, Crime in the United States, 2009

who receive the most serious sanction—a sentence of imprisonment in an adult prison—are not the serious offenders that one may imagine. The majority of youth held in adult prisons are not given extreme sentences such as life without parole, and 95% of youth will be released back to their communities before their

Juvenile Crime Has Been Declining for Years

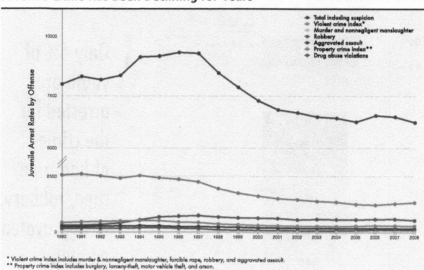

* Violent crime index includes murder & nonnegligent manslaughter, forcible rape, robbery, and aggravated assault.
** Property crime index includes burglary, larceny-theft, motor vehicle theft, and arson.

Source: National Center for Juvenile Justice; OJJDP Statistical Briefing Book

25th birthday.[14] Unfortunately, by virtue of being prosecuted in the adult system these youth are less likely to get an education or skills training, and their adult conviction will make it harder for them to get jobs.

Youth Are Often Housed in Adult Jails and Prisons

One of the most serious consequences of adult court prosecution is that youth can be housed in adult jails and prisons. On any given night in America, 10,000 children are held in adult jails and prisons.[15] State laws vary widely as to whether youth can be housed in adult facilities.

Although federal law requires that youth in the juvenile justice system be removed from adult jails or be sight-and-sound separated from other adults, these protections do not apply to youth prosecuted in the adult criminal justice system.[16] In fact, many youth who are held in adult jails have not even been convicted. Research shows that many never will. As many as one-half of these youth will be sent back to the juvenile justice system or will not be convicted. Yet, most of these youth will have spent *at least one month* in an adult jail, and one in five of these youth will have spent *over six months* in an adult jail.[17]

> If detained pre-trial, two-thirds of youth prosecuted as adults are held in adult jails.

Age-Specific Arrest Rates

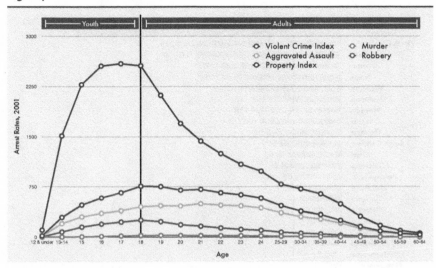

Source: Adapted from OJJDP Statistical Briefing Book

While in adult jails or prisons, most youth are denied educational and rehabilitative services that are necessary for their stage in development. A survey of adult facilities found that 40% of jails provided no educational services at all, only 11% provided special education services, and a mere 7% provided vocational training.[18] This lack of education increases the difficulty that youth will have once they return to their communities.

Youth are also in extreme danger when held in adult facilities. Staff in adult facilities face a dilemma: they can house youth in the general adult population where they are at substantial risk of physical and sexual abuse, or they can house youth in segregated settings in which isolation can cause or exacerbate mental health problems.

According to Sheriff Gabe Morgan of Newport News, Virginia:

The average 14-year-old is a "guppy in the ocean" of an adult facility. The law does not protect the juveniles; it says they are adults and treats them as such. Often they are placed in isolation for their protection, usually 23½ hours alone. Around age 17, we put [the youth] in the young head population, a special unit where all the youth are put together, and the 13- and 14-year-olds normally fall prey there as well.[19]

Youth who are held in adult facilities are at the greatest risk of sexual victimization. The National Prison Rape Elimination Commission found that "more

Youth Under 18 In Adult Prisons

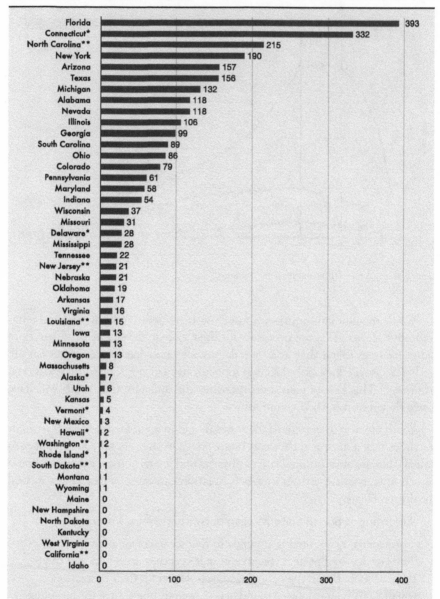

Florida	393
Connecticut*	332
North Carolina**	215
New York	190
Arizona	157
Texas	156
Michigan	132
Alabama	118
Nevada	118
Illinois	106
Georgia	99
South Carolina	89
Ohio	86
Colorado	79
Pennsylvania	61
Maryland	58
Indiana	54
Wisconsin	37
Missouri	31
Delaware*	28
Mississippi	28
Tennessee	22
New Jersey**	21
Nebraska	21
Oklahoma	19
Arkansas	17
Virginia	16
Louisiana**	15
Iowa	13
Minnesota	13
Oregon	13
Massachusetts	8
Alaska*	7
Utah	6
Kansas	5
Vermont*	4
New Mexico	3
Hawaii*	2
Washington**	2
Rhode Island*	1
South Dakota**	1
Montana	1
Wyoming	1
Maine	0
New Hampshire	0
North Dakota	0
Kentucky	0
West Virginia	0
California**	0
Idaho	0

* Prisons and jails form one integrated system. Data include total jail and prison populations.
** Counts include those held in privately-operated facilities.

Source: Bureau of Justice Statistics

than any other group of incarcerated persons, youth incarcerated with adults are probably at the highest risk for sexual abuse."[20]

Keeping youth away from other adult inmates is no solution either. Isolation has devastating consequences for youth—these conditions can cause anxiety, paranoia, and exacerbate existing mental disorders and put youth at risk of suicide. In fact, youth housed in adult jails are 36 times more likely to commit suicide than are youth housed in juvenile detention facilities.[21]

Prosecuting Youth in the Adult System Leads to More Crime, Not Less

All Americans have a stake in whether the juvenile and criminal justice system helps youth turn away from crime and build a productive future where they become an asset, rather than a liability, to their communities. Early interventions that prevent high-risk youth from engaging in repeat criminal offenses can save the public nearly $5.7 million in costs over a lifetime.[22]

Both conservatives and liberals agree that government services should be evaluated on whether they produce the best possible results at the lowest possible cost, but historically these cost-effective calculations have not been applied to criminal justice policies. Many states have begun to follow the lead of the Washington State Institute for Public Policy and examine the degree to which they are investing in juvenile programs with a proven track record. While states are starting to invest more in evidence-based programs, states have not always stopped using policies or programs that have demonstrated negative results. States should end practices that have the unintended consequence of hardening youth and making them a greater risk to the public than when they entered the system.

Trying youth as adults is an example of such a flawed policy. According to Shay Bilchik, a former Florida prosecutor who currently heads the Center for Juvenile Justice Reform at Georgetown University, trying youth as adults is "bad criminal justice policy. People didn't know that at the time the changes were made. Now we do, and we have to learn from it."[23]

Research shows that young people who are kept in the juvenile justice system are less likely to reoffend than young people who are transferred into the adult system. According to both the U.S. Centers for Disease Control and Prevention and the Office of Juvenile Justice and Delinquency Prevention, youth who are transferred from the juvenile court system to the adult criminal system are approximately 34% more likely than youth retained in the juvenile court system to be re-arrested for violent or other crime.[24]

These findings are not surprising. Youth in the adult system receive limited services and o ten become socialized into a culture where their role models are adult criminals and violence is a "routine part of institutional life."[25] Returning youth to juvenile court jurisdiction would save money for state correctional and judicial systems in the long run by decreasing reoffending and increasing the possibility that youth offenders could become productive members of society.[26]

Youth Have Lifelong Barriers to Employment

The negative consequences of prosecuting and sentencing youth in the adult system do not end when a youth avoids, or is released from, incarceration. An adult conviction can limit a youth's opportunities for the rest of his or her life. While most juvenile records are sealed, adult convictions become public record and, depending on the state and the crime, can limit a youth's job prospects for a lifetime. The Legal Action Center report, *After Prison: Roadblocks to Reentry: A Report on State Legal Barriers Facing People with Criminal Records*, has revealed several facts about legal barriers for people with criminal records:

- Most states allow employers to deny jobs to people arrested but never convicted of a crime;
- Most states allow employers to deny jobs to anyone with a criminal record, regardless of how old or minor the record or the individual's work history and personal circumstances;
- Most states make criminal history information accessible to the general public through the Internet, making it extremely easy for employers and others to discriminate against people on the basis of old or minor convictions, for example to deny employment or housing; and
- All but two states restrict in some way the right to vote for people with criminal convictions.[27]

When states make it difficult for youth to get jobs, states hamper their own economic growth. Given the diversity of state transfer laws, for many states it may also mean they are putting their own residents at a disadvantage when competing for jobs with youth from other states. For example, consider two 16-year-olds who are arrested for shoplifting. One is from North Carolina, the other from Tennessee. In Tennessee, a youth arrested for shoplifting is likely to be prosecuted in the juvenile system and probably would not have to report his or her youthful indiscretion. However, a youth arrested for the same crime in North Carolina will be charged as an adult and will have an adult criminal conviction for life.

[...]

FOUR TRENDS TO WATCH

As a society, we still have a long way to go to keep children out of the adult system. However, recent events indicate that we are finally on the right track. The past few years have seen a growing recognition by citizens, researchers, juvenile justice professionals, and policymakers that children do not belong in the adult system. Between 2005 and 2010, nearly half of the states have considered or passed legislation designed to help youth in the adult system. The four trends of change are:

[...]

Trend 1. States and Local Jurisdictions Remove Youth from Adult Jails and Prisons

Recognizing the many dangers youth face when incarcerated with adults, several states and local jurisdictions took action to protect youth. Three states (Maine, Virginia, and Pennsylvania) and one local jurisdiction (Multnomah Country, Oregon) either allow or require that youth in the adult system be held in juvenile, instead of adult, facilities. Colorado changed the criteria to determine whether to house youth in a juvenile facility, and also guarantees that youth will receive educational services in adult jails. Finally, New York City has asked the Department of Corrections to collect data on the dangers that youth face in adult jails.

[...]

Trend 2. States Raise the Age of Juvenile Court Jurisdiction

While the majority of states have drawn the line at age 18 for their juvenile justice systems, 13 states in the U.S. have set the line at a younger age. Currently, New York and North Carolina both end juvenile court jurisdiction at age 16. Eleven other states end jurisdiction at 17: Connecticut, Georgia, Illinois (felonies only), Louisiana, Massachusetts, Michigan, Missouri, New Hampshire, South Carolina, Texas, and Wisconsin. As a result of these laws, more than two million 16- and 17-year-olds residing in these 13 states would automatically be prosecuted in the adult system if charged with any offense,[28] regardless of the seriousness of the offense or any extenuating circumstances.

Three states (Connecticut, Illinois, and Mississippi) have raised the age of juvenile court jurisdiction and four additional states (North Carolina, Massachusetts, New York, and Wisconsin) seem poised to do so in the future.

[...]

Trend 3. States Change Transfer Laws to Keep More Youth in Juvenile Court

States have a variety of mechanisms for transferring children to the adult system. Some states exclude youth charged with certain offenses from the juvenile court. In other states, prosecutors make the decision whether to try a youth as a juvenile or adult. In most instances, juvenile court judges do not make the decision about whether a youth should be prosecuted in adult court, despite the fact that a juvenile court judge is a neutral player who is in the best position to investigate the facts and make the decision.

In the past five years, 10 states made changes to their transfer laws. Two states (Arizona and Utah) made it easier for youth who were tried as adults to get reverse waiver hearings to allow them to return to the juvenile court. Three states (Arizona, Colorado, and Nevada) changed the age requirements before youth can be tried as adults. Three states (Indiana, Virginia, and Washington) made changes to "once an adult, always an adult" laws. Four states (Connecticut, Delaware, Illinois, and Indiana) limited the types of offenses that required adult court prosecution or changed the presumptions for adult court prosecution. Several additional other states (Arizona, Maryland, Nevada, Texas, Virginia, and Washington) are currently contemplating changes to their state laws.

[...]

Trend 4. States Rethink Sentencing Laws for Youth

Youth who are prosecuted and sentenced in the adult criminal justice system have historically been subject to the same harsh sentencing laws as adults. Most states have some form of mandatory sentencing laws and few states have statutory exceptions for youth. This means that many states subject youth to harsh mandatory sentencing guidelines without allowing judges to take the child's developmental differences into account. However, in two recent United States Supreme Court cases, the Court explicitly held that youth are categorically less deserving of these punishments. In 2005, the Court abolished the juvenile death penalty in the case of *Roper v. Simmons*.[29] In 2010, the Court abolished life without parole sentences for youth convicted of nonhomicide crimes in *Graham v. Florida*.[30]

Several states (Colorado, Georgia, Texas, and Washington) reexamined how adult sentences are applied to youth and have recognized that youth have great potential for rehabilitation and that the developmental differences of youth should be taken into consideration in sentencing. In the wake of *Graham*, several additional states will likely be contemplating changes to prevent youth from being sentenced to extreme sentences.

[. . .]

NOTES

1. Griffin, Patrick. National Institute of Corrections Convening, June 18, 2010.

2. Deitch, Michele, et.al. (2009). *From Time Out to Hard Time: Young Children in the Adult Criminal Justice System*, Austin, TX: The University of Texas at Austin, LBJ School of Public Affairs.

3. National Juvenile Justice Network (2010), *Polling on Public Attitudes About the Treatment of Young Offenders*, Washington DC: National Juvenile Justice Network.

4. National Juvenile Defender Center Summaries of State Legislation from 2005, 2006, and 2007 available online at http://www.njdc.info/publications.php; National Conference of State Legislatures Juvenile Justice Bill Tracking Database available online at http://www.ncsl.org/default.aspx?tabid=12686.

5. Pew Center on the States (2008), *One in 100: Behind Bars in America 2008*, Washington, DC: Pew Center on the States.

6. Cohen, Mark A. and Piquero, Alex R. (December 2007). New Evidence on the Monetary Value of Saving a High Risk Youth, Vanderbilt Law and Economics Research Paper No. 08-07, available at SSRN: http://ssrn.com/abstract=1077214.

7. Eric Tucker, *RI Prosecutes 17-Year-Olds to Save Money*, USA Today, July 13, 2007.

8. S.B. 1141B, 2007 Gen. Assem. (R.I. 2007).

9. Federal Bureau of Investigation. Crime in the United States 2008. Washington, D.C.

10. Federal Bureau of Investigation. Crime in the United States 2008. Washington, D.C.

11. Federal Bureau of Investigation. Crime in the United States 2008. Washington, D.C.

12. Federal Bureau of Investigation. Crime in the United States 2008. Washington, D.C.

13. *The Consequences Aren't Minor: the Impact of Trying Youth as Adults and Strategies for Reform* (2007, March). Washington, DC: Campaign for Youth Justice.

14. Richard E. Redding, *Juvenile transfer laws: An effective deterrent to delinquency?* (Washington, D.C.: U.S. Department of Justice, Office of Justice Programs, Office of Juvenile Justice and Delinquency Prevention) (June 2010).

15. Minton, Todd D. (June 2010). *Jail inmates at midyear 2009*. Washington, DC: U.S. Department of Justice, Bureau of Justice Statistics. West, Heather C. (June 2010). *Prison inmates at midyear 2009*. Washington, DC: U.S. Department of Justice, Bureau of Justice Statistics.

16. *Jailing Juveniles* (2007, November). Washington, DC: Campaign for Youth Justice.

17. *Jailing Juveniles* (2007, November). Washington, DC: Campaign for Youth Justice.

18. Harlow, C.W. (2003, January). *Education and Correctional Populations*. Washington, D.C.: U.S. Department of Justice, Office of Justice Programs, Bureau of Justice Statistics.

19. Sheriff Gabe Morgan, National Institute of Corrections Convening, June 18th, 2010.

20. National Prison Rape Elimination Commission, Report 18 (June 2009), available at http://www.ncjrs.gov/pdffiles1/226680.pdf.

21. *Jailing Juveniles* (2007, November). Washington, DC: Campaign for Youth Justice.

22. Cohen, Mark A. and Piquero, Alex R., New Evidence on the Monetary Value of Saving a High Risk Youth, Vanderbilt Law and Economics Research Paper No. 08-07, available at SSRN: http://ssrn.com/abstract=1077214. (December 2007).

23. Sharon Cohen, Associated Press, *States Rethink Charging Kids as Adults*, Dec 16, 2007.

24. Centers for Disease Control and Prevention. (2007) Effects on Violence of Laws and Policies Facilitating the Transfer of Youth from the Juvenile to the Adult Justice System: A Report on Recommendations of the Task Force on Community Preventive Services. MMWR 2007; 56 (No. RR-9); Richard E. Redding, *Juvenile transfer laws: An effective deterrent to delinquency?* (Washington, D.C.: U.S. Department of Justice, Office of Justice Programs, Office of Juvenile Justice and Delinquency Prevention) (June 2010).

25. Campaign for Youth Justice, *Jailing Juveniles* 7–8 (2007).

26. Roman, J. (2005, July). *Assessing the economic consequences of juvenile versus adult justice.* Washington, DC: The Urban Institute, p. 39.

27. *After Prison: Roadblocks to Reentry: A Report on State Legal Barriers Facing People with Criminal Records.* (2004) New York, New York: The Legal Action Center. Updated here: http://www.lac.org/roadblocks-to-reentry/upload/lacreport/Roadblocks-to-Reentry--2009.pdf.

28. Office of Juvenile Justice and Delinquency Prevention. *Easy Access to Juvenile Populations: 1990–2008.* http://ojjdp.ncjrs.gov/ojstatbb/ezapop/asp/comparison_display.asp.

29. *Roper v. Simmons*, 543 U.S. 551 (2005).

30. *Graham v. Florida*, 130 S.Ct. 2011 (2010).

*Neelum Arya** is assistant professor of law at the Barry Law School. She was the research & policy director for the Campaign for Youth Justice, a not-for-profit organization in Washington, D.C., dedicated to ending the practice of trying, sentencing, and incarcerating youth under 18 in the adult criminal justice system. Neelum is a graduate of the Epstein Program in Public Interest Law & Policy at the UCLA School of Law and Harvard University's Kennedy School of Government.

Neelum Arya, "State Trends: Legislative Victories from 2005 to 2010—Removing Youth from the Adult Criminal Justice System" (Washington, DC: Campaign for Youth Justice, 2011). Excerpted and reprinted with permission.

Extreme Sentencing Of Youth In The United States: The Imposition of the Sentence of Life without the Possibility of Parole for Youth

by Allison Conyers, Shobha L. Mahadev, Caitlin Shay, and Sarah Silins*

There are more than 2,500 individuals in prison in the United States serving life without parole sentences for crimes they committed under the age of eighteen, and none in the rest of the world.[1] The juvenile justice system in the United States was founded on the belief that youth have the potential to grow and change. Yet our justice system has denied these young people the opportunity to prove reform or rehabilitation.

Young people are still developing mentally and neurologically. When young people commit serious crimes, they should be held accountable in a way that reflects their greater capacity to change.[2] Research confirms that adolescents do not have adult levels of judgment, impulse control, or risk assessment.[3] Because of their relatively unformed characters, young people are strong candidates for rehabilitation.

We also know that the practice of sentencing youth to life without parole affects entire communities. Victims of violent crime, people sentenced to life without parole, their family members and decimated neighborhoods robbed of productive citizens are all harmed by the sentence. The following article outlines the implementation of life without parole sentences for youth in the United States, the current legal landscape, and the stories of three people directly impacted by the sentence.

I. Background

For over a century since founding the first juvenile court in the United States in Illinois, juvenile courts across the country have recognized children's unique needs and capacity for rehabilitation. Despite this recognition, states have in recent decades begun to impose harsh punishments for children in a variety of circumstances—transferring them to adult criminal court and sentencing them for many years, often without any individualized consideration of the child's circumstances. Sentencing children to life imprisonment without the possibility of parole, the most extreme example of handing down harsh and lengthy sentences to young people under the age of 18, flouts the logic and rehabilitative goals of the juvenile court system and by its nature, abandons certain children as irreparable and irredeemable for the rest of their lives.

Despite the continued practice of imposing harsh sentences on youth, emerging research in adolescent brain development confirming that children's brains continue to grow until their early twenties has prompted courts to reevaluate the legitimacy of these sentencing schemes. In 2010, the United States Supreme Court in *Graham v. Florida*,[4] held that sentencing children under the age of 18 who do not commit a homicide to life without the possibility of parole, was cruel and unusual and therefore unconstitutional under the Eighth Amendment of the United States Constitution. In so doing, the Court recognized the rehabilitative capacity of children as compared with adults, and suggested that our criminal laws need to take into account the differences between children and adults. Notwithstanding the *Graham* decision, states continue to mete out extreme sentences for children and particularly, life without the possibility for parole for children who are involved in homicide cases.

Most juveniles sentenced to life without parole had never been previously convicted of a crime in the adult or juvenile system when they received their sentence.[5] Surprisingly, in eleven of seventeen years from 1985–2001, juveniles were more likely than adults to be sentenced to life without parole for committing the same crimes.[6] In most cases, the juveniles had adult codefendants when they committed their crimes.

Twenty-five percent of the people serving life without parole for a crime committed when they were under the age of eighteen were convicted of felony murder.[7] Felony murder occurs when an accomplice kills someone during the commission of a crime. This means a person may be convicted of felony murder even if that person never held a weapon, was not in the same room when the murder occurred, told the accomplice not to kill the person, did not know the other person had killed someone, or even did not know that the person had a weapon. Today, more than twenty-five percent of the people serving life without parole sentences committed felony murder.[8]

In the United States, thirty-nine states and the federal government permit life without parole for people under the age of eighteen.[9] Some of these states sentence youth to life without parole far more often than others. California, Florida, Louisiana, Michigan, and Pennsylvania have the most people serving the sentence. Except for California, all of these states require the person to be sentenced to juvenile life without parole ("JLWOP") if they are found guilty of certain crimes, regardless of what the jury or judge thinks is appropriate.[10]

II. A Watershed in JLWOP Sentences: *Graham v. Florida*

In 2010, the landscape of juvenile sentencing fundamentally changed. In May, the Supreme Court decided in *Graham v. Florida* that the Eighth Amendment's prohibition on "cruel and unusual punishment" means that states and the federal government are not allowed to sentence youth under the age of eighteen to life without parole when they do not commit a homicide.[11] However, *Graham* did not occur in a vacuum. Five years earlier, in *Roper v. Simmons*, the Supreme Court, relying on scientific evidence demonstrating that adolescents' brains continue to evolve throughout their teenage years and that youth were therefore "categorically" less blameworthy for their actions than adults, abolished the death penalty for juveniles under the age of eighteen.[12]

Once the death penalty was abolished for juveniles, it was clear that this was not the end of the issue. States seemed to be circumventing the reasoning in *Roper* by imposing an alternative type of death sentence on juveniles: life in prison without the possibility of parole.

And then, in 2010, the case of Terrance Graham came before the Supreme Court. Terrance Graham was born into a difficult life. Both of his parents were addicted to crack cocaine and he was diagnosed with attention deficit hyperactivity disorder when he was young.[13] Terrance also began drinking and using drugs as a teenager.[14] When he was sixteen, Terrance was involved in an armed burglary.[15] However, since it was his first offense, he agreed to a plea bargain with the prosecutor and was sentenced to three years of parole, with the first year in the county jail.[16]

Six months after he was released, Terrance participated in a home invasion robbery with two adults. Terrance and his accomplices knocked on the door of a home, forced their way in, and held a pistol to the chest of the man who opened the door.[17] After searching for money, the three barricaded the man and his friend into a closet, left, and then attempted a second robbery later that evening. After separating from the other two, one of whom had been injured, Terrance was arrested by the police, and subsequently sentenced to life in prison without the possibility of parole.[18]

Terrance appealed his case to the Supreme Court. Ruling in his favor, the Court relied on its past decisions about reduced teenage culpability due to psychological and brain development. Particularly, the Court noted that psychological evidence showed that teenagers have a harder time resisting their impulses than they will as adults.[19] The Court also acknowledged that neurological evidence demonstrated that teenagers have an extremely active amygdala, which controls their emotions.[20] The pre-frontal cortex, which controls rational decision-making, develops fully only for adults.[21]

The Court also considered the different purposes of imprisonment: deterrence, retribution, incapacitation and rehabilitation. Because teenagers act impulsively, it found that they are unlikely to be deterred by overly harsh sentences and life without parole is unduly severe for retribution purposes. Further, a life without parole sentence completely disregards the possibility of rehabilitation and incapacitates teens for life even if they no longer pose a threat to society.

The Supreme Court also examined what other states were doing. It recognized that even though most states technically allow life without parole for non-homicide crimes, only eleven states actually enforced the law and the Court could only identify 123 people in the country serving life sentences for non-homicide crimes committed when they were under the age of eighteen.[22] This data was enough for the Supreme Court to find a general national consensus against life without parole sentences for youth convicted of non-homicide crimes. Using this consensus, psychological evidence, and the lack of penological justifications for the punishment, the Supreme Court decided that life without parole sentences for youth are a cruel and unusual punishment for non-homicide crimes, in violation of the Eighth Amendment.

The *Graham* decision applied retroactively, meaning that anyone in the prison system who was serving a life sentence for a crime they committed before they were eighteen would now be eligible for parole.[23] However, the Supreme Court was not asked to consider whether youth who were convicted of murder are eligible for a life without parole sentence, even though the majority of youth serving life without parole were convicted of homicide (including youth who were convicted of felony murder or as accomplices). That question, and others surrounding extreme sentencing of youth, remains unresolved.

III. INTERNATIONAL HUMAN RIGHTS LAW

In the United States, all states and the federal government must adhere to the Constitution. While states are welcome to pass laws that protect individuals even more than the Constitution requires, they are never allowed to pass laws that would provide less protection. In addition to our domestic laws, the United States and the global community are governed by a set of international laws. In most cases, countries can decide whether to sign a treaty or to be bound by an international agreement. Once a country decides to sign and ratify a treaty, the country is required to follow the treaty much like states are required to follow our Constitution. In the United States, Article VI of the Constitution states that once the U.S. signs a treaty, that treaty becomes law, and all the states must follow what it says.[24]

Human rights are rights that all human beings must receive, just because they are human. These are our most basic minimum rights, like the ability to be free from torture. In order to ensure that these rights are protected, the United Nations has drafted many human rights treaties, including ones that protect children's rights.

The Convention on the Rights of the Child (CRC) is a human rights treaty that was specifically drafted in recognition of the fact that children are vulnerable and deserve special human rights protections. Article 37(a) of the CRC states, "Neither capital punishment nor life imprisonment without possibility of release shall be imposed for offences committed by persons below eighteen years of age."[25] It further states that children should only be put in jail as a last resort and should be released in the shortest amount of time possible.[26] The United States and Somalia are the only two countries in the entire world that have not ratified the CRC.[27] While it did initially sign the CRC, Congress never ratified it with a two-thirds vote. However, according to international law principles, countries still have to follow treaties they have signed, even if Congress has not yet ratified it.[28]

The United States has ratified the International Covenant on Civil and Political Rights (ICCPR), the Convention on the Elimination of all Forms of Racial Discrimination (CERD), and the Convention Against Torture (CAT), all of which consider children's rights. Life without parole sentences for youth violates all of these treaties.

The U.S. specifically agreed to the CRC, and other international agreements, which makes it obligated to follow those treaties. Until the U.S. abolishes life without parole sentences for youth, it will continue to be in violation of its commitments in international law.

IV. Growing Support for Abolition

Using the rationale in *Graham*, international human rights law, and their own sense of propriety, many individuals, groups, and organizations have publicly denounced JLWOP. Human rights advocates like Human Rights Watch and Amnesty International have publicly released reports arguing that life without parole sentences for youth violate constitutional and human rights guarantees.[29]

International human rights bodies like the Human Rights Council and the Committee against Torture have also indicated that the sentence does not conform to U.S. obligations under international law.[30] Other countries have agreed: Switzerland, Belgium, Austria and Slovakia all recommended to the Human Rights Council that the United States abolish the practice of sentencing youth to life without parole.[31]

In the United States, a coalition of prosecutors and judges has agreed that life without parole sentences for youth are unconstitutional and unduly expensive.[32] This coalition included a former state attorney general, assistant state's attorneys, and chief justices' of state supreme courts. Families of many victims have also made statements expressing their concern over the continued use of life without parole sentences for youth. Regarding the punishment of the teen that killed her husband, one woman commented, "Don't get me wrong, she should be punished severely for her crime, but there should be a light at the end of the tunnel."[33] Linda White, whose daughter was murdered by a teenager, said of one of the young men who committed the crime "My experience with Gary has taught me that we have a responsibility to protect our youth from the kind of childhood that Gary had, from treatment that recklessly disregards their inherent vulnerability. He is proof that young people, even those who have done horrible things, can be transformed."[34]

In the last few years, Colorado and Texas passed legislation to end the practice of sentencing youth to life without parole. Several other states are currently looking at ways to change their policies.[35] As developmental research continues to emerge, and prominent persons and organizations continue to speak out against the sentence, it is possible that Congress or the Supreme Court will eventually ban life without parole sentences for youth altogether.

V. The Journey to a Life Sentence: Real Stories from Youth Serving the Sentence

Because, as noted above, most of the young people who receive life without parole are first-time offenders,[36] it is clear that the sentence is not simply the logical result of the youth's involvement in an escalating life of crime. Rather, getting a juvenile life without parole sentence in the United States is often the result of a myriad of factors including geography, race, economics, resources, education, family circumstances, mental health and trauma, peer pressure and relationships, and just plain chance. Additionally, intricacies of local and state legal systems, including the attitudes and training of judges, prosecutors and defense lawyers play a huge role in what type of sentence a teenage defendant ultimately receives.

The following section briefly examines some of the factors that contribute to the JLWOP and then tracks the stories of two inmates serving the sentence, as well as one family's journey to come to terms with their child's imprisonment, and ultimately, to fight for review of the sentence.

Adolescent Development, Mental Health and Trauma

One reason that youth commit crimes is that their brains are not yet fully formed. As a result of the ways in which their brains develop, adolescents are more likely to act impulsively, neglect to consider long-term consequences of their actions and to act in groups than their adult counterparts. Our legal system, scientific and behavioral studies and own experience attest to these differences:

- The founding of our country's juvenile justice system was premised on the belief that children, even those who commit grave acts, are fundamentally different from adults and more amenable to treatment and rehabilitation.

- Other areas of our law recognize that developmental immaturity justifies age-based restrictions on rights and privileges such as voting, marriage, jury service and drinking.

- The United States Supreme Court agreed in *Roper v. Simmons* and *Graham v. Florida*, explaining in *Roper* that, "From a moral standpoint it would be misguided to equate the failings of a minor with those of an adult, for a greater possibility exists that a minor's character deficiencies will be reformed."[37]

- Trauma can have a profound effect on the development of the young mind, resulting in aggressive responses to frightening or violent situations and fear.[38]

Despite these differences, the sentence of life without parole, and other extreme sentencing of young people, disregards the fundamental differences between youth and adults. Many inmates who were sentenced to life without parole for crimes committed in their youth, particularly those who have served at least 10 to 15 years in prison, attest to the significant growth and learning they have experienced since their childhood.

Racial Disparity

The disproportionate imposition of JLWOP and other extreme sentences on youth of color begs reconsideration of its fairness. Even before sentencing, children of color in the United States are over-selected at every stage of the criminal justice process from arrest to detention to conviction; accordingly, later stages such as sentencing may reflect racial differences accumulated over earlier stages of processing. Studies regularly show that patterns of offending—that is, categories and levels of crime by various demographics—fail to sufficiently explain the rate at which Black children are arrested.[39]

Given these disparities, it should come as no surprise that Black youth disproportionately serve life without parole sentences. One out of every 8 African-American youth who are convicted of killing someone will be sentenced to life without parole, however this is the case for only one out of every 13 white youth convicted of murder.[40]

School "Push-out"

It likely comes as no surprise that many youth who end up in criminal court serving long sentences, including life without the possibility of parole, struggle in school and are often no longer attending school at the time the offense for which they are convicted occurs.[41] These children may face learning disabilities, mental health issues and circumstances at home that make it difficult for them to succeed in school.

Voices from Inside Prison Walls

No statistic can adequately capture the suffering and harm caused to victims, youth, families and communities as a result of the devastating crimes that led to these sentences and to the losses experienced by all sides. The following narratives of people serving life without parole for a crime committed in their youth and their families, provide a small window into the complexity of the issues involved, and offer a sense of the road to maturity, remorse and redemption for the youth involved.[42]

CASE STUDY

Julian—sentenced to life without parole for a crime committed when he was fifteen years old

Julian was raised by his mother and father, in Chatham—an almost all Black neighborhood on Chicago's southeast side. When he was a sophomore in high school his father died in a van fire on the shoulder of a Chicago expressway.

When asked about the neighborhood where he grew up, Julian said it really was not bad, but definitely rough. Julian was a good student and was admitted to one of the Chicago Public School's selective enrollment High Schools, a top school in the city. He had to travel over 2 hours each day to and from school. He was an A/B student prior to his father's death. He recalls being bored at school. School work and tests came easily for him, and he knew early on he could be successful on the tests even if he did not put time into the homework or coming to school.

After his father's death his performance in school decreased significantly. He says the worst advice that someone gave him the night his father died was that he was to be the "man" of the house now that his father was gone. He became immersed in the care of his younger brother and felt he was responsible for his family and his home. His brother had barely turned a year old when his father died. He decided that he needed to transfer to a high school closer to home, and soon after dropped out. He had been very involved in athletics. After his father passed away, he stopped playing sports outside of an occasional game at the park.

Julian said his father was very strict. Now looking back, he recognizes that conduct as abuse. Julian's father hit his children routinely, and his punishments were often extremely harsh. He said his dad tried to use the "scared straight" method of parenting and Julian feels that it backfired. His father had been abused as a child, and his mom said his dad once recalled being put in the dryer, by his own mother (Julian's grandmother) as a punishment. Julian said his father's abuse had begun to soften right before he died.

Julian says that around the time of the offense for which he is serving life without parole, he felt as though he was "drowning." He reached out to the family minister, telling him he thought he was going to hurt someone, and the minister offered to pray with him, which Julian feels was not an effective intervention.

Julian was convicted of killing two other young men, his girlfriend's current boyfriend and the boyfriend's friend, four days prior to his 16th birthday. He was drinking very heavily at the time. Julian was the first to call 911, and the first to respond to the victims, stripping down to just his underwear in order to use his clothing to try and stop the bleeding.

Julian has now been in prison for 21 years. He would like to be transferred to the prison that is closest to his mother, an hour outside of the city with public transportation directly to the prison. He does not like her making the five-hour drive from Chicago to see him. She does not own a car, so she rents one and comes only once or twice a year, but writes him regularly and sends him books. He also talks to his brother, the minister, every so often.

Julian is extremely regimented about his life in prison. He eats no sugar, no meat, exercises regularly, and does a tremendous amount of reading and writing. When asked why he is so focused on health, he says "I have to last, I cannot die in here."

Each year he reads the Bible and the Quran from cover to cover. He divided them both into 30 parts and reads each part over the course of a month. Each section takes him about 3–4 hours. He struggles a lot with what he reads, and asks questions and tries to investigate the aspects that he does not understand. He believes in God although he does not associate himself directly with organized religion. He says that he has had a tremendous amount of spiritual growth since he has been in prison. "When you are by yourself and have no one to talk to you are going to talk to god." His spirituality helps him to approach a life sentence.

Julian spends a lot of time trying to think of how he could apologize to his victim's family. He feels that sending them a letter would scare them, but he would like to be able to do something. He seems to have an incredible will to grow and improve himself. He seems dedicated to staying out of trouble. He seems to feel he will not get out. There is a tremendous subtext of sadness though he smiles occasionally, and the smiles seem very real.

If he got out of prison today Julian would appreciate the opportunity to talk to young people. He says, "they have the wrong people telling kids what they should not do, they are not showing them what they should do."

He says the hardest part is, "knowing I won't have a chance to test myself on who I consider myself to be. . . . I want a chance."

CASE STUDY

Liliana—Loss of childhood and a journey to redemption

In 1992, Liliana, along with two other young women, shot and killed two men in their 20s—members of a rival street gang. Liliana was 15 years old. Liliana takes full responsibility for this crime. She grieves for them and for the pain that her actions have caused.

> *"Not a day goes by that I don't wish it were me. They were human, they were somebody's father, they were somebody's child."*

The crime was one terrible chapter in a long story of inter-gang warfare in Liliana's neighborhood. This particular shooting was in retaliation for the rival gang's killing of a young deaf boy who lived in the neighborhood affiliated with Liliana's gang.

Liliana was groomed to be a gang "soldier" from a very young age—by her stepfather who was a gang leader himself. Cooking and selling drugs from the kitchen in their tiny home, her stepfather recalls sending Liliana out to deliver heroin when she was as young as 6 or 7.

He also recalls taking Liliana with him to collect debts for the gang, describing in particular one incident where Liliana sat terrified behind the wheel of the family van while her stepfather grabbed another man off the street, pulled him into the van and beat him until he was unconscious. Liliana was only 10 or 11 at the time.

Violence ruled in their home as well. The stepfather, who kept guns throughout the house, often turned them on Liliana's mother and admits to physically abusing all of the women in the household. Indeed, records from Illinois state child welfare agency confirm that Liliana's bruises eventually caused her teachers to contact the authorities to report the abuse. Liliana also took to self-abusive behaviors during this period—cutting herself, flinging her body into the walls of her apartment. Her stepfather recalls the round marks he would sometimes find in the drywall—places where Liliana had thrown her head into the wall with such force that the wall itself had given way.

Liliana suffered sexual abuse, too, at the hands of her stepfather and from a very young age. As she got older, he would often leave money by her bed on the nights he assaulted her.

At the same time, her stepfather insisted that Liliana "learn to be tough"—teaching her how to fight, encouraging her to do so, ensnaring her even further in the "family business" when she left school in the seventh grade.

Thus, Liliana grew up both hating this violent man and crafted in his image—when she left home, at 12, she joined a gang herself. Notably, though, the gang she chose was the rival of her powerful stepfather's; Liliana found a way to turn what he had made her into her best weapon against him.

None of this is to say, in any way, that the crime in Liliana's case is remotely excusable, but it does indicate, contrary to all the sensationalistic media coverage at the time, that it was not a monster who committed those murders but a terribly broken young woman.

"I did what they said I did, I'm not who they say I am."

Because of the charges against her, Liliana was automatically transferred to adult court, that foreboding rite of passage in which your age disappears and, whether you are 15 or 35, you are viewed as the same before the court. She received a mandatory life without possibility of parole sentence.

None of us is the same person at 35 that we were at 15, but Liliana's transformation has been truly astonishing. Even more so when you consider the circumstances in which she has had to grow, to literally grow up, to learn and to transform.

At 35, she has earned her high school degree as well as a number of college credits—nothing but the limited programming available to her has prevented her from doing all she can to become a productive person; she has taken virtually every single class offered at her prison. She is also a poet and deeply committed to helping young people, particularly those in thrall to the gang lifestyle she knows so well. Having long renounced her own gang affiliation, Liliana is an advocate for other prisoners and a mother figure to many of them.

Her most recent accomplishment is her graduation from a program in which inmates train service dogs for the disabled.

These changes were hard wrought and by no means instantaneous. When Liliana first arrived at adult prison—transferred on her 17th birthday per Illinois law—she was the youngest person in the entire prison system, forced to choose between being victimized and developing a reputation that would hopefully protect her from harm. She chose the latter. She also spent many of her early years openly defying prison rules—having been told, repeatedly, that she was to die in that prison, no matter what she did, no matter who she became, she had trouble finding any reason to do otherwise.

Eventually, Liliana came to realize that her future depended on rejecting the persona that had once been essential to her survival and forged a new identity as a protector of the younger inmates whose fear and fierceness she well understood. To visit her today is to see a true and committed leader—many of the inmates call her "mom."

CASE STUDY

Phillip and Juliet—Accidental Activists

Even amidst the most challenging of situations, Phillip and Juliet have attempted to parent their son James, sentenced to life without possibility of parole at the age of 15, from outside the prison walls. They visit, send him books, talk with him on the phone, copy board game cards and content into letters so James can recreate old favorite games out of the meager supplies allowed in prisons, toilet paper, cardboard, pencils. They are, as so many parents become, advocates, activists, and frequently, the sole lifeline to the outside world.

In Juliet's own words: Nothing in my life or upbringing prepared me to be living the life I am living.

Our son James is serving juvenile life without parole, in Menard Penitentiary—located in southern Illinois about 350 miles from our home. We are allowed five two-hour visits a month, and we have never missed a visit, in 16 years.

James was sentenced to life in prison with no possibility of parole, for a crime he was convicted of when he was 15 years old.

James is now 31 years old and has spent over half of his life behind bars.

I truly did not realize that this happened in our country, when James was arrested and we met with our attorney he told us that, if convicted, James would face the rest of his life in prison without ever having a chance for parole. Because of the sentence James would be serving in a maximum facility, on lockdown for 23 hours a day. You are locked in a concrete 6 × 8 cell with another person that you may or may not get along with or even like. Then they are given "yard" time—one day a week, provided the facility has not gone on lockdown.

My husband and I were raised on the Southwest Side of Chicago, we both come from working middle class blue collar families. We met in High School and got married about a year after graduation (that was 35 years ago), we then bought an old Chicago Bungalow right in the neighborhood where we both grew up. A few years later and we had our son James. Followed by another son Anthony and then our daughter Lily. We thought this is what we were supposed to do, we thought we were doing things right.

We sent our children to Catholic schools, believing that the supervision and religious upbringing would help us raise our children to be responsible, law abiding adults.

James was a very smart child, and I know all moms think this, but he was and still is, probably to his demise. James was also very slight and small of stature, which in hindsight, was also a problem. James did very well in grammar school, he had the grades to be on the honor roll every single semester, but he refused to do his homework, thus earning "checks" that kept him off the honor roll. We would battle almost daily in regards to homework. That was probably our biggest challenge during his first 13 years.

When James started High School (again a Catholic school), is when he began rebelling. Hanging out with older kids he began missing curfew times, and towards the end of his freshman year, skipping school. We were not ready for this, and we really didn't know where to turn for help. James, for as smart as he was, was immature and willful, never thinking of consequences, such as "if I miss too much school, I'll have to repeat my freshman year." Not uncommon teenage stuff.

James's friends were mostly older and they were not his grade school friends. So these boys formed a "gang." In the 90's gangs were very very fashionable. The gang became very important to James, like all teenagers his peers were the most important thing to him. What his parents wanted was not that important to him.

The day they came and took my son away in handcuffs, at the age of 15 never to see his home again, is one I relive over and over. Even in writing this 16 years later the pain is there and strong.

There were 7 defendants in James's case, James was the youngest, the next oldest was a 17 year old, the eldest was 23. 6 were convicted, 4 are serving life without parole, 2 will be eligible for parole in a few years, and one never went to trial

There were no winners in this, from the victims' families to the defendants' families, everyone lost. I wish there were some comfort I could give the other families, [but] there isn't anything. For some reason as a society we tell victims that someone needs to be punished, that will lessen their loss, this is of course not true, no matter how many people go to prison, the loss is still there.

So I ask, do we lock our children away for life as a punishment? To prevent them committing the same crime again? Because they are a danger to society?

These are not throw away children, many of them deserve a second chance, many of them can contribute something to society.

James has grown up in prison, but he has also grown up, he is a man now. He has a job in the prison, he also paints, is an avid reader and lives for visits from his family. He looks back when he was a teenager, which many of us do, and wishes he could change things, wishes he would have listened to those in his life that loved him. But, we can only move forward.

VI. Conclusion

A myriad of factors leads a young person to receive the sentence of life without the possibility of parole—the harshest punishment available for a child under the age of eighteen in the United States and indeed, around the world. At its core, the sentence asks us to consider whether people—especially teenagers—can change as they grow into adulthood. The United States Supreme Court's recent decision in *Graham v. Florida* strongly suggests that it is time to rethink the way in which we treat children in the criminal justice system—recognizing their right to childhood and inherent capacity to change and grow, while finding meaningful ways to address the serious harm caused to individuals, families and communities.

Acknowledgments

The authors would like to acknowledge Patricia Soung (National Center for Youth Law), Alison Flaum (CFJC), and Julie Anderson, who contributed to the writing of this article.

NOTES

1. Human Rights Watch & Amnesty International. (2005, October 11). The rest of their lives: Life without parole for child offenders in the United States, 39–44 . Retrieved from http://www. hrw.org/reports/2005/us1005/

2. Elizabeth Cauffman & Laurence Steinberg, (Im)Maturity of Judgment in Adolescence: Why Adolescents May Be Less Culpable Than Adults, 18 Behav. Sci. & L. 741,742 (2000).

3. E.g., Nitin Gogtay et al., Dynamic Mapping of Human Cortical Development During Childhood Through Early Adulthood, 101 Proceedings Nat'l Acad. Sci. 8174, 8177 (2004); see also Amicus Brief of the American Medical Society et. al., *Roper v. Simmons*, 543 U.S. 551, 1255 S.Ct. 1183 (2005) at 10, available at http://www.abanet.org/crimjust/juvjus/simmons/simmonsamicus/.

4. *Graham v. Florida*, 130 S. Ct. 2011 (2010).

5. Human Rights Watch, The Rest of Their Lives: Life Without Parole for Youth Offenders in the United States in 2008 (2008), http://www.hrw.org/sites/default/files/reports/us1005execsum.pdf.

6. *Id.* at 2.

7. *Ibid.*

8. *Ibid.*

9. *Ibid.*

10. *Id.*

11. *Graham v. Florida*, 130 S. Ct. 2011 (2010).

12. *Roper v. Simmons*, 543 U.S. 551 (2005).

13. *Graham*, 130 S. Ct. 2011 at 2018.

14. *Id.*

15. *Id.*

16. *Id.*

17. *Id.* at 2018–19.

18. *Id.* at 2019–2020.

19. American Psychiatric Association, *Diagnostic and Statistical Manual of Mental Disorders* 701—06 (4th ed. rev. 2000), *Roper*, 543 U.S. at 573 (2005).

20. Laurence Steinberg, *Age Differences in Future Orientation and Delay Discounting*, 80 Child Development 28, 40 (2009); Elkhonon Goldberg, *The New Executive Brain: Frontal Lobes in a Complex World* 175 (Oxford Univ. Press 2009).

21. Neir Eshel et al., Neural Substrates of Choice Selection in Adults and Adolescents: Development of the Ventrolateral Prefrontal and Anterior Cingulate Cortices, 45 *Neuropsychologica* 1270, 1270 (2007).

22. *Id.* at 1024.

23. *State v. Means*, No. FECR167295 (Sept.2010) available at http://www.angelareyeslaw.com/meansopinion.pdf.

24. U.S. Constitution, Article VI, clause 2.

25. General Assembly resolution 1386 (XIV), November 20, 1959.

26. Art. 37(b).

27. HRW, at 99.

28. See Vienna Convention on the Law of Treaties, art. 18, concluded May 23, 1969, 1155 U.N.T.S. 331 (entered into force Jan. 27, 1980).

29. HRW report.

30. HRW 2008, p. 9.

31. CFSY newsletter.

32. Campaign for the Fair Sentencing of Youth. (n.d.). Statement in support of elimination of juvenile life without parole sentencing. Unpublished letter.

33. Campaign for the Fair Sentencing of Youth. (n.d.). Not All Victims. Unpublished report.

34. Linda White, OnFaith Blog, Accessed July 26, 2011. Site: http://newsweek.washingtonpost.com/onfaith/guestvoices/2010/06/forgiving_my_daughters_killer.html

35. V.T.C.A., Penal Code § 12.31 (a)(1) (2011); http://ctjja.org/glossary.html; HRW report; http://www.law.com/jsp/article.jsp?id=1202446216111&More_States_Rethinking_Life_Sentences_for_Teens&slreturn=1&hbxlogin=1.

36. *See* note 6, *supra*.

37. *Roper v. Simmons*, 543 U.S. 551, 570 (2005).

38. *See* Frank W. Putnam, *The Impact of Trauma on Child Development*, 57 Juv. & Faro. Ct. J., Winter 2006, at 1, 1–7 (discussing the neurological effects of child maltreatment on youth); Henry R. Cellini, *Child Abuse, Neglect and Delinquency: The Neurological Link*, 55 Juv. & Fam. Ct. J., Fall 2004, at 1, 1–14 (discussing research showing the "clear connection" between child maltreatment and negative changes in a youth's neurological development); Julian Ford, et al., National Center for Mental Health and Juvenile Justice, *Trauma Among Youth in the Juvenile Justice System: Critical Issues and New Directions*, June 2007, at 3.

39. Barbara I. Williams, What Do the Numbers Tell Us about Crime and Children?, 71 *The Journal of Negro Education* 3, 127 (2002). One 2002 study, for instance, finds, "The numbers tell us, rather emphatically, that the prevalence of drug/alcohol use and violent behavior does not determine the rate at which Black children are arrested."

40. Human Rights Watch & Amnesty International. (2005, October 11). The rest of their lives: Life without parole for child offenders in the United States, 39–44. Retrieved from http://www.hrw.org/reports/2005/us1005/

41. ACLU of Michigan. (n.d.). Second chances: Juveniles serving life without parole in Michigan prisons, 6. Retrieved from http://www.aclumich.org/sites/default/files/file/Publications/Juv%20Lifers%20V8.pdf.

42. Names in this article have been changed in order to protect the confidentiality of the individuals profiled.

*Allison Conyers is the communications specialist at the Campaign for the Fair Sentencing of Youth.

Shobha L. Mahadev is a clinical assistant professor and project director of the Illinois Coalition for the Fair Sentencing of Children (ICFSC) at the Children and Family Justice Center (CFJC) at Northwestern University School of Law.

Caitlin Shay is a student at American University's Washington College of Law.

Sarah Silins is the Outreach Coordinator for the ICFSC.

DISCUSSION QUESTIONS

1. Should the trajectory of adolescent development be a factor in determining how to respond to juvenile crime?

2. What are the costs to society of prosecuting and sentencing children as adults? What are the benefits?

3. Should youth be placed in jail with adult prisoners? Why or why not?

4. Should youth who commit murder be sentenced to life without parole? What are some sentencing alternatives?

5. Should the justice system focus on rehabilitation of youth who commit serious crimes? Why or why not?

Chapter 5:

Populations Overreferred to the Juvenile Justice System

The juvenile justice system touches nearly every sector of adolescent life. Schools, which turned to "get tough" policies after events like the massacre at Columbine, in which 2 students killed 12 students and injured 21 others, now feed thousands of youth into juvenile courtrooms. Youth struggling with mental health problems often get trapped in the juvenile justice system as a result of their condition or because mental health resources are not available to them within their communities. Girls who are the victims of trauma and abuse are often prosecuted in systems that are unable, or unwilling, to understand the causes of their behavior and/or meet their unique needs. Each of these populations—schoolchildren, youth affected by mental health disorders, and girls—are examined in this chapter.

The first article, "Still Haven't Shut Off the School-to-Prison Pipeline: Evaluating the Impact of Florida's New Zero-Tolerance Law," released by the ACLU of Florida, the Advancement Project, and the Florida State Conference of the NAACP, assesses the damage caused by zero tolerance discipline policies in schools across the state. Next, in "Addressing the Mental Health Needs of Youth in Contact With the Juvenile Justice System in System of Care Communities: An Overview and Summary of Key Issues," Dr. Joseph Cocozza, Kathleen Skowyra, and Jennie Shufelt examine the challenges faced by youth with mental health disorders who enter the justice system. They present options for identifying youth with mental health needs before they are formally placed into the juvenile justice system. They also introduce a number of mental health and juvenile justice system collaborations aimed at effectively addressing the mental health needs of youth who are in conflict with the law. The chapter concludes with Francine Sherman's "Reframing the Response: Girls in the Juvenile Justice System and Domestic Violence," which explores the connection between family trauma and young girls' involvement in juvenile court. The author identifies practices that negatively affect girls and offers alternatives to incarceration for girls who have been victims of abuse.

Still Haven't Shut Off the School-to-Prison Pipeline: Evaluating the Impact of Florida's New Zero-Tolerance Law

by ACLU of Florida, Advancement Project,
Florida State Conference of the NAACP*

INTRODUCTION

It was only five years ago that two police officers pinned five-year-old kindergarten student Ja'eisha Scott down onto a table, handcuffed her, and dragged her out of school and into a police cruiser after throwing a tantrum during a jelly bean counting game.[1] They then refused to release Ja'eisha into her mother's custody, keeping her in the back of the car for hours.[2] The video that captured the infamous incident—showing the tears streaming down the tiny child's face and unmistakable look of fear in her eyes—has been forever imprinted in the minds of many who saw it.

Just two years later, in Avon Park, six-year-old Desre'e Watson was also handcuffed, arrested, and taken away from school in a police car after a tantrum in her kindergarten class.[3] Desre'e's wrists were so small that the handcuffs had to be placed around her biceps.[4] She was taken to county jail, fingerprinted, had a mug shot taken, and was charged with a felony and two misdemeanors.[5]

Many of the more than 20,000 referrals from Florida schools to the juvenile justice system that occurred each year were similarly outrageous. Many others were simply unnecessary. In response, a groundswell of grassroots advocacy emerged across the state, with youth, parents, and other community members speaking out against these harsh, "zero-tolerance" disciplinary practices and the School-to-Prison Pipeline that had been created in Florida.[6] These determined advocates demanded action from the legislature, and in the spring of 2009, Florida's lawmakers responded. They passed a new zero-tolerance law (SB 1540), which urged Florida schools to limit the use of law enforcement intervention and other severe punishments for school behavior.

Finally, after nearly a decade of embarrassing news reports and studies about the devastating effects of harsh school disciplinary practices in Florida schools,[7] the State was apparently moving in the right direction. Indeed, the law propelled Florida to the forefront of school discipline reform nationally.[8] The stage was set for meaningful reform of school discipline practices in Florida, with the hope that student misbehavior would once again be dealt with in less damaging and more developmentally appropriate ways. Yet sadly, just a few months after Governor Crist signed SB 1540 into law, in October 2009, a 14-year-old student in Lehigh Acres was tasered by a school resource officer during a schoolyard fight at her middle school.[9] And just this past October, we were reminded once again of the progress still to be made, as police were called to a Fort Pierce elementary school to handle yet another "unruly" five-year-old child having a tantrum.[10]

An analysis was launched to determine how effectively the changes made in Tallahassee were reaching the students in Florida's school districts. We reviewed and analyzed zero-tolerance policies and codes of conduct from 55 out of the 67 total districts within the state.[11] We also reviewed the available school discipline data from the last school year. Our key finding is:

> While there has been some encouraging progress, the implementation of Florida's new zero-tolerance law has fallen substantially short of what is needed to adequately address the over-criminalization of Florida's youth and the over-reliance on exclusionary discipline by Florida's schools.

After discussing the history of zero tolerance in Florida briefly below, we summarize our analysis and ultimately recommend additional steps that the legislature, state Departments of Education and Juvenile Justice, and school districts should take to ensure that the promise of SB 1540 is fulfilled so that Florida's children are no longer needlessly criminalized, deprived of their education, and pushed out of school by the misapplication of zero tolerance.

BACKGROUND

Florida enacted its first zero-tolerance school discipline law in 1997 and proceeded to rewrite it three times by 2002 to make it harsher.[12] Under that law, public schools were allowed to—and in some cases were required to—refer students to law enforcement agencies for a variety of school behaviors. Many districts decided to go even further than what the law required, broadening the array of school disciplinary matters that triggered very severe punishments. These harsh school policies and practices combined with the increased role of law enforcement in schools to create a School-to-Prison Pipeline throughout Florida's public school system.

The use of out-of-school suspensions, expulsions, and school-based arrests to address student misbehavior skyrocketed across the State, especially for minor incidents.[13] As a result, huge numbers of children and youth were pushed out of school and into the juvenile and criminal justice systems. Incidents that previously had been handled on the school campus by teachers, administrators, and parents were now handled by the police. For example, in 2004–05, over 28,000 students were arrested and referred to the Florida Department of Juvenile Justice (DJJ), and 63% of the referrals were for misdemeanor offenses.[14] And this "get-tough" approach to discipline turned many Florida schools into unwelcoming and even hostile environments for students, thus (1) making many schools less safe than before zero tolerance was implemented; and (2) jeopardizing the right of all Florida children under the state constitution to receive a high-quality education.[15]

The failure of this harsh, unforgiving form of discipline has been well-documented. In fact, national research demonstrates that zero-tolerance policies have not made schools any safer since the policies were first implemented.[16] There is also no credible evidence that zero-tolerance policies are an effective means for changing student behavior.[17] On the contrary, research has shown that zero-tolerance policies are associated with lower individual and schoolwide academic achievement, lower graduation rates, and worse school climate.[18] Zero tolerance has also been found to make students feel less "connected" to school, which is linked to increased likelihood of engaging in risky behaviors, violence, and alcohol or substance abuse.[19] And suspension and expulsion increase the likelihood that the child or youth will enter the juvenile or criminal justice systems.[20]

When students are brought into contact with the juvenile justice system, the effects can be even more severe and long-lasting. Students who are arrested or ticketed in school face serious consequences within the justice system, but also when applying for college, the military, or a job.[21] Students who miss school time are pushed farther behind their peers and are more apt to fall behind academically. They are also frequently traumatized by these experiences, and become more alienated from their schools, families, and communities.[22] Students arrested in school are also far more likely to drop out of school and ultimately to wind up being incarcerated.[23]

There are also huge economic costs to zero tolerance. It often costs schools districts (and taxpayers) millions of dollars for school police officers who spend most of their time disciplining students for conduct that should be addressed by classroom interventions, school programs, and counseling.[24] Moreover, the costs to the community of pushing these students out of school far exceed the costs of keeping them in school.[25]

Thus, these "get-tough" practices have had dire consequences for children, families, and communities across the country, and across Florida. In particular, students of color and students with disabilities have been disproportionately affected. These young people already have to struggle to catch up to peers who have been provided greater educational opportunities, and zero tolerance sets them back even further. For example, in 2008–09, Black students were nearly three times more likely to be referred to the juvenile justice system than their White peers, and the most recently available statewide suspension data shows that Black students were almost four times more likely to be suspended out-of-school.[26] Yet there continues to be no evidence that those disparities can be explained by differences in student behavior. To the contrary, there is considerable evidence that students of color are disciplined more harshly than their peers for identical behavior.[27]

In short, Florida's zero-tolerance approach to school discipline has been both ineffective and costly, and necessitated a dramatic change.

Florida's Revised Zero-Tolerance Law

In response to the overwhelming evidence of the failures and mounting social and economic costs of damaging zero-tolerance practices, on July 1, 2009, the Florida Legislature amended the state's zero-tolerance law.[28] The amendment, known as Senate Bill (SB) 1540, passed unanimously in both the House and Senate and was signed into law by Governor Crist. At the time of signing, the Governor aptly stated, "Florida's children are one of our most important resources for securing Florida's future, and we must ensure they have a safe, fair, and first-class education."[29]

SB 1540 makes six important changes:

1. It encourages schools to handle petty disciplinary infractions and misdemeanor offenses—such as disrupting a school function, disorderly conduct, simple assault or battery, affray, trespassing, theft (less than $300), and vandalism (less than $1,000)—without relying on police officers, prosecutors, and judges, and without expelling students from school.[30] It further says that zero-tolerance policies may not require the reporting of these offenses to law enforcement.[31]

2. The law encourages schools to use alternatives to expulsion and referral to law enforcement agencies, such as restorative justice.[32]

3. It addresses disparities in discipline by stating that zero-tolerance policies must apply "equally to all students, regardless of their economic status, race, or disability."[33]

4. The law pushes back against the "one size fits all" approach to discipline by requiring districts to take the particularized circumstances of the student's misconduct into account before punishing a student under a zero-tolerance policy.[34]

5. It requires districts to provide each student with an opportunity for review of any disciplinary action taken against the student pursuant to the school's zero-tolerance policy.[35] (Prior to the law's revision, only students who were expelled from school, not those who faced in-school or out-of-school suspensions, were afforded this basic due process right.)

6. The law requires districts with corporal punishment policies to review those policies every three years at district school board meetings in which public testimony is taken.[36]

The new law was undoubtedly a significant step forward. Nevertheless, it did not go as far as many advocates thought necessary to adequately address the problem. In fact, by merely encouraging districts to decriminalize certain behaviors, SB 1540 fell short of the Florida DJJ's Blueprint Commission's recommendation to eliminate the referral of students to law enforcement for misdemeanor offenses.[37] Thus, the potential impact of the law was limited from the start. But to better understand the impact SB 1540 actually had, an evaluation was undertaken of the implementation process.

FINDINGS

To assess the performance of Florida's school districts in implementing SB 1540, each Florida school district was asked to provide the new policies that they were instructed to write by the legislature, and then we analyzed the available policies (representing 55 out of 67 Florida school districts) for compliance.[38] Additionally, we reviewed the available data on school-based referrals to the juvenile justice system, provided by the state Department of Juvenile Justice (as of this writing, the Department of Education has not released suspension and expulsion data for 2009–10).[39] From that research we conclude that the results of SB 1540 implementation have been mixed. While there are certainly some encouraging signs, the overall performance of Florida school districts with regard to school discipline remains deeply concerning, and it appears that a substantial number of districts are not implementing SB 1540 as the state legislature intended. In fact, some districts appear to be in direct violation of the law.

Overall, for the 2009–10 school year, there were 18,467 referrals to DJJ, which represents a modest 8.7% drop statewide in the number of school-based referrals to the Department of Juvenile Justice, compared to the previous year.[40] However, almost half of all Florida districts—27—had more or the same number of referrals to the Department of Juvenile Justice following the passage of SB 1540 than they had the year before.[41] This indicates uneven implementation of the law. Perhaps most troubling is that 67% of school-based referrals to DJJ following the passage of SB 1540 were for misdemeanor offenses. It has been over two years since the Department of Juvenile Justice's Blueprint Commission recommended eliminating referrals of students to DJJ for misdemeanors, yet in the school year following the passage of SB 1540, there were still over 12,000 referrals for misdemeanor offenses.[42]

While the State deserves credit for the 34% drop in DJJ referrals since 2004–05,[43] it is important to point out that most of that change is due to statewide advocacy around this issue prior to the implementation of the new law. In fact, the drop in referrals this year is far lower than it was in many of the years prior to the passage of SB 1540.[44] More importantly, far too many districts have failed to demonstrate significant improvement, and far too many students are still finding themselves thrust into the juvenile justice system for minor misconduct. Thus, while the overall reduction in school-based referrals last year is a positive development, considering the many years SB 1540 was in the making and the far-reaching nature of the legislation, it would seem that the legislature intended a much more substantial reduction in the number of Florida students entering the juvenile justice system directly from schools. Indeed, even with the reduced number of referrals, Florida still has the highest documented number of school-based referrals to law enforcement in the country.[45] Clearly, much more is needed to dismantle Florida's School-to-Prison Pipeline.

Continued Overreliance on Referrals to Law Enforcement and Expulsion

Our analysis of the school discipline policies in 55 Florida school districts helps explain why the initial results of SB 1540 have fallen well short of what the law intended. For example, while the law requires each district to rewrite their zero-tolerance policies to define both "petty acts of misconduct" and "serious threats to school safety,"[46] 43 of the districts' policies we reviewed failed to comply.[47] That amounts to a direct violation of state law.

Additionally, while districts were instructed to rewrite their zero-tolerance policies to promote broader use of alternatives to expulsion and referrals to law enforcement for acts of petty misconduct and misdemeanors, most districts continue to allow for severe punishments for these acts. For example, SB 1540 listed eight examples of petty or misdemeanor offenses that should not be subject to zero tolerance: disorderly conduct, disruption of a school function, simple assault, simple battery, affray (fighting), theft of less than $300, trespassing, and vandalism of less than $1,000.[48] While these offenses may not trigger automatic referral to law enforcement or expulsion anymore, most districts' policies still allow for these excessively harsh punishments.

In fact, 44% of the districts analyzed had policies that permitted referral to law enforcement for all eight petty or misdemeanor offenses.[49] For seven of the eight offenses, at least 69% of the school districts analyzed allowed for law enforcement referrals.[50] "Simple battery," for example, can still result in referral to law enforcement in 84% of the districts analyzed. In other words, the vast majority of Florida districts appear not to have decriminalized these behaviors in their policies. As a result, a substantial percentage of school-based referrals to DJJ continue to be for these offenses; in fact, they account for three of the five most common offenses resulting in referral (misdemeanor assault/battery, disorderly conduct, and trespassing).[51]

Moreover, the vast majority of districts failed to change their policies to prevent students from being expelled from school for these behaviors. For example, 87% of the analyzed policies allow for fighting/affray to result in expulsion, and 83% of district policies analyzed say that students can be expelled for petty vandalism.[52]

Behind these data are a large number of policies that continue to over-rely on harsh, exclusionary disciplinary measures, contrary to the intent of SB 1540.

Percentage of Districts that Allow Students to be Referred to Law Enforcement for Minor Offenses 2009–2010

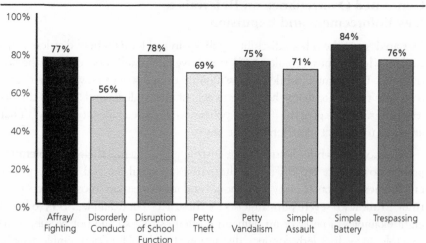

Percentage of Florida Districts Analyzed that Allow Students to Be Expelled for Minor Offenses 2009–2010

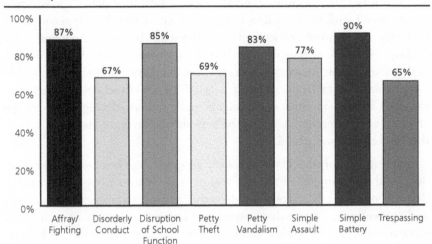

For example, Broward County Schools has a discipline "matrix" that it uses to advise school administrators about the appropriate consequences for disciplinary matters.[53] The matrix allows for law enforcement referrals following disruptions of school functions, trespassing, fighting, battery, and assault/threat, among many other types of student behavior.[54] It should be of no surprise that Broward had the most referrals to DJJ of any Florida county in 2009–10—1,668—as well as the largest increase from the previous year.[55]

Many other districts also appear not to have taken SB 1540 seriously. For example, within the discipline policy of Bay District Schools it states:

"All felonies and violent misdemeanors, whether committed by a student or adult, and delinquent acts that would be felonies or violent misdemeanors if committed by an adult, shall be reported to law enforcement."[56]

Because simple battery and affray/fighting are, by definition, "violent misdemeanors," Bay is in direct violation of SB 1540 by requiring referrals to law enforcement for misdemeanors.[57] Again, it is not surprising that the Bay School District had 20% more DJJ referrals in 2009–10 than it did the previous year.[58]

In short, Florida must take dramatic action—at the state and local levels—to end the unnecessary use of law enforcement referrals and expulsions for its students.

Continuing Racial Inequities

SB 1540 states "the Legislature finds that zero-tolerance policies must apply equally to all students regardless of their...race."[59] Florida's lawmakers were evidently, and rightfully, concerned about the state's history of disciplining students of color far more harshly than their peers. However, even after the passage of the new law, the implementation of school discipline continues to be highly inequitable along racial lines. In fact, racial disparities in school-based referrals worsened in 2009–10. Students of color actually comprised a higher percentage of school-based referrals to DJJ after the implementation of the law—65%—than they did before it was passed.[60]

While it certainly should not have been expected that these persistent disparities would be eliminated in the first year of implementation, we are concerned that not enough has been done to address this very serious problem. For example, we have seen no evidence that a significant number of districts are collecting, reporting, and analyzing school discipline data disaggregated by race, or holding school administrators accountable for reducing those disparities. Moreover, the vast majority of districts have not altered the other policy conditions that make racially disproportionate discipline possible, such as:

- Allowing severe punishments for highly subjective offenses, like "disobedience," "defiance," and "disrupting a school function."

    - For example: Martin County Public Schools permits referral to law enforcement, in addition to suspension and expulsion, for engaging in classroom "disruption," "insubordination," "defiance," "disorderly conduct," and any other "serious" misconduct.[61]

- Granting excessive discretion to school officials to impose harsh punishments for low-level behavior.

    - For example, in Hendry County Schools, the code of conduct states that a wide range of offenses—including many low-level behaviors extremely common among children and youth—can be punished through suspension, expulsion, or an "alternative" like corporal punishment. Additionally, the code allows principals and teachers to "take additional or more severe administrative action if, in his/her opinion, the nature of the misconduct warrants it."[62]

While discriminatory and unfair school discipline can be caused by a number of factors, research shows that the worst disparities are evident for subjective offenses.[63] And of course the severity of racial disparities in discipline increases dramatically when such life-altering consequences like long-term out-of school

Discretion and Subjectivity in Discipline Policy

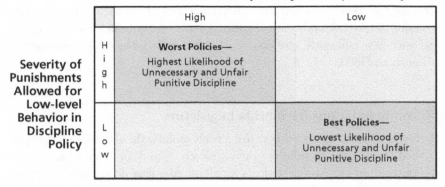

		High	Low
Severity of Punishments Allowed for Low-level Behavior in Discipline Policy	H i g h	**Worst Policies—** Highest Likelihood of Unnecessary and Unfair Punitive Discipline	
	L o w		**Best Policies—** Lowest Likelihood of Unnecessary and Unfair Punitive Discipline

suspension, expulsion, and referral to law enforcement are being used for relatively minor behavior. These conditions put students of color in a particularly precarious situation, and simply must be eliminated for the goals of SB 1540 to be realized. As the chart above illustrates, Florida school districts with a history of racial disparities in school discipline should instead be implementing policies with low levels of discretion and subjectivity, as well as less severe punishments for low-level behavior.

It is also worth noting that some districts add even more barriers for students. For example, while the Lake County School District offers some alternatives to suspension, it informs students and parents that "Any fees from counseling on anger management, substance abuse, tobacco education, prevention or treatment programs that are stipulated in a student's alternative placement or alternative to suspension plan, as part of a disciplinary action, are the responsibility of the student and parent/guardian."[64] By requiring payment to avoid suspension, it is blatantly obvious that low-income students will be unfairly subjected to punitive, unproductive consequences, while wealthier students will benefit from non-punitive alternatives where they can learn appropriate behavior and gain additional life skills.

RECOMMENDATIONS

Because Florida's students continue to have their educational opportunities—and thus, their life chances—limited by the over-use of harsh and unfair school discipline, there is an urgent need for action, at both the state and local levels. Fortunately, schools and districts across the country have already shown the way forward, and have pursued highly-effective strategies that can serve as a model for Florida.[65] If implemented, the recommendations below can reduce Florida's dropout rate, build safer and more effective schools, limit the number of youth entering the juvenile and criminal justice systems, use the State's law enforcement agencies more efficiently, save taxpayer dollars, and build healthier communities throughout Florida.

Recommendations for Florida Legislature

1. Strengthen the text of SB 1540 to expressly prohibit the arrest, citation, expulsion, disciplinary referral to an alternative school, and out-of-school suspension longer than five days of students for all offenses that do not pose a serious, ongoing threat to the safety of students or staff, which should be limited to the following:
   a. Capitol felonies;
   b. Life felonies;
   c. First degree felonies;
   d. Second or third degree felonies involving a firearm, weapon, or use of fire or explosives;
   e. Bringing a firearm or other deadly weapon to school, any school function, or on school-sponsored transportation;
   f. Possessing a firearm at school;
   g. Making a false report or threat related to explosives or weapons of mass destruction and involving school or school personnel's property, school transportation, or a school-sponsored activity;
   h. Aggravated battery;
   i. Aggravated battery against school personnel; and
   j. Dealing or delivering in controlled substances.

2. Implement an accountability structure under which state funding can be withheld from districts that: (a) repeatedly refer students to the Department of Juvenile Justice for offenses that do not pose a serious, ongoing threat to school safety; (b) demonstrate a continuing over-reliance on out-of-school suspensions, expulsions, and referrals to disciplinary alternative schools; and (c) have persistent racial disparities in the use of exclusionary school discipline and have not developed and implemented a plan for addressing them.

3. Hold law enforcement officials accountable for reducing the use of school-based arrests for school disciplinary matters by making funding for school-based law enforcement contingent on reductions in arrests and reductions of racial disparities.

4. Provide resources for the formation of local or regional councils comprised of parents, youth, and representatives from school systems, juvenile courts, law enforcement agencies, social service agencies, and non-profit community organizations that would be charged with developing comprehensive strategies for addressing the School-to-Prison Pipeline in specific communities. In particular, the councils should be focused on the allocation of public resources and how they can be optimized to ensure that every child and youth in the community receives a full and equal opportunity to receive a high-quality education.

5. Allocate additional funding, and divert funding used for law enforcement and security infrastructure, to support proven and promising school-based discipline frameworks to be implemented in a culturally relevant manner, such as restorative justice/restorative practices, Positive Behavior Interventions and Supports, and other educational purposes, such as additional guidance counselors, social workers, and school psychologists.

6. Prohibit the use of corporal punishment in schools.

7. Enhance the public reporting system for school discipline data, to ensure that all schools—including charter schools and alternative schools—are reporting data on the use of exclusionary discipline, referrals to law enforcement, school-based arrests that is disaggregated by offense, age, gender, grade, race/ethnicity, disability, school, and result.

Recommendations for Florida Departments of Education and Juvenile Justice

1. Provide all districts with a model discipline policy designed to create more effective, caring, and supportive learning environments for students by eliminating policies and practices that unnecessarily push students out of school through the use of suspensions, expulsions, referrals to alternative schools, referrals to law enforcement, and school-based arrests.

2. Provide all districts with a model memorandum of understanding between schools and law enforcement agencies that provides guidance on limiting the involvement of law enforcement and security personnel in schools to conduct that poses a serious, ongoing threat to the safety of students or staff.

3. Issue a report detailing "best practices" from around the state and country on alternatives to zero tolerance and reducing racial disparities in discipline.

4. Provide trainings to district administrators, teachers, and staff on the adverse effects of zero tolerance, child and adolescent development, effective classroom

management, restorative justice/restorative practices, Positive Behavior Interventions and Supports, conflict resolution, disciplinary alternatives, and student engagement through challenging and culturally relevant curricula.

5. Provide trainings to school-based law enforcement officers on the adverse effects of zero tolerance, child and adolescent development, restorative justice/restorative practices, Positive Behavior Interventions and Supports, conflict resolution, and cultural competence.

Recommendations for Florida School Districts

1. Create working groups of stakeholders within the community—including parents, students, teachers, principals, and other community members—to craft school discipline policies and alternatives that limit the use of exclusionary discipline and reduce the flow of students to the juvenile justice system. The focus of the working groups should be on the following:

   a. Limiting the use of out-of-school suspensions longer than five days, expulsions, disciplinary referrals to alternative schools, referrals to law enforcement, and school-based arrests to conduct that poses a serious, ongoing threat to the safety of students or staff.

   b. Limiting short-term out-of-school suspensions to serious misconduct or to when other interventions have been unsuccessful in addressing low-level misconduct.

      i.   Using a graduated approach to assigning consequences.
      ii. Eliminating long-term suspensions and placing caps on the duration of all suspensions, especially for low-level infractions.
      iii. Ensuring that students are provided academic work during suspension periods and are not penalized academically for suspensions.
      iv. Limiting the use of suspensions for conduct that occurs away from school.
      v.   Substituting in-school suspensions for out-of-school suspensions.

   c. Eliminating racial disparities in the use of suspensions, expulsions, disciplinary referrals to alternative schools, referrals to law enforcement, and school-based arrests.

   d. Strengthening the protection of parents'/guardians' and students' due process rights during all disciplinary proceedings and placements, especially around the rights to be notified of disciplinary actions, to be heard throughout the disciplinary process, to have representation at hearings, and to file an appeal for all disciplinary proceedings.

e. Ensuring that all students and parents/guardians are educated on their rights under the discipline policies, and that all school officials and staff are trained on how to implement the new policies.

2. Implement an accountability structure under which school officials are held responsible for:
   a. reducing the use of out-of-school suspensions, expulsions, referrals to alternative schools, referrals to law enforcement, and school-based arrests; and
   b. eliminating racial disparities in exclusionary discipline measures, and law enforcement officials are held responsible for:
   c. reducing the use of school-based arrests for school disciplinary matters; and
   d. eliminating racial disparities in school-based arrests.

3. Clarify the roles and responsibilities of school police through a memorandum of understanding between the school district and police department.
   a. Limit police involvement to felony offenses that pose an ongoing, serious threat to the safety of students or staff.
   b. Require that school resource officers receive training on the adverse effects of zero tolerance, child and adolescent development, restorative justice/restorative practices, Positive Behavior Interventions and Supports, conflict resolution, and cultural competence.

4. Increase funding for guidance counselors, social workers, and school psychologists who are available to address students' academic and behavioral issues, and consider diverting funding for school resource officers, security guards, and security equipment within schools toward those purposes or toward proven prevention and intervention programs like Positive Behavioral Interventions and Supports and restorative justice/restorative practices.

5. Implement a district-wide training program for all school administrators, teachers, police and security officers, and school staff on the adverse consequences of the zero-tolerance approach, effective classroom management techniques, adolescent development, conflict resolution, restorative justice/restorative practices, Positive Behavioral Interventions and Supports, disciplinary alternatives, and student engagement through challenging and culturally relevant curricula.

6. Create a public reporting system for school discipline data, including referrals to law enforcement and school-based arrests, disaggregated by offense, age, gender, grade, race/ethnicity, disability, school, teacher/school staff, and result. Data should also be used within districts to track program success, identify areas of improvement, and develop alternative programs tailored to the disciplinary issues that exist.

7. Establish school discipline oversight committees, which would include school personnel, parents, students, and interested community members. The responsibilities of these committees could include: handling complaints about school discipline practices; handling complaints about the conduct of security and police officers; reviewing discipline and arrest statistics; and evaluating the school district's efforts to maintain safety in a fair and nondiscriminatory manner.

8. Eliminate the use of corporal punishment.

CONCLUSION

The state of Florida took a significant step forward by adopting SB 1540 and amending its harsh zero-tolerance law. But the job is far from complete. Meaningful reform has still not reached most of the schools across the state, which means Florida's children, families, and communities continue to suffer from the devastating effects of zero tolerance. We know these "get tough" strategies are ineffective. We also know how to do it better, and that many school districts throughout the country already do better. So it is time to complete the work that was started to dismantle Florida's School-to-Prison Pipeline once and for all.

NOTES

1. Tobin, T. (2005, April 22). Video shows police handcuffing five-year-old. *Tampabay.com*. Retrieved November 11, 2010, from http://www.sptimes.com/2005/04/22/Southpinellas/Video_shows_police_ha.shtml.

2. Advancement Project, Florida State Conference NAACP, & NAACP Legal Defense and Educational Fund. (2006, Spring). *Arresting development: Addressing the school discipline crisis in Florida*, 14. Retrieved October 5, 2010, from http://advancementproject.org/sites/default/files/full%20report.pdf.

3. Herbert, B. (2007, April 9). Six-year-olds under arrest [Opinion-Editorial]. *The New York Times*. Retrieved March 30, 2009, from http://select.nytimes.com/2007/04/09/opinion/09herbert.html?pagewanted=print.

4. Id.

5. Id.

6. *See, e.g.*, Advancement Project, et al. (2006, Spring), 6, 18.

7. *See, e.g.*, Advancement Project, et al. (2006, Spring); Advancement Project. (2005, March). *Education on lockdown: The schoolhouse to jailhouse track*, 37–42. Retrieved November 11, 2010, from http://www.advancementproject.org/sites/default/files/publications/FINALEOLrep.pdf; Advancement Project. (2003, May 14). *Derailed: The schoolhouse to jailhouse track*, 13–14, 21–28. Retrieved November 10, 2010, from http://advancementproject.org/sites/default/files/publications/Derailerepcor_o.pdf.

8. Dorell, O. (2009, January 2). Schools' zero-tolerance policies tested. *USAToday.com*. Retrieved November 11, 2010, from http://www.usatoday.com/news/nation/2009-11-01-zero-tolerance_N.htm.

9. Teen tasered by school resource officer, arrested for assault. (2009, October 15). *TheGrio.com*. Retrieved October 15, 2010, from http://www.thegrio.com/news/teen-tasered-by-school-officer.php.

10. Jones, E. (2010, October 13). Police called after Fort Pierce 5-year-old throws toy at classmate, kicks teacher and principal. *TCPalm.com*. Retrieved October 21, 2010, from http://www.tcoasttalk.com/2010/10/13/police-called-after-fort-pierce-5-year-old-throws-toy-at-classmate-kicks-teacher-and-principal/.

11. As of February 2, 2011, the authors did not have a full set of 2009-10 policies for 12 districts. Therefore, they were excluded from the analysis.

12. Tarbutton, M. R. (2006, December 4). *Redefining zero tolerance in Florida schools: An analysis of options*, 5. Retrieved October 24, 2010, from http://www.askew.fsu.edu/current/masters/actionreport/fa2006/Michelle%20Tarbutton%20-%20Redefining%20Zero%20Tolerance%20In%20Florida's%20Schools.pdf.

13. Advancement Project. (2010, March). *Test, punish, and pushout: How zero tolerance and high–stakes testing funnel youth into the school-to-prison pipeline*, 32–34. Retrieved October 24, 2010, from http://www.advancementproject.org/sites/default/files/publications/rev_fin.pdf; Advancement Project, et al. (2006, Spring); Advancement Project. (2005, March), 37–42; Advancement Project. (2003, May 14), 13–14, 21–28.

14. Id.

15. Advancement Project. (2010, March), 32–34; Advancement Project, et al. (2006, Spring).

16. American Psychological Association (APA) Zero Tolerance Task Force. (2006, February 1). *Are zero tolerance policies effective in the schools? An evidentiary review and recommendations*. (on file with authors). *See also* APA. (2008, December). Are zero tolerance policies effective in the schools? An evidentiary review and recommendations. *American Psychologist*, 63(9), 852–62. Retrieved October 24, 2010, from http://www.apa.org/pubs/info/reports/zero-tolerance.pdf, 853.

17. Id.

18. Id.

19. Blum, R. W. & Rinehart, P.M. (2001). *Reducing the risk: Connections that make a difference in the lives of youth*, 21–24. Retrieved January 10, 2009, from http://www.cpc.unc.edu/projects/addhealth/faqs/addhealth/Reducing-the-risk.pdf; The Public Policy Research Institute. (2005). *Study of minority overrepresentation in the Texas juvenile justice system final report*, 24–27. Retrieved March 30, 2009, from http://DMCFinalReport.tamu.edu; Kentucky Center for School Safety. (n.d.). *School characteristics related to the use of suspension*, 1, 4–6. Retrieved March 30, 2009, from http://www.kysafeschools.org/pdfs-docs/clearpdf/issuesbriefs/EDJJresearch.pdf. 20APA. (2008, December), 856.

20. APA. (2008, December), 856.

21. Advancement Project. (2005, March), 17.

22. APA. (2008, December), 856.

23. Blum, R. et al. (2001); National Center for Education Statistics. (2006, June 1). *The conditions of education 2006*, Table 27–2. [Data File]. Retrieved July 4, 2009, from http://nces.ed.gov/pubs2006/2006071_App1.pdf.

24. Advancement Project. (2010, March), 17, 24.

25. Levin, H., Belfield, C., Muennig, P. & Rouse, C. (2007, January). *The costs and benefits of an excellent education for all of America's children*, 5–18. New York: Center for Benefit-Cost Studies of Education, Teachers College, Columbia University. Retrieved March 30, 2009, from http://www.cbcse.org/media/download_gallery/Leeds_Report_Final_Jan2007.pdf; APA Zero Tolerance Task Force. (2006, February 1), 82–85. Alliance for Excellent Education. (2007, October). *The high cost of high school dropouts*, 1–2, 4. Retrieved December 9, 2010, from http://www.all4ed.org/files/archive/publications/HighCost.pdf, 1–2, 4.

26. Florida Department of Juvenile Justice. *Delinquency in Florida's Schools: A five-year study* (2004–05 to. 2008–09), 7. Retrieved November 7, 2010, from http://www.djj.state.fl.us/Research/School_Referrals/FY-2008-09-Delinquency-in-Schools-Analysis.pdf; SESIR Discipline Data Reports.

(2006–07). Florida Department of Education. Retrieved November 11, 2010, from http://www.criminologycenter.fsu.edu/sdfs/reports-pubs-SESIR results.php?Discipline=1&year=2004&district=00; Florida Department of Education. *Florida School Indicators Report 2008–09*. Retrieved November 7, 2010, from http://www.fldoe.org/eias/eiaspubs/0809fsir.asp.

27. *See, e.g.*, Skiba, R. et al. (2000, June). *The color of discipline*, 2–4, 14–19. Indiana Education Policy Center. Retrieved December 1, 2010, from http://www.indiana.edu/~safeschl/cod.pdf

28. Fla. Stat. 1006.07 (2010).

29. *Governor Crist signs DJJ priority legislation enhancing zero tolerance in schools.* [Press Release]. (2009, June 17). Retrieved October 24, 2010, from http://www.djj.state.fl.us/zero-tolerance/index.html.

30. Fla. Stat. §1006.13(1) (2010).

31. Fla. Stat. § 1006.13(4)(c) (2010).

32. Fla. Stat. §1006.13(1) (2010).

33. Fla. Stat. § 1006.13(1) (2010).

34. Fla. Stat. § 1006.3(7) (2010).

35. Fla. Stat. § 1006.3(2)(e) (2010).

36. Fla. Stat. § 1002.20(4)(c)(2) (2010).

37. Florida Department of Juvenile Justice Blueprint Commission. (2008, February). *Getting smart about juvenile justice in Florida*, 18. Retrieved October 2, 2010, from http://www.djj.state.fl.us/blueprint/documents/Report_of_the_Blueprint_Commision.pdf. The Commission recommended decriminalizing all misdemeanor offenses.

38. We analyzed discipline policies from 55 out of 67 districts. Of those that are included, in some cases, an online search was conducted for the district's Student Code of Conduct, Student Handbook, or Zero-Tolerance policy, and that was included in the study.

39. As of February 2, 2011, the Florida Department of Education had not released any school discipline data from the 2009–10 school year.

40. Florida Department of Juvenile Justice. (2010, November). *Delinquency in Florida's schools: A six-year study (2004–05 through 2009–10)*, 3. Retrieved December 5, 2010, from http://www.djj.state.fl.us/Research/School_Referrals/FY-2009–10-Delinquency-in-Schools-Analysis.pdf.

41. Id. Florida Department of Juvenile Justice. (2009, November), 4–5.

42. Florida Department of Juvenile Justice. (2010, November), 8. Florida Department of Juvenile Justice Blueprint Commission. (2008, February), 66.

43. Florida Department of Juvenile Justice. (2010, November), 3.

44. Id.

45. Currently, this data is not collected nationwide. Many individual states report this information, but no other state reports as many school-based referrals to law enforcement as Florida.

46. Fla. Stat. § 1006.13 (2)(b)(2010); Fla. Stat. § 1006.13 (2)(c) (2010).

47. This is based on zero-tolerance policies collected by public records requests that were conducted by the ACLU of Florida and the codes of conducts, student handbooks, and zero-tolerance policies that were found through an online search.

48. Fla. Stat. § 1006.13(1) (2010).

49. This is based on 2009–2010 zero-tolerance policies collected by public records requests that were conducted by the ACLU of Florida and the codes of conducts, student handbooks, and zero-tolerance policies for 2009–2010 that were found through an online search. A sampling of the districts' policies, 55, was analyzed.

50. Id.

51. Florida Department of Juvenile Justice. (2010, November), 8.

52. *Supra* note 49. With regard to expulsions, our analysis included 52 districts instead of 55 districts because the information regarding expulsion was incomplete in 3 districts.

53. Broward County Public Schools Administrative Discipline Matrix. Retrieved September 15, 2010, from http://www.browardschools.com/schools/pdf/secondary_matrix.pdf.

54. Id.

55. Florida Department of Juvenile Justice. (2010, November), 5.

56. 2009–2010 Bay District Schools Student Code of Conduct, 4. Retrieved September 2, 2010, from http://www.bay.k12.fl.us/LinkClick.aspx?fileticket=EA%2bIAdPvE8c%3d&tabid=1760.

57. Fla. Stat. § 1006.13(4)(c) (2010).

58. Florida Department of Juvenile Justice. (2009, November), 5; Florida Department of Juvenile Justice. (2010, November), 5.

59. Fla. Stat. §1006.13(1) (2010).

60. Florida Department of Juvenile Justice. (2010, November), 7.

61. 2009–2010 Martin County School District Student Conduct and Discipline Code, Secondary. Retrieved October 5, 2010, from http://www.sbmc.org/new/docs/repository/2009/2009-2010-secondary_student_conduct_and_discipline_code.pdf.

62. 2009–2010 Hendry County Schools Student Code of Conduct. (on file with authors).

63. Skiba, R. et al. (2000, June), 13.

64. 2009–2010 Lake County School District Code of Student Conduct & Policy Guide. Retrieved October 5, 2010, from http://lake.k12.fl.us/16511031010632497/lib/16511031010632497/2009-2010_Code_of_Conduct.pdf.

65. Advancement Project. (2010, March), 34–43.

*American Civil Liberties Union of Florida works to defend individual rights and personal freedoms guaranteed by the Constitution and the Bill of Rights.

Advancement Project is a multi-racial civil rights organization that uses innovative strategies and strong community alliances to tackle issues of inequity and inspire and strengthen movements.

Florida State Conference of the NAACP works to ensure that the voices of African Americans are heard. The fundamental goal of the NAACP's education advocacy agenda is to provide all students with access to quality education.

ACLU of Florida, Advancement Project, and Florida State Conference of the NAACP, "Still Haven't Shut Off the School-to-Prison Pipeline: Evaluating the Impact of Florida's New Zero-Tolerance Law" (March 2011), http://www.advancementproject.org/digital-library/publications/still-haven%E2%80%99t-shut-off-the-school-to-prison-pipeline-evaluating-the-imp. Adapted and reprinted with permission.

Addressing the Mental Health Needs of Youth in Contact With the Juvenile Justice System in System of Care Communities: An Overview and Summary of Key Issues

by Joseph J. Cocozza, Ph.D., Kathleen R. Skowyra, and Jennie L. Shufelt, M.S.*

BACKGROUND

More than 2 million youth are arrested every year in the United States; more than 600,000 are processed through juvenile detention centers; and more than 93,000 are placed in secure juvenile correctional facilities (Snyder & Sickmund, 2006). The majority of these youth—65 to 70 percent—have a diagnosable mental health disorder (Shufelt and Cocozza, 2006; Wasserman, McReynolds, Lucas, Fisher, & Santos, 2002; Teplin, Abram, McClelland, Dulcan, & Mericle, 2002). The mental health needs of these youth are often severe and complex. According to a recent study by the National Center for Mental Health and Juvenile Justice (NCMHJJ), 27 percent of youth in detention, correctional, and community-based placements experience disorders so severe that their ability to function is highly impaired. Furthermore, youth in the study often met criteria for multiple disorders. Of those youth who met criteria for at least one mental health disorder, more than 60 percent met criteria for three or more diagnoses, and nearly 61 percent had a co-occurring substance use disorder (Skowyra & Cocozza, 2007).

Many youth with mental health needs end up in the juvenile justice system not because of the seriousness of their offenses but because of their need for mental health treatment that is otherwise unavailable to them in the community (Skowyra & Cocozza, 2007; Casey Strategic Consulting Group, 2003). During a survey by the National Alliance on Mental Illness (NAMI, 1999), 36 percent of parents reported that their children were placed in the juvenile justice system because mental health services were unavailable in the community. In a similar manner, a U.S. General Accounting Office report found that, in 2001, parents placed almost 13,000 children in the child welfare or juvenile justice systems in an effort to access mental health treatment (U.S. General Accounting Office, 2003). The undesirable trend of parents' turning to the juvenile justice system as a last resort for treatment was confirmed during a series of focus groups convened in 2004 by NCMHJJ and the Federation of Families for Children's Mental

Health (Osher & Shufelt, 2006). Furthermore, a 2004 study of juvenile detention facilities across the country found that two-thirds of facilities reported holding youth because they needed mental health treatment that was not available in the community (U.S. House of Representatives, 2004).

The unfortunate irony of using the juvenile justice system to access mental health care is that the mental health services within the juvenile justice system are frequently inadequate or completely unavailable. Investigations by the U.S. Department of Justice into the conditions of confinement in juvenile detention and correctional facilities have documented consistent and pervasive failures in the provision of adequate mental health services to youth in their care (U.S. Department of Justice, 2005). Similarly, a 2004 study of 698 detention centers found that a quarter of all facilities provided poor or no mental health treatment to youth, and more than 50 percent had inadequate levels of staff training (U.S. House of Representatives, 2004). This is particularly troubling for youth of color, who are overrepresented in the juvenile justice system (Drakeford & Garfinkel, 2000), underrepresented in outpatient mental health treatment (U.S. Department of Health and Human Services, 2001), and more likely than white youth to have their mental health problems identified through the juvenile justice system (National Mental Health Association, 2004).

For youth with serious and complex mental health needs, involvement with the juvenile justice system can have profound and devastating effects. Placement in juvenile justice facilities can exacerbate a youth's mental health symptoms and, among those youth with a history of traumatic experiences, can trigger memories and reactions to previous traumatic experiences (Mahoney, Ford, Ko, & Siegfried, 2004). Involvement with the juvenile justice system can also be detrimental to a youth's family. Families may feel increasingly anxious and concerned about the safety and well-being of their children, powerless to help their children or manage their treatment, and resentful and angry over the unavailability of other services that might have prevented the involvement of their child with the juvenile justice system (Osher & Hunt, 2002). Families often report feeling "dismayed and bitterly disappointed with the care and treatment their children . . . received" while involved with the juvenile justice system (Osher & Shufelt, 2006).

THE ROLE OF SYSTEMS OF CARE

The multitude of communities across the country that receive funding through the Comprehensive Community Mental Health Services Program for Children and Their Families, commonly referred to as the "system of care initiative," have a significant opportunity to change the stories of youth in their community who have mental health needs and have become involved with the juvenile justice system. For those communities that take on this challenge, the success of their effort will require the following:

1. *Recognition that youth with mental health needs are more often than not found outside the traditional children's mental health system.* Youth with mental health needs are now seen in multiple systems and contexts beyond the traditional mental health setting, including the juvenile justice, child welfare, education, and health care systems. The President's New Freedom Commission Report on Mental Health recognized this trend and called for a "fundamental transformation" of the nation's mental health system into a system that can face this reality and provide access to mental health services *in these various contexts* (The President's New Freedom Commission on Mental Health, 2003). We now know that the vast majority of youth in the juvenile justice system have mental health needs. The system of care initiative, at its core, encourages the formation of multiagency partnerships to provide a wraparound strengths-based approach to mental health care that is driven by the needs of youth and their family. Therefore, systems of care are ideally positioned to embrace such a transformation.

2. *Commitment to enter into meaningful partnerships with the juvenile justice system to jointly examine the extent of overrepresentation of youth with mental health needs in the juvenile justice system at key stages of processing, and to develop joint ways to respond.* These partnerships are not always easy. However, this issue cannot be solved by any single agency or system, and collaboration is critical. A multisystem planning committee is vital to building consensus around a select number of priority issues (e.g., reducing school-based referrals to the police, providing preadjudicatory mental health diversion services to juvenile probationers, strengthening aftercare planning for youth coming home), and such a committee allows a community to strategically select its target group and its focus. Starting small and building on achieved success creates a foundation for future and potentially more ambitious collaborations.

3. *Use of system of care funding to create more community-based, evidence-based mental health treatment capacity for youth in contact (or at risk of contact) with the juvenile justice system.* This targeted capacity-building effort could be used to accomplish the following:

   a. Prevent involvement with the juvenile justice system by providing services for youth that are accessible by parents, schools, and police

b. Create more diversion opportunities for youth with mental health needs so that they can be safely and appropriately diverted from the juvenile justice system and into community-based mental health treatment

c. Create aftercare services for youth with mental health needs who are transitioning out of juvenile justice system placement and back to their homes and communities

CHALLENGES TO SYSTEM OF CARE—
JUVENILE JUSTICE PARTNERSHIPS

The juvenile justice system has been identified as a "critically important component" in the system of care initiative (System of Care Evaluation Brief, 2000). The Substance Abuse and Mental Health Services Administration (SAMHSA) has gone so far as to encourage the prioritization of youth in the juvenile justice system. Additionally, they require applicants to demonstrate substantial planning, support, and input from a variety of state and local stakeholders, including representatives from juvenile justice when developing their programs. Despite the declaration that at-risk youth or youth involved in the juvenile justice system represent a priority population for the system of care communities, the focus on serving these youth varies widely and has not been a priority for many sites.

Data from a national cross-site evaluation of the system of care program indicates that only about 15 percent of all referrals in the system of care sites come from the juvenile justice system. Juvenile justice referrals ranged from 0 to 83 percent across the sites, with half the funded sites receiving fewer than 5 percent of their referrals from juvenile justice (Cocozza, 2004). This suggests that, for the most part, youth in contact with the juvenile justice system remain underserved within many system of care communities. In some cases, this is due to the presence of competing priorities and limitations on resources. In others, it is due to a number of barriers and challenges associated with such partnerships. Under any circumstance, this kind of effort can be difficult. Some of the most common barriers to partnership between the juvenile justice system and systems of care are discussed below.

Difficulties Associated With Collaboration. Critical to the establishment of any partnership is some degree of trust between the involved systems (Skowyra & Cocozza, 2007). A lack of a collaborative history between the mental health and juvenile justice systems can make it hard for these two systems to trust each other. Collaboration can be challenging for a number of reasons. The juvenile justice and mental health systems have very different goals (rehabilitation and the implementation of sanctions versus treatment), philosophies (families in some way are responsible for their children's misbehavior versus family-driven care), and language (holding youth accountable versus strength-based treatment planning). Separate funding streams and accountability measures make blending or braiding funding difficult. Uncertainty about the limits and appropriateness of information sharing, and perceptions that the "other" agency is attempting to avoid responsibility often complicate collaborative relationships.

Complexity of Needs. Youth in contact with the justice system commonly present with multiple and complex needs. Many of these youth have multiple mental health disorders and/or co-occurring substance use disorders (Shufelt & Cocozza, 2006). In addition, these youth are likely to have educational, developmental, and behavioral challenges. Coupled with the fact that these youth have come into contact with the juvenile justice system as a result of delinquent behaviors, many community mental health service providers perceive these youth as dangerous or violent and are unwilling to accept and treat them. Reluctance on the part of community service providers to engage these youth results in even fewer service options.

Public/Political Support. Many youth in the juvenile justice system have complex mental health needs that are best addressed through diversion to community mental health services (Skowyra & Cocozza, 2007). A significant portion of these youth have committed minor, nonviolent offenses, and had it not been for the lack of access to community services, they would not be in the juvenile justice system in the first place. Unfortunately, the service needs of youth in the juvenile justice system are often not a high priority for policymakers, despite the significant potential for cost-savings by reducing institutional placement costs. Without strong advocacy and community awareness efforts, programs that serve these youth are often cut during times of fiscal shortfalls. This uncertainty and lack of prioritization can be a significant challenge to communities looking to establish a stable and sustainable system of care.

Lack of Treatment Capacity. The reality for most system of care sites is that the need for mental health services far outstrips the capacity of the community to provide services, because of a lack of qualified providers, inadequate funding, or other barriers. As a result, these communities must make difficult decisions about which populations of youth to prioritize. Unfortunately, because of the often limited political and public support for serving youth involved with the juvenile justice system, and the challenges associated with collaboration, lack of service capacity often results in the prioritization of other youth populations.

Opportunities for Partnership. While certainly more the exception than the rule, it is possible to create strong partnerships between the juvenile justice system and systems of care. It has been done in a small number of sites—Wraparound Milwaukee, Central Massachusetts Communities of Care, the Dawn Project in Indianapolis, IN, and Project Hope in Rhode Island are all examples of instances where such partnerships have worked exceptionally well. Arguably, the first step in undertaking a collaboration with the juvenile justice system is *understanding* the juvenile justice system, and the key opportunities for system of care collaboration. The juvenile justice system can be complicated and difficult to understand, thus frustrating efforts by the mental health system to meaningfully connect.

In 2007, NCMHJJ released its "Blueprint for Change: A Comprehensive Model for the Identification and Treatment of Youth with Mental Health Needs in Contact with the Juvenile Justice System" (Skowyra & Cocozza, 2007). This technical assistance document, prepared for the Office of Juvenile Justice and Delinquency Prevention (OJJDP), provides a framework for examining the juvenile justice system in its entirety and offers recommendations and guidelines for improving collaboration, identification, diversion, and treatment for youth with mental health needs who are involved with the system. A key component of the Blueprint is the identification of Critical Intervention Points, which are discrete processing points in the juvenile justice continuum that can be used as a framework for thinking about where opportunities for enhanced collaboration between the juvenile justice and mental health systems exist. [. . .]

The following sections describe each critical intervention point in the continuum and provide examples of existing collaborative initiatives that target youth at this particular intervention point. Some examples are of juvenile justice/system of care collaboratives; others are of innovative programs or strategies that have been developed to improve the response to youth with mental health needs. Both types of examples provide illustrations of how mental health collaboration, identification, diversion, and treatment can be improved at key juvenile justice processing points.

Initial Contact and Referral. When a youth is suspected of committing an offense, the police are often the first to intervene. Law enforcement officers respond to calls from schools, parents, the concerned public, and victims of a suspected offense. When responding to a call involving youth with mental health needs, law enforcement officers typically have discretion about how best to respond. Common responses include: informal "adjustment," either on site or at the station house; diversion of youth from formal processing based on certain conditions; or filing of a formal complaint or charges. Increasingly, law enforcement departments are partnering with community mental health agencies to assist police responding to crises involving individuals with mental health needs, by co-responding with police officers, co-training police on how to respond to youth experiencing some type of mental health crisis, or providing a place for law enforcement officers to take youth in need of mental health evaluation and services. System of care communities can partner with law enforcement on such efforts, to ensure that youth in a mental health crisis receive immediate and effective crisis services.

Program Example:

Central Massachusetts Communities of Care (CMCC) accepts referrals from various points within the juvenile justice system, including the police. The goal of CMCC is to "decrease and prevent youth with serious emotional disturbance from becoming involved with the courts and to reduce the seriousness and duration of juvenile justice involvement" (Wenz-Gross & DuBrino, 2008). CMCC operates two Family Centers that provide a range of services from prevention to intervention, as well as evidence-based practices, such as Trauma-focused Cognitive Behavioral Therapy and Positive Behavioral Interventions and Support.

Sometimes a school will refer youth to the police. Many schools do not want to make this referral, particularly for a youth who is suspected of having a mental health need of some sort. However, they are often left with very few options. A new response that has developed over the last few years involves the use of mental health responders who are assigned to specific school buildings and are available to respond to school-based incidents among youth with suspected mental health disorders, in lieu of a referral to the police. These mental health responders provide immediate crisis intervention, arrange for parents to be contacted and evaluations to be performed, make referrals for treatment planning and service provision, and provide case management services.

Program Example:

Mobile Urgent Treatment Teams (MUTT), *Wisconsin,* created as an offshoot of Wraparound Milwaukee, provide mobile crisis response services to schools in the Milwaukee School District. These teams provide a range of crisis-intervention and treatment-planning services to youth, and work with schools on safety plans that will allow youth to stay in school while they receive mental health treatment for the behavioral health issue that brought them to the attention of the MUTT. This model has been replicated in other states participating in the John D. and Catherine T. MacArthur Foundation's Models for Change Mental

Health/Juvenile Justice Action Network, including Connecticut, which is implementing a high-fidelity wraparound responder model in two middle schools, as well as Washington State, which is using Three Rivers Wraparound as its mental health responder for youth in middle schools in Benton and Franklin counties.

Intake. "Intake" generally refers to the process that occurs after a formal referral by law enforcement, during which an assessment process is initiated to determine whether a case should be dismissed, handled informally, or referred to juvenile court for formal intervention. While the general function of intake is consistent, its structure varies significantly across jurisdictions. Intake may be the responsibility of probation, juvenile court, the prosecutor's office, a state juvenile justice agency, or a centralized intake center, known as a "juvenile assessment center." Because of the nature of intake, and the discretionary decisions made at this time, intake represents a significant opportunity to identify mental health needs among youth and to divert and/or refer youth for community-based treatment. By working with intake units to provide assessment services and diversion opportunities, system of care sites can ensure that the mental health needs of youth are identified early and that youth are diverted (when appropriate) in the early stages of the juvenile justice processing continuum, before youth and their families experience many of the negative effects of system contact.

Program Example:

Beaver County System of Care: Optimizing Resources, Education and Support (BC-SCORES), Pennsylvania, serves youth between the ages of 10 and 21 in Beaver County, PA, who have mental health and co-occurring substance use disorders and who are involved with the juvenile justice system. Referrals come from the Juvenile Services Division, which is responsible for juvenile court intake and probation supervision. Services provided through BC-SCORES include case management, Multi-Systemic Therapy (MST), family-based therapies, individual psychotherapy, medication management, and a range of support services. Family coordinators are available to help families understand and access available resources.

Program Example:

Special Needs Diversionary Program (SNDP), Texas, is a probation-based collaborative program targeting youth who meet specific mental health diagnostic criteria. SNDP serves as both a diversion program and a reentry program for youth released from secure care. Colocated Probation/Licensed Practitioners of the Healing Arts (LPHA) teams of four provide joint case management, service coordination, and supervision to caseloads of anywhere from 12 to 15 youth. After an initial MAYSI-2 screen and a clinical assessment and family interview, treatment plans are developed and services are provided using a wraparound philosophy.

Detention. The most common use of secure detention facilities is as a short-term "holding" facility for youth while they await adjudication. However, some states also use detention as a holding facility for youth awaiting disposition or placement after adjudication, and a few use detention facilities as a postadjudication placement. Because of the short length of stay common in detention facilities (approximately 15 days), and their preadjudicatory, temporary nature, as well as overcrowding and staff shortages, many of these facilities fall short of providing quality mental health care. Given the fact that these facilities often represent a youth's first separation from his or her parents or caregivers, and can result in interruptions in medication and therapeutic services, mental health assessment and treatment for youth in detention is particularly critical. System of care sites can provide assistance by partnering with detention to provide community-based mental health assessment and services to youth.

Program Example:

The Illinois Mental Health/Juvenile Justice Initiative (MHJJI) was created in 2000 as a way to target youth in juvenile detention who have the most serious of disorders. Funds are provided to the community mental health agency to support "system liaisons" who serve as care coordinators to identify youth in detention appropriate for MHJJI, conduct eligibility assessments and develop care plans, seek approval from the court to release the youth from detention to participate in the program, and link the youth and their families to services for 6 months. Once the plan is in place, services are provided on the basis of a wraparound model.

Judicial Processing. Judicial processing encompasses two major steps that occur within juvenile court: adjudication and disposition. "Adjudication" refers to the process of conducting a hearing, considering evidence, and making a delinquency determination. If a youth is found delinquent during the adjudicatory process, a dispositional plan is developed. The dispositional plan is similar to sentencing within the adult system. This plan details the consequences of the youth's offense (e.g., probation, placement in a juvenile correctional facility, restitution). Development of the plan is based on a detailed history of the youth and assessment of available support systems and programs, and can include psychological evaluations and diagnostic testing. There are many opportunities within judicial processing for system of care sites to work with the courts. System of care sites can provide diagnostic and evaluation services, collaborate with the justice system to establish diversion options for youth with mental health needs, and establish community-based programs and services that can be incorporated in a dispositional plan.

Program Example:

Mental Health Diagnostic and Evaluation (D&E) Units, Jefferson County, Alabama, established through a system of care grant, serve youth through four D&E Units located in schools, child welfare, and the juvenile court. The juvenile court D&E Unit conducts assessments and develops individualized service plans for youth who meet criteria for serious emotional disturbances, have either experienced a previous separation from the family or significant functional impairments at home, and are at risk of placement. Referrals to the court D&E unit are made by both probation intake and the family court judge. This unit also provides a range of services, including medication management, crisis services, case management, and outpatient therapy.

Program Example:

Crossroads, Summit County, Ohio, is a specialized, postdispositional court for youth with mental health and co-occurring substance use disorders who meet specific diagnostic and juvenile justice criteria. The court's psychologist conducts assessments of youth, and treatment is provided primarily by specific community providers, although youth and families have the option of choosing their treatment providers. Some youth, whom the court's suitability committee deems most in need of home-based services, receive Integrated Co-Occurring Treatment (ICT). Crossroads probation officers serve as case managers and are responsible for the community supervision of youth. If a youth successfully completes treatment, his or her admitting charge and any related probation violations are expunged from their record.

Secure Correctional Placement. Placement in a secure juvenile correctional facility is the most restrictive disposition that a youth in the juvenile justice system can receive. Although all juvenile correctional facilities are designed to impose a sanction on the youth, protect the public, and provide some type of structured rehabilitative environment (Bilchik, 1998), the characteristics of these facilities vary significantly. Because of their secure nature and long-term custody of youth, these facilities are responsible for providing a range of services to youth. However, these facilities have been criticized as being sterile, inappropriate for rehabilitative programming, and fostering abuse and maltreatment (Greenwood,

Model, Rydell, & Chiesa, 1996). There are real concerns about the quality and availability of mental health care for youth in correctional settings (Bosman, 2010), and a sense among mental health experts that it is preferable to treat youth with serious mental health disorders outside institutional settings in general and outside correctional settings in particular (Koppelman, 2005). Furthermore, these facilities frequently do not allow for youth to maintain connections with their families and ecological support systems, making it very difficult for the effects of any type of therapeutic intervention to be sustained. Despite these very real challenges and concerns, youth with mental health needs who end up in correctional placement should be afforded access to effective, evidence-based mental health treatment.

Program Example:

The Integrated Treatment Model (ITM), Washington, is an umbrella term for a combination of approaches used by Washington State's Juvenile Rehabilitation Administration within the state's residential programs and parole aftercare services. ITM combines a set of evidence-based cognitive behavioral therapy (CBT) approaches shown to reduce recidivism and improve clinical outcomes for troubled youth. The skills addressed in treatment reflect the clinical needs of the youth. All residential staff are trained in these principles and parole staff are trained in Functional Family Parole, which focuses on family and community reintegration. A preliminary evaluation of the ITM model indicates that it has had a positive impact on functioning and recidivism (Lucenko & Mancuso, 2009).

Probation Supervision. Probation supervision is the most common disposition within the juvenile justice system. Probation supervision is frequently accompanied by other court-imposed conditions, such as community service, restitution, or participation in community treatment services. For youth with mental health needs on probation supervision, this can be an important opportunity to provide needed mental health services. Partnerships with system of care sites can ensure that there are a range of services and programs available to meet the mental health needs of youth on probation supervision.

Program Example:

Harris County Systems of Hope, Texas, accepts referrals of adjudicated youth on probation that meet criteria for an Axis-I disorder according to the Diagnostic and Statistical Manual of Mental Disorders (DSM IV) and have an IQ of at least 70. Assessments are completed by juvenile probation, and appropriate youth are sent to Systems of Hope. Once a referral is received, youth are either offered participation in a juvenile mental health court or wraparound services. A dedicated care team works with youth participating in the 6-month juvenile mental health court program.

Reentry. Reentry is the final point in the juvenile justice processing continuum, and incorporates programs and services that assist youth transitioning from juvenile justice placement back into the community (Geis, 2003). An effective reentry program that involves collaboration between the juvenile justice and mental health systems begins well in advance of a youth's release and ensures that the youth is linked with effective community-based services, which can be critical to his or her long-term success. Since one of the goals of reentry planning is to link youth with community mental health services that will be available after contact with the juvenile justice system ceases, reentry is a logical point in the juvenile justice system for a partnership with a system of care. System of care sites may be able to partner with correctional facilities to provide reentry planning and services to youth who will continue to need mental health care on their release. These efforts need to begin early—shortly after the youth enters the facility ("think exit at entry")—and should, whenever possible, involve the youth, his or her family, and representatives from the community-based agencies that will be working with the youth on release from care.

Program Example:

Project Hope, Rhode Island, which began as a system of care site, is an aftercare program for youth diagnosed with a mental health disorder who are leaving the Rhode Island Training School (RITS). Reentry planning begins 90 to 120 days prior to a youth's discharge from RITS, and is a coordinated effort between the RITS clinical social worker and Project Hope Family Service coordinators, who work together to plan for a youth's service needs and community safety concerns. Case managers oversee service plan implementation for 9 to 12 months postdischarge.

CONCLUSION

All too often, youth with mental health needs are unnecessarily referred to the juvenile justice system because community-based mental health services are unavailable to them. Many of these youth are in the juvenile justice system for relatively minor, nonviolent offenses and would be more appropriately served in community settings that allow them access to effective treatment, and give them the chance to stay connected to their families, schools, and communities.

Unfortunately, the reality is that for many youth, these treatment options do not exist and referral to the juvenile justice system becomes their last and only resort.

System of care communities, in partnership with the juvenile justice system, have the potential to change this course. By helping create more community-based treatment capacity and establishing linkages between the community mental health system and the juvenile justice system at key points of opportunity, communities have the potential to make a great difference in the lives of many children and youth. While such partnerships must confront and address a number of unique challenges, these challenges are by no means insurmountable. With careful planning and open communication, these challenges can be avoided or overcome, and successful and sustainable systems of care can be built to serve youth with mental health needs in the juvenile justice system.

REFERENCES

Bilchik, S. (1998). *Mental health disorders and substance abuse problems among juveniles*. Washington, DC: U.S. Department of Justice, Office of Justice Programs, Office of Juvenile Justice and Delinquency Prevention. Retrieved from http://www.ncjrs.gov/pdffiles1/fs9882.pdf on July 15, 2010.

Bosman, J. (2010, February 10). For detained youth, no mental health overseer. *New York Times*. Retrieved from http://www.nytimes.com/2010/02/11/nyregion/11youth.html on July 15, 2010.

Casey Strategic Consulting Group. (2003). *Reducing juvenile incarceration in Louisiana*. New Orleans, LA: Joint Legislative Juvenile Justice Commission. Retrieved from http://www.correctionsproject.com/tallulah/pressRoom/reports-rulings/caseyReport.pdf on July 15, 2010.

Cocozza, J. (2004). *Mental illness and juvenile justice: An overview of issues and trends*. Presentation at the Developing Systems of Care Training Institutes, San Francisco.

Drakeford, W., & Garfinkel, L. (2000). Differential Treatment of African American Youth. *Reclaiming Children and Youth: The Journal of Emotional and Behavioral Problems*, 9(1), 51–52.

Geis, S. (2003). *Aftercare services*. Washington, DC: U.S. Department of Justice, Office of Justice Programs, Office of Juvenile Justice and Delinquency Prevention. Retrieved from http://www.ncjrs.gov/pdffiles1/ojjdp/201800.pdf on July 15, 2010.

Greenwood, P., Model, K., Rydell, C., & Chiesa, J. (1996). *Diverting children from a life of crime: Measuring costs and benefits*. Arlington, VA: RAND Corporation. Retrieved from http://www.rand.org/pubs/monograph_reports/MR699-1/ on July 15, 2010.

Koppelman, J. (2005). *Mental health and juvenile justice: Moving toward more effective systems of care*. Washington, DC: National Health Policy Forum. Retrieved from http://www.nhpf.org/library/issue-briefs/IB805_JuvJustice_07-22-05.pdf on July 15, 2010.

Lucenko, B., & Mancuso, D. (2009). *Integrated Treatment Model improves employment and re-arrest outcomes for youth served by Washington State's Juvenile Rehabilitation Administration*. Olympia, WA: Washington State Department of Social and Health Services. Retrieved from http://www.dshs.wa.gov//pdf/ms/rda/research/2/22.pdf on July 15, 2010.

Mahoney, K., Ford, J., Ko, S., & Siegfried, C. (2004). *Trauma-focused interventions for youth in the juvenile justice system*. Los Angeles: National Child Traumatic Stress Network. Retrieved from http://www.nctsnet.org/nctsn_assets/pdfs/edu_materials/trauma_focused_interventions_youth_jjsys.pdf on July 15, 2010.

National Alliance on Mental Illness. (1999). *Families on the brink: The impact of ignoring children with serious mental illness*. Arlington, VA: Author. Retrieved from http://www.nami.org/Content/ContentGroups/CAAC/Families_on_the_Brink.pdf on July 15, 2010.

National Mental Health Association (2004). *Mental Health treatment of youth in the juvenile justice system: A compendium of promising practices*. Washington, DC: Author. Retrieved from https://www.nttac.org/views/docs/jabg/mhcurriculum/mh_mht.pdf on July 15, 2010.

Osher, T., & Hunt, P. (2002). *Involving families of youth who are in contact with the juvenile justice system*. Delmar, NY: National Center for Mental Health and Juvenile Justice. Retrieved from http://www.ncmhjj.com/pdfs/publications/family.pdf on July 15, 2010.

Osher, T., & Shufelt, J. (2006). *What families think of the juvenile justice system: Findings from the OJJDP multi-state study*. Focal Point: Summer, 2006. Retrieved from http://www.rtc.pdx.edu/PDF/fpS0607Corrected.pdf on July 15, 2010.

The President's New Freedom Commission on Mental Health. (2003). *Achieving the promise: Transforming mental health care in America* (Final Report, DHHS Pub. No. SMA-03-3832). Rockville, MD: U.S. Department of Health and Human Services. Retrieved from http://www.mentalhealthcommission.gov/reports/FinalReport/downloads/FinalReport.pdf on July 15, 2010.

Shufelt, J., & Cocozza, J. (2006). *Youth with mental health disorders in the juvenile justice system: Results from a multi-state prevalence study*. Delmar, NY: National Center for Mental Health and Juvenile Justice. Retrieved from http://www.ncmhjj.com/pdfs/publications/PrevalenceRPB.pdf on July 15, 2010.

Skowyra, K., & Cocozza, J. (2007). *Blueprint for change: A comprehensive model for the identification and treatment of youth with mental health needs in contact with the juvenile justice system*. Delmar, NY: National Center for Mental Health and Juvenile Justice. Retrieved from http://www.ncmhjj.com/Blueprint/pdfs/Blueprint.pdf on July 15, 2010.

Snyder, H. N., & Sickmund, M. (2006). *Juvenile offenders and victims: 2006 National Report*. Washington, DC: U.S. Department of Justice, Office of Justice Programs, Office of Juvenile Justice and Delinquency Prevention.

System of Care Evaluation Brief. (2000). *Juvenile justice characteristics and outcomes of children in systems of care*. Rockville, MD: Substance Abuse and Mental Health Services Administration, U.S. Department of Health and Human Services. Retrieved from http://systemsofcare.samhsa.gov/newinformation/docs/2000/Nov00.pdf on July 15, 2010.

Teplin, L., Abram, K., McClelland, G., Dulcan, M., & Mericle A. (2002). Psychiatric disorders in youth in juvenile detention. *Archives of General Psychiatry, 59*(12), 1133–1143.

U.S. Department of Health and Human Services. (2001). *Mental health: Culture, race and ethnicity—A supplement to mental health: A report of the Surgeon General*. Rockville, MD: U.S. Department of Health and Human Services, Public Health Service, Office of the Surgeon General. Retrieved from http://www.surgeongeneral.gov/library/mentalhealth/cre/sma-01-3613.pdf on July 15, 2010.

U.S. Department of Justice. (2005). *Department of Justice activities under the Civil Rights of Institutionalized Persons Act: Fiscal year 2004*. Washington, DC: Author. Retrieved from http://www.justice.gov/crt/split/documents/split_cripa04.pdf on July 15, 2010.

U.S. General Accounting Office. (2003). *Child welfare and juvenile justice: Federal agencies could play a stronger role in helping states reduce the number of children placed solely to obtain mental health services*. Washington, DC: Author. Retrieved from http://www.gao.gov/new.items/d03397.pdf on July 15, 2010.

U.S. House of Representatives. (2004). *Incarceration of youth who are waiting for community mental health services in the United States*. Washington, DC: Committee on Government Reform. Retrieved from http://hsgac.senate.gov/public/index.cfm?FuseAction=Files.View&FileStore_id=bdb90292-b3d5-47d4-9ffc-52dcd6e480da- on July 15, 2010.

Wasserman, G., McReynolds, L., Lucas, C., Fisher, P., & Santos, L. (2002). The Voice DISC-IV with incarcerated male youths: Prevalence of disorder. *Journal of the American Academy of Child and Adolescent Psychiatry, 41*(3), 314–321.

Wenz-Gross, M., & DuBrino, T. (2008). *Crafting community created systems of care strategies: Applying a theory of change approach to support implementation, evaluation, and strategic planning.* Presentation at the 21st Annual Research Conference, Tampa, FL. Retrieved from http://logicmodel. fmhi.usf.edu/narrations/presentations/CentralMass/ on July 15, 2010.

*Joseph Cocozza is the director of the National Center for Mental Health and Juvenile Justice at Policy Research Associates, an organization that strives to increase awareness of youth with mental health needs in the juvenile justice system and improve policies and practices for these youth.

Kathleen Skowyra is the associate director of the Mental Health/Juvenile Justice Action Network, which is based within the National Center for Mental Health and Juvenile Justice at Policy Research Associates. The Action Network is part of the MacArthur Foundation's Models for Change initiative.

Jennie Shufelt is an associate in the Litigation and Health Law departments at Hinman Straub. She formerly served as the associate director of the National Center for Mental Health and Juvenile Justice at Policy Research Associates, where she assisted in project management.

Joseph J. Cocozza, PhD, Kathleen R. Skowyra, and Jennie L. Shufelt, MS, *Addressing the Mental Health Needs of Youth in Contact With the Juvenile Justice System in System of Care Communities: An Overview and Summary of Key Issues,* Juvenile Justice Resource Series (Washington D.C.: Technical Assistance Partnership for Child and Mental Health, 2010). This publication was authored by the National Center for Mental Health and Juvenile Justice in partnership with the Technical Assistance Partnership for Child and Family Mental at the American Institutes for Research. The work was funded by the U.S. Department of Health and Human Services (Substance Abuse and Mental Health Services Administration, Center for Mental Health Services, Child, Adolescent, and Family Branch) under contract #HHSS280200800003C.

Reprinted by permission.

Reframing the Response: Girls in the Juvenile Justice System and Domestic Violence

*by Francine T. Sherman**

"With my hands behind my back
And a million knives through my chest
There are still flowers in my eyes
As I wait for the day to wash away these memories
And become the shining light I once was
I am forever waiting for my chance to be FREE!"

— Jasmine T., Age 15

In 1992, the Juvenile Justice and Delinquency Prevention Act, the federal legislation most directly influencing state juvenile justice policy, mandated that states analyze and plan to deliver gender-specific treatment and prevention services.[1] Since that time, research on the needs of girls in the juvenile justice system and gender-responsive approaches to addressing those needs has increased dramatically. We have learned that childhood trauma, family chaos, mental and physical health issues, and educational failure are all associated with delinquency in girls. Moreover, we are discovering that, in addition to contributing to delinquency, these needs can also become system triggers that pull girls who are victims of trauma into the juvenile justice system.

Juvenile justice policy has moved in cycles reflecting ongoing tension between its dual goals—social welfare and social control. The juvenile justice system, along with the child welfare system, began with an exclusive focus on social welfare, exercising authority as *parens patriae* to protect youths whose parents were unable or unwilling to do so. Young people involved with crime were categorized along with neglected and abused youths as in need of the guidance of the court and its related services. However, over the last century public protection, through accountability measures such as incapacitation and punishment, has been increasingly competing, and at times overtaking, social welfare as a guiding principle for juvenile justice systems.

Nevertheless, state juvenile justice purpose clauses continue to reflect the social welfare origins of juvenile justice. Many retain the original language of rehabilitation, describing a system of "...care, custody and discipline of children...," one that "...approximate(s) as nearly as possible that which they should receive from their parents . . . (and treats them). . . not as criminals but as children in need of aid, encouragement, and guidance."[2] More recently, state purpose clauses have adopted a modern iteration of this theme in the restorative justice concept of promoting individual competencies. Despite these clearly stated goals, however, the mechanics of the juvenile court and juvenile justice system—detention, probation, warrants, waiver, disposition—are largely designed to hold juveniles accountable and enforce the criminal laws, but not to treat the trauma or illness which often underlies delinquent behavior. This accountability orientation is the wrong framework to address the constellation of needs and strengths common among system-involved girls.

The experience of girls in the juvenile justice system illustrates how ill-suited the prevailing accountability model is for youths who have significant needs but pose little threat to public safety and how laws, policies, and practices can sweep the most vulnerable into that system. This experience also illustrates the potential for strengths-based, contextual frameworks, such as Positive Youth Development, to organize integrated systems that capitalize on youths' resiliencies.

A Profile of Girls in the Juvenile Justice System

The connection between trauma and later delinquency is well-established and particularly significant for girls. Recent research, building on findings from the late 1980s,[3] confirms the link between childhood trauma and future delinquency, finding high rates of trauma and family chaos in the profiles of girls in the delinquency system.[4] Although the connection between childhood trauma and later delinquency is present for boys as well, it is particularly striking for girls who are more often victims of sexual abuse and who are less likely than boys to be violent in the absence of childhood trauma. Girls' experiences of trauma, including domestic violence, are predictive of involvement in health risk behaviors and delinquency.[5]

For girls, family chaos and later delinquency are further connected by findings that girls in the delinquency system more often have parents convicted of a crime, siblings who are institutionalized, and multiple out-of-home placements. Out-of-home placements are connected to girls' histories of abuse and neglect, which result in foster care and residential placements.[6] The significant overlap of girls in both the child welfare and delinquency systems has been attributed to the shared risk factors of trauma and family chaos as well as to system issues such as the lack of communication between child welfare systems and the police, probation, or juvenile court.

While both boys and girls in the juvenile justice system have high rates of mental illness, substantial research shows that these girls have higher rates of mental illness than their male counterparts. In particular, system-involved girls suffer from prost-traumatic stress disorder, depression, and anxiety disorders.[7]

The connection between girls' trauma and their involvement in the delinquency system has multiple levels. Trauma is related to mental health issues, for which the juvenile justice system is the system of last resort. Moreover, trauma leads girls to risk-taking behaviors, which in turn result in delinquency. An additional and sometimes overlooked part of the equation is the system responses themselves which play a role in criminalizing girls who are trauma victims.

THE ROLE OF GENDER IN JUVENILE JUSTICE PROCESSING

Although the proportion of girls arrested and entering the juvenile justice system has increased over the last two decades, arrest patterns for girls continue to differ from those of their male counterparts. In 2006, prostitution and running away continued to be the only two offenses for which girls comprised the majority of juvenile arrests (74% of arrests for prostitution and 57% of arrests for running away). The next greatest share of girls' arrests included property offenses such as embezzlement (45% of arrests) and larceny-theft (41% of arrests). While girls comprised 17% of arrests for violent crime in 2006, this was largely due to arrests for aggravated assault (23% of juvenile arrests). In 2006, girls comprised approximately one-third of juvenile arrests for crimes such as liquor law violations, driving under the influence, disorderly conduct, and curfew violations.[8]

Along with these differing arrest patterns, detention is utilized differently for girls than for boys. In 2006, 41% of detained girls were held for technical violations (violating rules of probation or parole) or status offenses (behavior that would not be an offense for an adult), as compared with 26% of boys. The overuse of detention for girls with significant needs but minor crime is facilitated, but not excused, by the role of detention at the front end of the juvenile justice process, to hold pre-adjudicated youths without the requirement of a finding of delinquency. At the back end of the juvenile justice process, once a delinquency finding is required, the percentage of girls committed for technical violations or status offenses is reduced somewhat to 32% of all girls committed. However, the gender difference remains, with the share of girls' commitments for technical violations and status offenses almost twice that of boys (32% of all girls versus 17% of all boys).[9]

Although more research is needed to understand the correlates of delinquency, arrest, and detention utilization for girls, existing research suggests that these gender differences are in part the result of efforts by juvenile justice decision makers to protect girls. That protective impulse reflects gender bias as it sweeps girls into the system for more minor offenses than boys and triggers heightened responses to girls' failures to comply once in the system.[10]

This effort to protect is behind "bootstrapping" in which status offenses, which alone cannot result in locked confinement, become delinquency through probation violations, contempt, and charging decisions. Essentially, a girl brought into court on the status offense of running away or disobeying her parent, is told to obey a curfew, report to probation, and attend school regularly as conditions of her probation. When she violates her curfew or runs away again, she is held in detention for violation of court order, contempt, or AWOL, thereby bootstrapping the delinquency offense onto the underlying misbehavior. Alternatively girls can be charged with minor delinquency, such as disorderly conduct, for status type behaviors, allowing their detention and processing in the delinquency system.

Although these practices are consistently criticized, and bootstrapping has been found to violate law in some states, they remain commonplace ways in which juvenile courts and probation seek to control girls' behaviors. While courts need to be able to enforce their orders, girls often run and act out in response to family chaos and abuse; therefore, criminalizing this behavior penalizes girls for their attempts at survival without addressing the underlying family circumstances.[11]

The increase in arrests of girls for assault of the last decade illustrates the way laws are being applied to the detriment of vulnerable girls in this case by sweeping girls into the juvenile justice system as perpetrators when they are actually the victims of abuse, neglect, and domestic violence.

❏ **No Father**

I was always told that I have no father. That the one I've known all my life was just a donor. It's his fault I can't sleep. When I was little I had to hide under the sheets, because I tired of seeing my mother get beat. One day he disappeared and never came back. I was made to believe he was dead. To this day I still see my mother get hit and I can't get that out of my head. So now I still have no father to hug. Just my beautiful mother to care for until the day she's gone.

—Kassandra, Age 13

ASSAULT, DOMESTIC BATTERY, AND GIRLS

While girls' proportion of violent offenses has remained relatively low compared to their male counterparts (accounting for 11% of burglary arrests, 10% of arrests for weapons offenses, 9% of robbery arrests, and 5% of murder arrests in 2006),[12] their arrests for simple and aggravated assault have increased significantly in the past decade. This increase is particularly striking in comparison to boys. From 1996 to 2005, girls' arrests for simple assault increased 24% while boys' arrests declined 4%; girls' arrests for aggravated assault declined 5.4% while boys' arrests declined 23.4%. Overall arrests of girls for violence remained stable in relation to boys except for arrests for assault.[13] A similar gender difference was seen in assault arrests among adults. Between 1997 and 2006, adult male arrests for aggravated assault fell 14% while adult female arrests fell 2%; adult male arrests for simple assault fell 10% while adult female arrests rose 8%.[14]

These data have led observers to question the notion that girls are "getting more violent" and look for explanations linked to gender roles and law enforcement practices.

A recent report commissioned by the Office of Juvenile Justice and Delinquency Prevention concluded that the increase in arrests of girls for assault over the past decade was in large part a reflection of changed enforcement and increased visibility of domestic violence cases, which is sweeping in girls whose violence often occurs in the home.[15] In support of this conclusion, the report notes:

- The ratio of simple assault arrests is much higher for girls than for boys indicating that girls' violence is of a less serious nature than boys;
- Arrests of girls for assault increased during this time but arrests of girls for other violent offenses did not;
- Trends in female self-reported assault over the same time period remained stable;
- Victim-reported assaults over the same time period showed no difference between male and female trends, both of which dropped in recent years.[16]

The study offers a contextual explanation noting that changes in law enforcement policies and social services responses to domestic violence have coincided with the increase in arrests of girls for assaults. It points to a lowered threshold for reporting and classifying behavior as assault and to zero tolerance policies in schools, which result in arrests for behavior that was not formerly subject to arrest; both give the impression of an increase in assaults.[17]

Notably, the report cites shifts over the past decade in a number of practices related to domestic violence which have had a disproportionate and unintended impact on girls. While both boys' and girls' violence is most often perpetrated against same-sex peers, the second most common victim of girls' violence is a family member. In fact, one study found girls three times as likely as boys to assault a family member, often their mother.[18] Thus, less discretion and stricter enforcement of domestic violence laws is likely to disproportionately affect girls. A number of states and localities have adopted mandatory arrest or mandatory hold policies in cases of domestic disturbance. Moreover, family violence, which formerly might have been referred to family services, is now more likely to be handled by law enforcement as a domestic disturbance. The result is net-widening—more cases are classified within domestic violence laws and those laws have become stricter and more criminal in nature.

NEVADA'S DOMESTIC BATTERY REFORMS

These findings came to life recently when two counties in Nevada discovered that girls were being disproportionately and inappropriately affected by a Nevada statute which required a 12-hour mandatory hold in secure detention for any child charged with domestic battery.

As part of their efforts to reform detention practices and reduce the inappropriate use of secure detention, Washoe and Clark counties reviewed all detention data for girls. Both counties discovered that a significant number of girls were being detained for domestic battery and that the impact of the law fell disproportionately on girls. In 2006 in Clark County (Las Vegas), girls comprised 22% of overall detentions but 43% of detentions for domestic battery; in Washoe County (Reno), girls accounted for 28% of all detentions but 40% of detentions for domestic battery. In Washoe County, 69% of girls' person-offense detentions in 2006 were for domestic battery.[19]

Law enforcement described responding to domestic disturbances involving multiple family members, including parents, but routinely charging the teenager rather than the parent because there were younger children in the home who required a parent to be present. In these cases, the girl was not necessarily more culpable, she was simply more convenient.

Moreover, although the Nevada statute required a 12-hour hold, girls' average length of stay in detention for domestic battery was longer. Once a girl was detained, she remained in detention for the judicial detention hearing, and as a result of processing delays, continued to be detained for an average of 8 days.[20] Moreover, while girls were detained, few if any services were mobilized to address the domestic violence behind the initial charges, so when the girl was returned home she was returned to a chaotic family in which the violence was not addressed.

As a result of the efforts of a coalition of Nevada's juvenile justice departments, law enforcement agencies, and the domestic violence community, the Nevada state legislature amended this law effective August 2007. The new law requires a youth arrested for domestic battery to be released unless he or she otherwise qualifies for detention. Moreover, the law favors provision of family services to maintain the child in the home and respite or other out-of-home alternative if needed to protect the child from injury.[21]

The amended law has allowed a revised approach to youths involved in domestic disturbance. In the year after the law became effective, Washoe County detained 13% of girls charged with domestic battery as compared with 100% in the preceding year [...]. Moreover, the amended law is providing the impetus to strengthen family services, including respite care and family counseling, and to restructure case management to better assess the complex needs of girls and their families.

INCORPORATING POSITIVE YOUTH DEVELOPMENT

The accountability response for girls involved in domestic violence or for girls who run away from chaotic families penalizes them for their attempts to survive, criminalizing their efforts to assert control over chaotic home lives. The accountability response also exclusively targets the girl for legal and service interventions, allowing systems to ignore needs within the family and community which contribute to domestic violence and family chaos. Finally, the accountability response reflected in common juvenile justice interventions, such as detention, revictimizes girls who have already suffered trauma.

Positive Youth Development (PYD), which has been gaining traction as a framework for juvenile justice since the mid-1990s, offers an ecological approach to youth services with a goal of helping young people grow into successful adults. PYD recognizes that the spheres in which youths develop have positive as well as negative elements. A PYD approach promotes those positive elements, fostering youths' strengths in their families, communities, and society rather than focusing disproportionately on their deficits. Common goals of juvenile justice PYD programming would be promoting healthy family and peer relationships, developing leadership skills, job training, and promoting civic engagement. To achieve these goals, a juvenile justice system organized around PYD would be integrated with other child-serving and public health systems to promote strengths and resiliency factors in youths' families and communities.[22] This strengths-based frame is a challenge to the prevailing treatment and accountability models in juvenile justice. Yet, it fits girls in the juvenile justice system well because much of girls' offending is linked to family, community, and societal issues.

For example, PYD might re-frame a "domestic battery" case as a girl's attempt to survive, and running away as her attempt to exert control over a chaotic family situation. PYD might be incorporated into the front-end of juvenile justice systems through diversion, designed to move a youth whose charges arise in the family context out of the justice system and provide family services designed to address the issues creating the context for the offense and support the youth's social supports so she has safe alternatives.

Pima County, Arizona's Domestic Violence Outreach Center (DVOC) is an example of this sort of innovation. The DVOC is an effort to address cases of youths charged with domestic violence related crimes more comprehensively outside of the accountability mechanisms of traditional juvenile justice. The Center works as a partnership among law enforcement, juvenile court, probation, and child protective and mental health services. It strives to identify community resources to address the individual and family issues central to domestic violence charges thus diverting the youth from detention and the formal juvenile justice system.

CONCLUSION

Girls who have experienced significant trauma and family chaos are being swept into the delinquency systems as an unintended consequence of juvenile justice laws, policies, and practices. Yet that system, based largely on an accountability model, is poorly designed to address these girls' needs and foster their strengths. Although institutional impediments to a PYD framework throughout juvenile justice systems are great, it offers a positive, forward-looking alternative to the accountability model and is a good fit for girls whose delinquency must be understood in family, community, and societal contexts.

NOTES

1. 42 U.S.C.A. section 5633, et seq.
2. 119 Mass. Gen Laws 53.
3. Widom, C., & Maxfield, M. (2001). An update on the "cycle of violence," Research in Brief. Washington DC: U.S. Department of Justice, Office of Justice Programs, National Institute of Justice.

4. Chamberlain, P. (2002). Treatment foster care, in Burns, B. & Hoagwood, K. (Eds.), *Community treatment for youth*, (pp. 117–138). New York: Oxford University Press.

5. Smith, D. Leve, L., & Chamberlain, P. (2006). Adolescent girls' offending and health-risking sexual behavior: The predictive role of trauma, *Child Maltreatment*, *11*(4), 346–353.

6. *Supra* note 4.

7. Cauffman, E., Lexcen, F.J., Goldweber, A., Shulman, E.P., & Grisso, T. (2007). Gender differences in mental health symptoms among delinquent and community youth, *Youth Violence and Juvenile Justice*, *5*(3), 287–307.

8. Snyder, H. (2008). Juvenile arrests 2006, Juvenile Justice Bulletin. Washington, DC: U.S. Department of Justice, Office of Juvenile Justice and Delinquency Prevention.

9. Sickmund, M., Sladky, T.J., Kang, W., & Puzzanchera, C. (2008). *Easy access to the census of juveniles in residential placement*, available at http://www.ojjdp.ncjrs.gov/ojstatbb/ezacjrp/

10. Bishop, D. & Frazier, C. (1992). Gender bias in juvenile justice processing: Implications of the JJDP Act, *Criminology*, *82*, 1162–1186.

11. Humphrey, A. (2004). The criminalization of survival attempts: Locking up female runaways and other status offenders, *Hastings Women's Law Journal*, *15*, 165–184.

12. *Supra* note 8.

13. Zahn, M. et al. (2008). *Violence by teenage girls: Trends and context*. Washington, DC: U.S. Department of Justice, Office of Juvenile Justice and Delinquency Prevention.

14. *Supra* note 8.

15. *Supra* note 13.

16. *Id.*

17. *Id.*

18. *Id.*

19. Sherman, F. (2007). Nevada amends domestic battery hold for juveniles, *JDAI News*. Annie E. Casey Foundation.

20. Washoe County Department of Juvenile Justice. (2006).

21. Nevada Rev. Stat. 62C.020 (2008).

22. *See, e.g.*, Fratbutt, J., Di Luca, I., & Graves, K. (2008). Envisioning a juvenile justice system that supports positive youth development, *Notre Dame Journal of Law, Ethics, and Public Policy*, *22*, 107–125.

*Francine T. Sherman is a clinical professor and director of the Juvenile Rights Advocacy Project at Boston College Law School.

Reprinted by permission of the National Council of Juvenile and Family Court Judges, *Juvenile and Family Justice Today* 18, no. 1 (Winter 2009).

Poetry is used with permission of Artistic Noise www.artisticnoise.org.

DISCUSSION QUESTIONS

1. Do you think that zero-tolerance policies actually keep students safe? If so, do you think that the benefits of these policies outweigh the documented consequences? What are some alternative approaches that would help keep children safe without pushing students out of school and/or into the courts?

2. Should schools have on-duty police officers? Why or why not?

3. What sorts of resources are available to youth with mental health disorders before they enter the justice system? Are these resources effective?

4. Should the fact that a child suffers from a mental illness excuse him from criminal responsibility? Why or why not?

5. Should girls be treated just the same as boys in the juvenile justice system? Why or why not?